# READING SEMINAR XX

SUNY series in Psychoanalysis and Culture
Henry Sussman, Editor

# READING SEMINAR XX

Lacan's Major Work on Love,
Knowledge, and Feminine Sexuality

EDITED BY

Suzanne
Barnard

Bruce
Fink

STATE UNIVERSITY OF NEW YORK PRESS

Published by
STATE UNIVERSITY OF NEW YORK PRESS
ALBANY

For information, address
State University of New York Press,
90 State Street, Suite 700, Albany, NY 12207

Production, Laurie Searl
Marketing, Anne M. Valentine


Library of Congress Cataloging-in-Publication Data

Reading Seminar XX : Lacan's major work on love, knowledge, and
feminine sexuality / Suzanne Barnard & Bruce Fink, editors.
      p. cm.—(SUNY series in psychoanalysis and culture)
   Includes bibliographical references and index.
   ISBN 0-7914-5431-2 (alk. paper)—ISBN 0-7914-5432-0 (pbk. : alk. paper)
    1. Psychoanalysis.  2. Lacan, Jacques, 1901–   I. Barnard, Suzanne,
1963–  II. Fink, Bruce, 1956–  III. Series.

BF173 .R3657 2002
150.19'5—dc21                                             2002017727

        10     9     8     7     6     5     4     3     2

# CONTENTS

# INTRODUCTION

*Suzanne Barnard*

*Encore*, or Seminar XX, represents the cornerstone of Lacan's work on the themes of sexual difference, knowledge, *jouissance*, and love. In this landmark seminar, Lacan maps a critical terrain across philosophy, theology, history, linguistics, and mathematics, articulating certain exemplary points at which psychoanalysis provides a unique intervention into these discourses. Arguing that the subject of psychoanalysis is a consequence of the Enlightenment's rejection of reality in pursuit of the real, Lacan sets out in Seminar XX to articulate how a *psychoanalytic* science of the real might transform accepted ideas about sexual difference, being, and knowledge. With his predictable rhetorical flair, expansive reach, and provocative wit, Lacan exposes the founding fantasies of historically dominant systems of thought, illuminating, for example, the Eros characteristic of philosophical and religious assumptions about the "One" of being or God, the ambivalence about the loss of a synthetic cosmology attending modern science, and other key philosophical and scientific assumptions about the subject, the body, causality, and determinism. Psychoanalysis itself is not exempt from scrutiny in *Encore*, as Lacan finds many of these same preoccupations haunting both Freudian and various neo-Freudian texts. By the end of the seminar, it is clear that *Encore* contains significant revisions of Lacan's own ideas as well.

Historically, Seminar XX has been known to many (if not most) readers as Lacan's treatise on feminine sexuality. While this fact is clearly overdetermined by current disciplinary and broader cultural preoccupations, it can be attributed in large part to the delay in *Encore*'s complete translation. Existing English-language scholarship on Seminar XX has been based, until quite recently, on the snapshot of the Seminar provided by partial translations of two chapters in

1

*Feminine Sexuality*,[1] hence, its almost exclusive popularization as a text on sexual difference to the neglect of its other interventions into philosophy and science. With the advent of the recent translation of *Encore* by Bruce Fink,[2] English-speaking audiences now have access to a complete translation of the Seminar, one informed by recent scholarship and including detailed footnotes explaining Lacan's more obscure cultural and theoretical references. Its complete version[3] reveals as much concern on Lacan's part with the post–Cartesian status of the subject—and the implications of this status for the limits and possibilities of knowledge and jouissance—as it does with sexual difference, and it arguably represents the most sustained and sophisticated work on these themes in Lacan's oeuvre.

The chapters of Seminar XX presented in *Feminine Sexuality* have come to occupy a prominent place in contemporary debate concerning sexual difference across an impressive range of disciplines. In fact, they are routinely cited in contemporary psychoanalytic, philosophical, literary, political, and film theory discussions of sexual difference—of which the most obvious example is the ongoing debates between Lacanian psychoanalysis and feminist theories concerning feminine sexuality. Given the limited perspective on *Encore* that these chapters represent, their prominence among the texts informing these debates is profoundly ironic and problematic. While the debates have obviously had a certain use-value for both psychoanalysis and feminism, the overreliance in feminist scholarship on such a circumscribed familiarity with *Encore* has made it a "straw-text" for feminist critique. This circumstance is additionally complicated by the relative lack of Anglophone scholarship on Lacan's engagement with his "Other" (Freud), particularly scholarship that does justice to Lacan's uncanny knack for reading Freud beyond himself.

While feminist suspicions about the impact of Freud's patriarchal legacy are quite legitimate, in the case of Lacan they too often have been enacted in the form of a superficial glossing and dismissal of what—in contrast to classical analytic appropriations of Freud—is a quite nontraditional reading. Hence, we encounter the unfortunate, though not unrelated, consequence that the best known of Lacan's remarks on femininity also are some of the most easily misread out of context. Readings of Lacan that perseverate on the more scandalous sounding of Lacan's claims to the exclusion of their context and meaning-effects domesticate the more radical moments—of which there are many—in Lacan's text. Invoking statements such as, "Woman cannot be said. Nothing can be said of woman" (Seminar XX, 75/81), or, "A woman can but be excluded by the nature of things . . . [and] if there is something that women themselves complain about enough for the time being, that's it. It's just that they don't know what they're saying—that's the whole difference between them and me" (Seminar XX, 68/73), and citing them as evidence of Lacan's phallocentrism short-circuits the potential for a more engaged and potentially fruitful exchange between psychoanalysis and feminist theories. Doubtless such remarks betray that Lacan took a certain surplus satisfaction in being provocative. However, when closely read in its entirety, Seminar XX represents a serious and profoundly original attempt to go beyond both the patriarchal dimensions of Freud's corpus and the banalities concerning feminine sexuality characteristic of neo-Freudian revisionism.

Beyond the the translation lag, the reception of *Encore* in the United States has been complicated by the fact that it is among the more difficult of Lacan's quintessentially challenging seminars. In particular, his arguments often revolve around relatively obscure philosophical references (e.g., Bentham's *Theory of Fictions*) and theories (e.g., number theory, set theory, topology) that are inaccessible to one uninitiated into the idiosyncracies of Lacan's later work. The difficulty of the Seminar also underscores the importance of understanding the evolution of Lacan's ideas across the span of his seminars. For example, Lacan's arguments concerning sexual difference in Seminar XX rely integrally on his work on ethics and the structure of courtly love in Seminar VII, as well as on his treatment of anxiety in Seminar X. His conceptualizations of sexual difference, jouissance, and the body develop significantly over the course of his oeuvre, beginning with a position more closely allied with Freud[4] and ending up with a position that diverges from Freud's in critical ways.[5] Finally, Seminar XX assumes some familiarity with Lacan's shift in emphasis from desire to drive; this shift is most clearly marked beginning with Seminar XI, and it involves significant transformations in his understanding of the subject, causality, and jouissance. Hence, some understanding of the developmental trajectory of Lacan's ideas across his seminars is indispensable for grasping how he situates himself vis-à-vis traditional philosophy and science in Seminar XX.

That said, however, it is obvious that the different readings of *Encore* both within and beyond the United States cannot be reduced to differential access to the text in translation or to its conceptual density and complexity. As Lacan himself never tired of reminding his audience, knowledge and jouissance are inextricably related; even in an ideal communication situation (e.g., a "complete" text or an "entire" oeuvre), interpretation confronts the limits constituted by the particularity of the subject's jouissance—the way in which a given subject "gets off" on (in this case) a text.[6] Lacan's caveat underscores the obvious point that readers come to his texts with very different interests, motivations, and strategies of reading. Even when readers are defined by a common interest—for example, those interested in questions of feminine sexuality— they approach the text with quite different preoccupations. A clear example of this can be seen in the significant differences in the preoccupations of French feminist readings of *Encore* (and the Anglophone readings inspired by those readings) and those emerging from the Ecole de la Cause freudienne (ECF). Many of the theorists writing from within the context of the ECF have been a part of the French academic culture in which Lacan was a major figure, and they continue to participate in the clinical subculture in which he played a primary structuring role. Consequently they are more often preoccupied with questions of sexual difference as they emerge out of or are relevant to clinical praxis. While French feminist theorists—Julia Kristeva and Luce Irigaray, for example—have been immersed in much the same academic, clinical, and cultural milieu, they have been relatively more concerned with the relationships between sexual difference and epistemology, as well as between sexual difference, social structure, and politics. As many Anglophone theorists have approached Lacan's work via French feminism (suggesting a certain jouissance found there), they have tended to mirror its concern with sociohistorical and political influences on the theorizing of sexual difference.

While French feminists, particularly Kristeva and Irigaray, are well acquainted with the "later Lacan," their more accessible readings of his work center on the problematics of sexual difference prior to *Encore*.[7] As a result, Anglophone feminists have focused more on the role of the imaginary and symbolic in the constitution of sexual difference and less on the role of the real. This trend has been reinforced by the way in which the imaginary and symbolic dimensions of sexuation lend themselves to correspondence with terminology in dominant discourses of sex and gender in the United States, discourses that are almost always framed in terms of either natural science, phenomenology, or forms of sociohistorical analysis and cultural studies (or some hybrid of these perspectives). Within some of these perspectives, the imaginary can be understood as correlative to constructs such as gender identity and embodiment (i.e., the "lived body") and the symbolic to aspects of the body and sexuality that are "socially constructed." However, there is no concept in these discourses that aims at anything like the Lacanian real (hence, the common misconception of the "real" as biological sex). As a result, Lacan's account of sexuation cannot be grasped via dominant academic discourses of sex and gender. In fact, the Lacanian real can be understood precisely as the traumatic cause on account of which any attempt to reduce sexual difference to biology, phenomenology, or cultural construction is doomed to fail. Seminar XX ultimately represents Lacan's attempt to trace the impact of this trauma—manifest as the gap between the symbolic and real—on the functioning of the symbolic itself. For him, then, the question of sexual difference is coextensive with the question born of the rupture between reality and the real produced by modern science, a rupture Lacan frames as the "frontier" between "knowledge and truth" (*Écrits*, 797/296).[8] It is because Lacan understands psychoanalysis to provide a unique intervention into the space of this question that he claims, "[I]t is perhaps here [at the border between knowledge and truth] that psychoanalysis signals its emergence, representing a new seism that occurred there" (ibid.).

It is in the spirit then of unsettling the prematurely familiar ground from which Lacan has been interpreted, and (re)introducing readers to the compelling originality and use-value of his later work on sexuation, knowledge, jouissance, and love that the contributors to this book "read" Seminar XX. With these ends in mind, many of the chapters offer a simple point of entry to Seminar XX and present clear exposés of basic concepts deployed therein—gestures sure to be appreciated by readers less well acquainted with Lacan's work. However, the chapters operate on several levels at once, clarifying elementary notions while simultaneously offering the reader familiar with Lacan the reward of a sophisticated working-through of the more challenging and obscure arguments in *Encore*—often through tracing their historical development across Lacan's oeuvre and/or by demonstrating their relation to particular philosophical, theological, mathematical, and scientific concepts. For example, the chapters collected here cover much of the terrain necessary for understanding sexual difference—not in terms of chromosomes, body parts, choice of sexual partner, or varieties of sexual practice but in terms of one's position vis-à-vis the Other and the kind of jouissance one is able to obtain. In so doing, they make significant interventions into the more recalcitrant structures of debate regarding sex, gender, and sexuality in feminist theory, philosophy, queer theory, and cultural studies. The chapters also address the intertwining of Lacan's account of sexual difference with the approaches to ethics, epistemology, and the science of "being" that he articulates in Seminar XX, particularly through articulating the specific relationships between knowledge, jouissance, and the body that emerge from the "splitting" of the Other into its "whole" and not-whole parts. In the process, they also engage with certain questions central to current discussions in the philosophy of science and science studies.

Each chapter also elaborates (more or less extensively) on the logic of Lacan's formulas of sexuation and the elements in the accompanying schema.

**FIGURE 1**
**The Formulas of Sexuation**

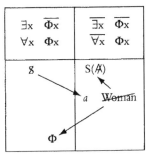

For the uninitiated, the intelligibility of these terms can be approached from several possible directions, each of which is taken up by one or more of the authors represented here. For some, the formulas of sexuation and the relations that obtain between them will be most accessible through understanding their connections to Lacan's broader discussions of subjectivization, being, jouissance, and the body. For others, they will be most easily grasped via Lacan's interventions into theories of causality, ontology, and epistemology. For more clinically inclined and/or feminist readers, Lacan's formulas of sexuation are perhaps most easily engaged by beginning with Lacan's reading of Freud's account of sexual difference, particularly the latter's discussion of femininity, and proceeding to Lacan's discussion of the failure of the sexual relationship and its implications for masculine and feminine structure. Whatever one's initial point of engagement, the book as a whole provides a comprehensive and studied introduction to the complexity of Lacan's ideas in Seminar XX. In the end, it is our hope that this book will facilitate important exchanges already begun between French, broader European, Latin American, and English-speaking readers of Lacan, as well as advance the ongoing interdisciplinary dialogues between psychoanalysis, feminist theory, and queer theory, between the philosophy of science and science studies, and between philosophy, political theory, and cultural studies.

## SEXUATION

Perhaps the most (in)famous of the claims that Lacan makes in Seminar XX is the one regarding the impossibility of founding (*poser*) a sexual relationship (Seminar XX, 14/9). Despite its centrality in Lacan's teachings on sexuation, it is commonly misread as referring to the "reality" of the relationship between the sexes. For example, in an otherwise lucid entry on Lacan in a literary theory guide, one finds the statement, "Thus Lacan claims flatly in Seminar XX that there is no such thing as sexual relations"![9] That such remarks appear in print with regularity is symptomatic of a certain fundamental confusion about key concepts in Seminar XX. When Lacan suggests that there is "no such thing" as the sexual relationship, he is *not* referring to sexual relations. Rather, as presented by Lacan in his formulas of sexuation, the impossibility of founding the sexual relationship is strictly coextensive with the conundrum of sexual difference. Indeed, one can best understand the formulas of sexuation as the product of Lacan's attempt to formalize and articulate the specific implications of the sexual relationship's *impossibility*.

Why has such a basic thesis been so susceptible of misreading? Perhaps the most obvious reason is the aforementioned incommensurability between the Lacanian logic of sexual difference and the logic subtending the sex-gender debates. While psychoanalytic theory in general is recognized as warranting conceptual distinction from both natural scientific and sociohistorical modes of analysis, this distinction often is cashed out in terms of a hybrid "part-biological/part-cultural" discourse, hence, the disenchantment with psychoanalysis voiced by biomedicine (it is not "scientific" enough), feminist essentialism (it does not offer an autonomous definition of woman), and feminist constructionism and cultural studies (it is too biologically, psychologically, and/or socially deterministic). It is not that the sex-gender distinction has not been useful in many obvious ways, but when applied to understanding Lacan's framework for articulating sexual difference, it creates more confusion than clarity. This is all too apparent in the long-standing debates concerning the status of the phallus in Lacan. Thus just as sexual difference is refracted through the lenses of sex and gender, so is the phallus read in terms of the opposition between the biological and the symbolic.

In their respective chapters, Colette Soler ("What Does the Unconscious Know about Women?"), Renata Salecl, and Geneviève Morel demonstrate—albeit with different emphases—the manner in which Lacan's translation of Freud's discourses on femininity and sexuality into the language of the symbolic, imaginary, and real renders problematic the accepted logic of sex and gender, particularly as these terms have structured the essentialist-constructionist debates among American feminist and gender theorists. In so doing, they clarify how Lacan's "translation" of Freud can be applied toward understanding the formulas of sexuation, as well as the particular modes of failure of the sexual relationship characteristic of subjects with masculine and feminine structure. Morel's and Soler's focus on Lacan's earlier work on feminine sexuality in "Signification of the Phallus" and "Guiding Remarks for a Convention on Feminine Sexuality" also serves as a bridge in understanding the significant revisions in Lacan's own position, found in Seminar XX.

In her chapter "What Does the Unconscious Know about Women?" Colette Soler notes several important parallels in Freud's and Lacan's accounts of feminine sexuality, while simultaneously elaborating on critical points of Lacan's departure from Freud's ultimately patriarchal account. So, for example, while Lacan is consistent with Freud in positing the partial nature of the drive, the importance of castration for sexual difference, and the absence of a feminine mark of difference in the unconscious, the logic of Lacan's formulations of these concepts diverges acutely from Freud's. Soler traces the logic behind Lacan's reconfiguration of Freud's binary between "having or not having" (the penis) to that of a "having or a being . . . the phallus" (*Écrits*, 694/289); she also articulates Lacan's rejection of Freud's exclusive definition of woman in terms of her relation to a male partner. In her reading of Lacan's earlier work on feminine sexuality, Soler discerns an affirmation of and implicit response to certain feminist critiques of Freud. She develops several of the more compelling aspects of these critiques, as well as the gist of Lacan's response—in particular highlighting the way in which his distinction between the symbolic and the imaginary facilitates a differentiation between the aspects of women's sexual alienation that are a function of demand and those that are a function of desire, hence her claim that "Lacan succeeded more than Freud in isolating the logical constraints of structure and their difference from ideal norms."

In "Feminine Conditions of Jouissance," Geneviève Morel takes up more specifically one of the controversial aspects of Freud's account of sexual development—the function of castration—in order to articulate its role in Lacan's discussion of feminine conditions of jouissance. Lacan's own account has been the target of much scrutiny and criticism, as he maintains the language of both castration and the phallus in his theory of sexuation. In her discussion of what psychoanalysis has to offer regarding the ways in which a woman (a feminine subject) experiences jouissance with a man (a masculine subject), Morel focuses in particular on the condition of jouissance that Lacan describes as the figure of the "castrated lover" or "dead man" (*Écrits*, 733/95). Her argument engages Lacan's claim that the phallic function and castration are required for a woman to experience jouissance in relation to a man. She mobilizes central elements of Lacan's discussion of frigidity in support of this claim. In contrast to Freud, Lacan understands frigidity—or the absence of "sexual" jouissance in a feminine subject—to be a structural, epistemic dilemma rather than an anatomical dysfunction or sign of an underdeveloped sexuality. More specifically, Lacan understands frigidity as consequent upon an imaginary identification with the phallus, an identification that inhibits the circulation of jouissance. Morel demonstrates the role of castration and the phallic function in women's sexual jouissance by elucidating the rather complicated set of structural relations between the feminine subject, her sexual partner, and the symbolic Other that Lacan presents in "Guiding Remarks for a Convention on Feminine Sexuality."[10] In so doing, she sheds light both on the sense of Lacan's remark in Seminar X, that "only love allows jouissance to condescend to desire" (March 13, 1963), and on his rewriting of this structure in Seminar XX via a splitting between phi (desire) and S($\cancel{A}$) (love). What is at stake in this shift in emphasis is, essentially, the elaboration of what Lacan refers to in *Encore* as the "other" face of the Other. In other words, what he discusses in "Guiding Remarks" as a form of sexual jouissance related to the figure of the dead man (or castrated lover) is further differentiated in Seminar XX into two modes of possible jouissance in women—phallic (sexual) jouissance and Other jouissance, the latter being related to the real or the "God" face of the Other.

While Morel focuses on the dynamics of sexual jouissance in the feminine subject, Renata Salecl provides an analysis of the specific ways in which the sexual relationship *fails*. More particularly, she examines the ways in which it fails differently for masculine and feminine subjects, and thus how they are each traumatized in exclusive ways. Beginning with Lacan's schema of masculine and feminine structures, she elaborates on the consequences of the fact that men and women do not relate to what their partners relate to in them. She links these consequences to certain hyperbolic expressions of masculinity and feminity as they are manifest both at the level of the individual—for example, vulnerability to certain modes of psychic distress—and at the level of social norms. In taking object *a* as his partner, that is, taking as object of desire that which he is not, man becomes especially vulnerable to the perceived inability to assume his symbolic role. In the language of the formulas of sexuation, he seeks to maintain his existence in the symbolic through obsessive labor in service of the "One" of the phallic exception. Woman, in contrast, is concerned with "what she doesn't have as such"; what she does not have is the object that man sees in her, and which thus constitutes her object of desire. Salecl suggests that the fear of not possessing this object provokes a ceaseless questioning of the Other's desire, leading the feminine subject to "wonder what is in her more than herself." The feminine subject, then, is likely to respond to loss of love not by ever-greater attempts to shore up the symbolic but by withdrawal and "immersion in melancholic indifference." Why? Again, in terms of the formulas of sexuation, one could say that the lack in the symbolic that her loss reveals becomes fixed in the imaginary, becoming an obstacle to the establishment of the signifying bonds that might mediate her sadness. However, for Salecl, this latter explanation raises the interesting question of the difference between the feminine mystic and the feminine melancholic. Salecl hypothesizes that this difference can be understood through articulating the ambiguous potential of Other jouissance for mediating the loss of herself as Other, a loss that the loss of her partner may represent. While Lacan clearly underscores the way in which feminine loss exceeds the phallic loss of the object, his account of the potential for feminine jouissance to compensate for this "plus of melancholy" is less definitive. Salecl suggests that the plus of sadness of the feminine melancholic might be accounted for by the fact that feminine jouissance does not pass through the unconscious and, therefore, cannot support the woman finding herself there.

Through tracing the development of Lacan's early work on feminine sexuality to his sustained engagement with the question in *Encore*, Salecl's, Morel's, and Soler's chapters illuminate certain distinctions between "reality" and the real that are critical in understanding Lacan's account of sexuation. To begin with, Lacan argues that what we take to be the reality of the sexual relationship depends for its integrity on a function of "seeming" or semblance, a phantasmatic propping up necessary to sustain the illusion of sexual complementarity within a closed circuit of desire and exchange. This assertion of the phantasmatic dimension of sexuality is one of the ways in which Lacan's treatment of sexual difference diverges markedly from Freud's account, as well as from contemporary essentialist approaches to sex and gender. For example, while Freud was clearly aware that the various essentialisms of his time had obscured certain interesting and persistent questions concerning sexuality and sexual difference, his own conflation of the phallus and the penis ultimately condemned him to share many of their blind spots. Hence, Freudian theory, while taking important steps toward a "denaturing" of sex and gender (as both Morel and Soler suggest), ultimately maintains a naive reliance on just the sort of phantasmatic grounding of reality that Lacan renders problematic.

In his own work, Lacan proposes that the fantasy-support of reality, especially where accepted notions of sex and sexuality are concerned, operates as a defense against the intrusion of the real into our everyday experience. Given this claim, it is ironic that readers of Lacan have often confused the "reality" of biological sex with his notion of the real. Under this misreading, the real is assumed to be a kind of material bedrock that either fundamentally resists symbolic inscription or is given shape through symbolic construction. However, in Lacan's formulation, sexual difference is not the manifestation of a fundamental materiality or an immutable biological difference but a function of one's position with respect to the Other. Hence, he unambiguously claims that "in the psyche, there is nothing by which the subject may situate himself as a male or female being . . . the human being always has to learn from scratch from the Other what he has to do, as man or woman" (Seminar XI, 204). Because they are inadequate to specify the real of sexual difference, and its implications for the subject's situation vis-à-vis the Other, the terms *sex* and *gender* are rarely used in Lacanian parlance. When they are referenced, *sex* is usually understood as an imaginary-symbolic construct deployed in certain contexts to mark the subject's "civil status" as a sexed subject, or else to refer to concrete sexual acts; *gender* is typically understood as a function of identification with idealized norms regarding sex. While anatomical differences are not irrelevant to the manner in which cultural ideals regarding sex and gender are transmitted and reproduced, they are not the foundation of sexual difference.

One of the more important implications of Lacan's argument that sexual difference is a function of one's position vis-à-vis the Other is that there is no stable basis for sexual complementarity or psychic harmony between masculine and feminine subjects. Morel, Salecl, and Soler all elaborate on the important consequences of Lacan's claim that there exists no unmediated, direct relationship between masculine and feminine subjects. Lacan describes the obstacle to such a relation as a function of the Other, where the Other comes between men and women in the form of a signifier; he designates this as the phallic signifier. However, rather than denoting any positive meaning (e.g., as related to cultural ideals regarding the *meaning* of phallic sexuality, etc.), the phallic signifier functions as an empty signifier that effects a "difference." This difference is not a difference between the sexes as such but the difference between the One and the not-one. In other words, the phallic signifier does not signify essential sexual difference but is an empty signifier that stands ultimately for the impossibility of signifying sex. As such, it can be understood to represent both a traumatic failure of meaning and the impossibility of ever fundamentally anchoring or positivizing the symbolic order. Revolving as it does around the signifier of the One, the symbolic also is irretrievably asymmetrical. This asymmetry marks the lack of reciprocity or harmony of structure between sexed subject positions and determines that masculine and feminine subjects relate to each *other* in terms of what they lack in relation to the *Other* (the Other here as the Other of the signifier). This asymmetry in the symbolic also illuminates Lacan's claim that sexual difference hinges on either a "having" or a "being" the phallus and, hence, that "strictly speaking, there is no symbolization of woman's sex as such" (Seminar III, 176).

In Seminar XX, Lacan relates this impossibility of signifying sexual difference to the structure of a double loss in the subject's potential for being. In his early work, he elaborates primarily on the loss correlative to the subject's accession to the symbolic. Beginning with Seminar XI, he becomes increasingly preoccupied with a logically prior loss, one he characterizes as a consequence of sexed reproduction. The loss associated with the former corresponds to what Lacan calls the subject of the signifier, and that associated with the latter to the subject of drive. In each case, however, it is not a matter of the subject losing a form of being that he or she already possessed but of retroactively losing the possibility of becoming a certain sort of being. Thus sexual difference must be understood in terms of a loss *inherent* in the structure of the subject rather than something that is imposed on the subject from the outside. It is, then, the nature of the losses constituting subjectivity as such that precludes one ever wholly becoming one's sex, ever achieving one's gender, or ever accomplishing one's sexuality. Hence, sexual difference can be understood to stand for that which forever eludes the grasp of normative symbolization. The obsessive individual and cultural reiterations of the "surface" of sexuality—the seeming reality of the sexual relationship, as it is divided into binaries such as male and female, masculine and feminine, hetero- and homosexuality, and so on—only cover over this fundamental dehiscence of the sexual subject.

## SUBJECTIVITY, KNOWLEDGE, AND JOUISSANCE

In Seminar XX, Lacan engages in a sustained interrogation of the implications of the subject's "double lack" for understanding jouissance and knowledge. Bruce Fink's, Colette Soler's ("Hysteria in Scientific Discourse"), and Slavoj Zizek's chapters present some of Lacan's most innovative interventions on these themes by first situating his account of sexuation in relation to the shifts in his conceptions of subjectivity and the Other, which can be discerned beginning in Seminar XI. Each author traces certain important nuances in Lacan's distinction between the subject of the signifier and the subject of drive; Fink, in particular, focuses on the relation between the forms of jouissance and knowledge production that Lacan associates with each. Lacan links the synthetic and universalizing tendencies of Western philosophy, religion, and science to the "phallic" attempt to make a knowledge adequate to the One. However, his development of the logic of feminine structure in Seminar XX suggests a knowledge and a jouissance "beyond the phallus"—a relation to the not-whole part of the Other that allows for what Lacan calls the "path of love." These authors discuss the implications of this Other jouissance for science, culture, and ethics.

In "Knowledge and Jouissance," Bruce Fink begins with a lucid discussion of Lacan's distinction between the subject of the signifier and the subject of drive in Seminar XI. He then links the subject of the signifier to the fantasy implicit in Antiquity's "prescientific" worldview of adequation or harmony between elements composing the world (say, form and matter), or between its governing principles (say, masculine and feminine). As Fink suggests, this subject also is characterized by a certain (phallic) jouissance, one that never quite makes good on its promise, which always comes up short in relation to the fantasy of a "whole" jouissance. This fantasy—which Fink argues is, in the end, the fantasy of copulation or "of an inscription of the sexual link" (Seminar XX, 76/82)—motivates a particular kind of knowledge formation. This is the kind of knowledge motivated by a deficiency of jouissance. However, Lacan claims that the "revolutions" modern science attributed to Copernicus[11] introduced the possibility for a kind of "knowledge" beyond fantasy, an "unknown" knowledge that can only be discerned in and through its effects. This "other" knowledge is one that Lacan describes in Seminar XX as a "reduction to letters"—that is, a reduction to the sort of formalization found in number theory, set theory, and topology—which he believed provided the basis for a nonimaginary approach to the field of the subject. Lacan associates the subject of affect, or drive, with the potential for this other form of knowledge production—the form made possible by the "decentering" effect of modern science. And while the subject of drive and feminine structure are not one and the same, the Other jouissance that Lacan suggests is possible for the feminine subject is associated in Seminar XX with this new science of the letter. Thus one finds the feminine subject as represented in the formulas of sexuation by the possibility of a jouissance sustained not in relation to object $a$ as a "stand in" for the "One" of Antiquity but, paradoxically, by a lack in the Other as real. This jouissance does not exist because it cannot be represented; it can, however, be traced in the history of its effects.

Soler's interest in "Hysteria in Scientific Discourse" intersects Fink's in its engagement with sexual difference, science, and the history of knowledge production. Rather than focusing on jouissance explicitly, however, she recounts the role played by hysteria as a structural component of shifts in knowledge, both across history and in (post)modern culture. She invokes Lacan's thesis that the hysteric's provocation can be found at the heart of the quest for knowledge from which science emerged. Soler also marks the reemergence of hysteria as a symptom paralleling—not coincidentally—the increasingly obvious cracks in the Enlightenment project manifest in Vienna between the two wars. As such, we also find hysteria at the root of the psychoanalytic desire to know. The sequelae of this intervention, this "breathing life" into science at its moments of imminent demise, are numerous. One of the most compelling, according to Soler, is the current happy intersection between science and capitalism—the universalizing tendencies of science being reinforced by capitalism's investment in the proliferation and hyper-dissemination of goods. Citing Lacan's early recognition of this paradox, Soler thus underscores how the hysteric's complaint—associated ultimately with the alienation attending the emergence of the speaking subject—can now only be compounded by the increasing instrumentalization of life. While this instrumentalization is not new, it penetrates the body of the individual and the social field more directly and completely than ever, to the detriment of a jouissance not amenable to the structure of production. This latter jouissance is antithetical to that produced by being the object of desire (i.e., by being man's symptom, what hysterics refuse). Thus Soler questions the consequences of this paradox both for the hysteric and for science. She suggests that the outcome will be overdetermined by the fact that all subjects, but most significantly women, are increasingly interpellated as universal, unisexual workers; as a result, women have greater access than ever to the phallic jouissance of "having" and producing. While not all women are hysterics and not all hysterics are women, the effects of cultural and economic shifts towards the unisexual worker decrease the Other jouissance in which the hysteric has a certain stake. Consistent with Lacan's remarks on hysteria in Seminar XX, Soler suggests that—while the analyst and the hysteric both represent the incarnation of what remains irreducible to phallic jouissance—it remains to be seen whether or not hysterics will be content with the aporia of sex that psychoanalytic science presents as a potential alternative to the phallic circuit of production and consumption.

Slavoj Zizek also is concerned with feminine jouissance, particularly in its role in subjectivization and what Lacan describes as the path of love. In "The Real of Sexual Difference," he suggests that one finds two points in Lacan's later work at which the status of the Other is significantly altered. Reading the formulas of sexuation with a particular emphasis on the illusory nature of the phallic exception and on the feminine logic of the not-whole, Zizek underscores how Lacan's interest in the real represents a passage in priority from the masculine logic of law and transgression to the feminine logic of love. Zizek's elaboration of the logic of feminine jouissance lays the groundwork for an understanding of Lacan's identification of the feminine subject as the subject *par excellence*. His exposé of feminine jouissance also clarifies the role of the real in producing what he refers to as the "deadlock" of sexual difference. By working though several examples of this deadlock—for example, Levi-Strauss' notion of the zero institution—Zizek sketches a framework that allows him to differentiate between Lacan's positing of the real dimension of the Other (and its implications for an "a-historical-ness" of sexual difference) and certain historicist critiques of Lacan (most notably that of Judith Butler);[12] this framework also allows him to distinguish between Lacan's "ethics of the real" (and its implications for ethical and political action) and common "postsecular" conflations of Lacan's ethics with Derridean- and/or Levinasian-inspired versions.[13]

Together, Zizek's, Fink's, and Soler's chapters clarify what is at stake in claiming specificity for a Lacanian response to certain questions concerning subjectivity, epistemology, and ethics dominant in contemporary interdisciplinary debates. While Lacan's emphasis on the subject's positioning vis-à-vis the Other is consistent with current interdisciplinary trends, his introduction of the subject of drive and its real Other reorients the structure of such debates significantly. It suggests that one cannot consider questions of, say, epistemology or ethics, without also considering their founding fantasies and attendant modes of jouissance. Regarding ethics, Lacan cites as a historical example the inherent despotism of Bentham's relentless and interminable cataloguing of human utility. He raises the question of the jouissance that at once motivates and eludes such a project, a question concerning the invincible optimism of the utilitarian reformer. Lacan's analysis of Bentham's project ultimately suggests that within the circuit of pleasure and pain there emerges an excess—a certain *en plus* of jouissance that cannot be reduced to utility. This is jouissance of the sort that "serves no purpose" (Seminar XX, 10/3). Lacan poses the jouissance behind Antigone's (decidedly nonutilitarian) gesture as a counterexample to the phallic jouissance implicit in Bentham's project. Zizek takes up the question of Antigone's jouissance to illustrate the specificity of Lacan's "ethics of the real," particularly in relation to contemporary debates in philosophical ethics. Lacan claims that it is only a refusal to recognize the negativity or gaps in being corresponding to gestures such as Antigone's that has allowed ethics to ground itself in ontology. In taking this position, Lacan is closely allied with philosophical positions such as Derrida's or Levinas'. However, as Zizek elaborates, contemporary articulations of Derrida's and Levinas' ethics often subtly retrieve this negativity in favor of a subject who "decides" (e.g., on a particular course of action), albeit as a response to the Other's decision "in" the subject. Zizek's Lacanian reading of Antigone's act—as one in which she does not merely relate to the Other-Thing but, in a sense, *becomes* it—underscores the specificity of the Lacanian subject's relation to the real for current work in philosophical and political ethics.

With respect to epistemology and jouissance, both Fink's and Soler's analyses suggest that modern science remains, at best, deeply ambivalent about its inaugural gesture of rejecting reality in favor of the real. Hence, we find fantasies of a "whole" jouissance alive and well in the academy and behind recent theoretical impulses as diverse as the attempts at grand synthesis in science and some of the more utopian formulations of identity politics in interdisciplinary theory. Perhaps most significantly, the recent partnership of science and capitalism referenced by Soler has produced the conditions for pursuit of the One on a hitherto unprecedented scale; the human genome project is perhaps the paradigmatic instance of this recent trend. For Soler, the question that arises in the wake of this science-capitalism merger is one concerning the role of the hysteric's provocation, specifically in its function as the real's "representative." As noted above, science has historically manifested the structure of the master's discourse, presented as a (dogmatically) metaphysical system of Truth. However, the hysteric's challenge to its integrity, and her revelation of its lack, has, paradoxically, often rejuvenated a flagging scientific enterprise, allowing for a perpetual reincarnation of science as the "whole" Truth. Ironically, this dialectic between hysteria and science also is well suited to reproducing the kind of jouisssance mobilized within increasingly globalized, capitalist modes of consumption. However, as Lacan suggested in 1975, the structure of the hysteric's discourse is closely allied with the structure of scientific discourse as alternatively constructed within quantum physics and formal mathematics—disciplines that exemplify what Lacan calls a "science of the real." The question that remains to be answered, then, is whether hysteria will be co-opted by the phallic jouissance of capitalist science or whether it will remain invested in the Other jouissance that drives the science of the real.

## THE BODY, BEING, AND THE LETTER

As one delves more deeply into Seminar XX, it becomes apparent that Lacan's reformulations of the drive, the object, and jouissance also perform a radical subversion of the classical Western binary between mind and body. Historically, most approaches to ontology, epistemology, and ethics have left this binary intact, neglecting in particular a consideration of the body's stake in knowledge. Feminist theories have by now rendered commonplace the notion that this binary is implicitly gendered and hierarchical. However, feminist theories of the body have been haunted by a related binary—that between essentialism and constructionism—and have expended significant labor in attempting to work it through. Paul Verhaeghe's, Andrew Cutrofello's, and my own chapters address the specificity of Lacan's engagement with the intransigence of these binaries, particularly via his use of number theory, set theory, topology, and other figurative means of indicating the role of the real in their subversion. Using these means, Lacan ultimately articulates what Verhaeghe calls a "nonhomologously structured" model of the subject—one that subverts both traditional notions of causality and conventional distinctions between mind and body, self and other, essential and constructed, and so on. The genesis of this alternative model is supported by Lacan's further articulation of feminine structure, particularly in its relation to the lack in the Other as real. By the end of the seminar, this development allows Lacan to adumbrate the sort of knowledge and being implied by a psychoanalytic science of the letter.

In "Lacan's Answer to the Classical Mind/Body Deadlock: Retracing Freud's *Beyond*," Paul Verhaeghe addresses Lacan's attempt in Seminar XX to move beyond the mind/body dualism of modern science and philosophy and to articulate the consequences of this move for understanding knowledge, jouissance, and the body. He focuses explicitly on the dynamics of "incarnation" of a jouissance "beyond" the phallus (i.e, what the hysteric represents). Verhaeghe illustrates—via a measured tacking back and forth between Freud and Lacan, and between texts within Lacan's oeuvre—the nonhomologous structure that Lacan produces in place of the classical binary between mind and body. Verhaeghe argues that, inspired by the topological models that confound accepted corporeal terms of "inside" and "outside" (e.g., the Möbius strip), Lacan articulates a "circular but non-reciprocal relationship" between the two terms. He invokes Lacan's formulation of the impossible but necessary relation of *tuché* and automaton as producing the retroactivity and incompleteness of this circuit from "*a* to body, to ego, to subject" to sexuation. In Seminar XX, *tuché* and automaton, correlated with the real and symbolic, respectively, are translated by Lacan into the deadlock of formalization represented by the "being" of the *letter* and the truth of the signifier.

In "The Ontological Status of Lacan's Mathematical Paradigms," Andrew Cutrofello takes up the notoriously difficult "Rings of String" chapter in

Seminar XX in order to explicate the status of the late Lacan's "mathemeatical" project. By a deceptively simple maneuvering through key moments of modern science and philosophy, Cutrofello proceeds to reconcile Lacan's seemingly contradictory claims that "[m]athematical formalization is our goal" and "[t]he analytic thing will not be mathematical." He provides a series of incisive examples of the central preoccupations of modern science, rendering the various attempts at mapping the possible relations between *aisthesis* (being) and *noesis* (thinking) as a response to anxiety over the ontological status of the sexual relationship. In so doing, Cutrofello sheds light on Lacan's interpretation of Cartesian doubt as "caused" by anxiety over the loss of the sexual relationship, this loss being implied in the shift from a science of reality to a science of the real. He claims that Cartesian science introduces a mathematical signifier whose destination is a science of the real—a destination that forces a choice between *aisthesis* and *noesis*. In its radical break with the realm of perceptible being, the Cartesian "thought experiment" produces the cogito as a being of pure *noesis*. Cutrofello ultimately invites us to frame psychoanalysis itself as the staging of a thought experiment that subjects the cogito to something wholly other. In other words, Cutrofello challenges us to think the psychoanalytic situation (and the social link it produces) as one in which something happens via a "revelation of a radical dis-affinity"—or, the emergence of an uncanny real that the subject cannot deny.

The relation between the "revelation of a radical dis-affinity" that Cutrofello invokes and the feminine subject's relation to S($\cancel{A}$) is one I explore in my chapter, "Tongues of Angels: Feminine Structure and Other Jouissance." I begin by introducing the overlapping lacks that Lacan proposes[14] to situate the subject of desire in relation to the subject of drive. In addressing the structure of drive, Lacan emphasizes the "death in life" that the advent of the subject via sexual reproduction represents. Through invoking the metaphor of meiosis— a process in which creation of "life" emerges in simultaneity with the expulsion of "dead" remainders—Lacan suggests that the subject of drive comes into being in relation to an object whose ontological status is situated somewhere between death and life, in a zone of the "undead." I mobilize this characterization of object *a* to facilitate a certain reading of the formulas of sexuation in Seminar XX—particularly as they are relevant in understanding Lacan's situation of the feminine subject as radically Other in relation to man, and in the feminine subject's relation to S($\cancel{A}$). Lacan claims that exploring the implications of the "not-whole" of feminine structure might put us on a path toward understanding how "that which until now has only been a fault (*faille*) or gap in jouissance could be realized" (Seminar XX, 14/8). With this in mind, I suggest several implications of his engagement with the figures of the *être-ange* (angel-being) and the spider web—figures he uses to suggest the structure of such a "real-ization." These implications allow for a further articulation of the feminine subject's relation to the signifier of the lack in the Other, a relation that—again following Lacan's lead—might be characterized as the space of *poesis*, or the production of a knowledge of the letter.

In their shared interest in Lacan's intervention into the radical gap that Descartes introduced between truth and being, Verhaeghe's, Cutrofello's, and my own chapters each speak to a dimension of Lacan's subversion of the mind/body binary historically sustained by this gap. Traditionally, Descartes' dualism has been understood as an especially flagrant instance of the body's denigration in Western philosophy. According to Lacan, however, in its disassociation with the "reality" of the body (as sensing and as an object of perception) and its retreat into the realm of pure thought, the Cartesian cogito actually opens up a space within which the *real* of the body (and, hence, a different sort of "being") might emerge.

As Cutrofello underscores, the split between being and truth can be seen as an attempt by modern science to deal with its anxiety over the ontological status of the sexual relationship. In Descartes' assertion of the heteronomy of this split, however, Lacan reads a certain recognition that, appropos of sexual difference, "when one gives rise to two, there is never a return. They don't revert to making one again, even if it is a new one" (Seminar XX, 79/86). Hence, staking his claim with the mathematical signifier introduced by Descartes, and with the impossibility of the sexual relationship with which it is coextensive, Lacan takes up the question of the cogito's implications for the subject of psychoanalysis. In Seminar XI, Lacan reads the split between *aisthesis* and *noesis* not as a dualism but in terms of an internal splitting produced by a forced choice between the two. In other words, the loss in being implied by the repudiation of the link between being and truth produces an inherently divided subject, albeit a subject divided in one of two possible ways. Here (Seminar XI) Lacan articulates the forced choice between being and truth as one that comes down on the side of thought; access to the realm in which "we can permit everything as a hypothesis of truth" (Seminar XI, 36) is paid for by a loss in being.[15] However, in Seminar XIV (1966–1967, unpublished), Lacan suggests that the cogito also can come down on the side of being, where the choice of being necessitates the exile of thought to the unconscious.

As Zizek elaborates elsewhere,[16] these two ways of reading the split can be mapped onto Lacan's formulas of masculine and feminine structure. Ironically, the properly Cartesian choice is ultimately the latter one; the rendering of the cogito as a thinking substance, as *res cogitans*, can be read as a "saving" of the subject by choosing existence as thinking "being" ("I am, therefore it thinks"). This corresponds to Lacan's formula for masculine structure, where the subject exists within the realm of the symbolic, but only on the basis of an exception that founds it—an exception that is itself not subject to symbolic law. The former version of the cogito, the choice of thinking over being, corresponds to feminine structure. In this instance, thinking is not substantialized but represents the vacant point of the pure "I think" ("I think, therefore it ex-sists").

Feminine structure is constituted not on the basis of an exception to the symbolic but on the basis of the feminine subject being in the symbolic "altogether"; as Lacan states, "[s]he is *not* not at all there. She is there in full" (Seminar XX, 71/77). Hence, through her identification with the contingency of the signifier, the feminine subject chooses thought over existence—or, in other words, over the sort of being to be had within the symbolic order.

From this vantage point, we can understand Lacan's gradual working through of the formulas of sexuation in Seminar XX as marking a return of his preoccupation with the cogito as an inaugural moment in the science of the real. In linking masculine structure to the Other of the signifier, Lacan suggests that it remains limited to the truth that can be articulated via the signifier, a truth always only half told and which tends toward a reduction of knowledge to the One. Lacan links feminine structure, on the other hand, to its exclusion from the "reality" of being (she "does not exist"), as well as to an identification with the signifier in its radically contingent, rather than exceptional, character. As Verhaeghe notes, this articulation of feminine structure simultaneously marks the trajectory in Seminar XX of a radical alteration in Lacan's understanding of *being* and the body.

In addressing himself to the question of the body's being, Lacan wants to avoid the imaginary pitfalls that have led philosophy and science to ground the body in a Being "behind" being. Hence, while he recognizes that "in point of fact everything called philosophy has to this day hung by this slender thread—that there is an order other than that along which the body thinks it moves," he also suggests that "the body is no more explained for all that" (*Feminine Sexuality*, 163–64). Lacan takes up the question of this "other" order of the body with his account of feminine structure. As conditioned by her identification with the contingency of the signifier, the feminine subject "ex-sists" with respect to the signifier of the One. It is in this very ex-sistence, however, that Lacan "locates" another sort of being, a being that requires, not One, but infinity (Seminar XX, 15/10). This being, while it is material and, as such, could be said to be of the body, ex-sists in relation to the material-ized, sexualized body—in other words, the body as signified. Lacan is here indicating that the shape and consistency given to the body (as a "lived" corporeal unity, extended across time) via the imaginary and symbolic are insufficient to fully account for the body. This not-whole of the (sexualized) body is what Lacan suggestively calls the *encore* of the *en-corps*, the enjoying substance that comes from beyond the signifier and its repetitive circuit of phallic jouissance. As I elaborate in my chapter, the "place" of this en-corps cannot be inscribed within a Euclidean geometric frame and must be figured through the elliptical geometric and topological means that Lacan deploys in Seminar XX to trace the effects of the real in the constitution of the body. These alternative means of figuration allow Lacan to relate the en-corps to the "being" of the letter—not in its signifying capacity but in its "signifierness" (Seminar XX, 67/71). In its signifierness, the letter manifests traces of a certain, Other jouissance; while in and of itself, the letter does not signify anything about this jouissance—"[one should not] too quickly associate its function with so-called messages"—it nevertheless has effects . . . it "reproduces, but never the same, never the same being of knowledge" (Seminar XX, 89/97). In other words, the letter does not transmit a sexualized knowledge of this jouissance but, like the germ cell or the atom, produces what can be called "being effects."

As Lacan suggests, "[W]riting is thus a trace in which an effect of language can be read. This is what happens when you scribble something. I certainly don't deprive myself of doing so, for that is how I prepare what I have to say" (Seminar XX, 110/121). It is in a similar spirit, then, that the following chapters are offered—as manifestations of a certain "cross-sighted" reading between the signifier and the letter, articulation and writing, and truth and being. It is our hope that, beyond what they offer of what can be said about Lacan's Seminar XX, they might also engender certain . . . effects.

## NOTES

1. See Juliet Mitchell and Jacqueline Rose, eds., *Feminine Sexuality: Jacques Lacan and the École Freudienne*, trans. J. Rose (New York: W. W. Norton & Co., 1982).

2. See *The Seminar, Book XX, Encore, On Feminine Sexuality: The Limits of Love and Knowledge*, trans. Bruce Fink (New York: W. W. Norton & Co., 1998). All page references to Seminar XX in this chapter are first to the French edition (Paris: Seuil, 1975) and then to the English translation.

3. There are eleven chapters in the Seminar.

4. See "Guiding Remarks for a Convention on Feminine Sexuality" and "Signification of the Phallus," *Feminine Sexuality: Jacques Lacan and the École Freudienne*, trans. J. Rose (New York: W. W. Norton & Co., 1982).

5. See "L'Etourdit," *Scilicet* 4 (1973), pp. 5–52, and Seminar XX.

6. In a related vein, Lacan often cautions his audience about the imaginary pitfalls of secondary elaboration, the ensnarements awaiting those who fixate on the knowledge contained "in" language rather than on the effects of language on the subject of jouissance.

7. Luce Irigaray published two essays in direct response to *Encore*, "Cosí Fan Tutti" and "The 'Mechanics' of Fluids." They are among her more challenging writings on Lacanian psychoanalysis and require the sort of familiarity with *Encore* not common among Anglophone readers. They are translated and published together in *This Sex Which Is Not One*, trans. C. Porter and C. Burke (Ithaca, N.Y.: Cornell University Press, 1985).

8. All references to *Écrits* here are first to the French edition (Paris: Seuil, 1966) and then to the English translation, trans. Alan Sheridan (New York: Norton, 1977).

9. See Michael Groden and Martin Kreiswirth, eds., "Jacques Lacan," *The Johns Hopkins Guide to Literary Theory and Criticism* (Baltimore: Johns Hopkins University Press, 1994), p. 453.

10. See "Guiding Remarks for a Convention on Feminine Sexuality" and "Signification of the Phallus," *Feminine Sexuality: Jacques Lacan and the École Freudienne*, trans. J. Rose (New York: W. W. Norton & Co., 1982).

11. Lacan credits Kepler instead.

12. See, for example, "Arguing with the Real," in *Bodies That Matter* (New York: Routledge, 1993), pp. 187–222 and *The Psychic Life of Power* (Stanford: Stanford University Press, 1997).

13. See, for example, Simon Critchley's "*Das Ding*: Lacan and Levinas" pp. 198–216 and "The Original Traumatism: Levinas and Psychoanalysis," pp. 183–197 in his *Ethics, Politics, Subjectivity* (New York: Verso, 1999).

14. See *Seminar XI, The Four Fundamental Concepts of Psychoanalysis* (New York: W. W. Norton & Co, 1978), p. 205.

15. See also Cutrofello's discussion of Lacan's analysis of the cogito's implications for the subject in this book.

16. Slavoj Zizek, *Tarrying with the Negative: Kant, Hegel, and the Critique of Ideology* (Durham: Duke University Press, 1993), p. 59.

# KNOWLEDGE AND JOUISSANCE

*Bruce Fink*

Psychoanalysis shares a problem with a number of the social sciences and humanities, though this may not be immediately apparent.[1] Psychoanalysts, in their work with patients, often find that, despite myriad interpretations and explanations—which both analyst and analysand may find convincing, and even inspired—the patients' symptoms do not go away. A purely linguistic or interpretative analysis of the events and experiences surrounding the formation of the symptom does not suffice to eliminate it.

Freud noticed this early on in his work and even formalized it initially by saying that analysis falls into two stages: one stage in which the analyst presents the patient with fine explanations of her symptoms, and a second in which change finally occurs, the patient taking up the material of her own analysis herself. Later, Freud formulated the problem differently, in terms of what he called "an economic factor": a powerful force must be holding the patient's symptom in place—the patient must be deriving considerable satisfaction from it (even if it is, as Freud qualifies it, a "substitute" satisfaction).

This brings up the fundamental distinction that Freud makes between representation and affect. For example, if we hypnotize a patient, we can elicit all kinds of representations from him—we can get him to remember the most minute details of events that he cannot remember at all while awake, we can get him to put into words many aspects of his history—but often nothing changes. When we wake him up from hypnosis, he remembers nothing more than before, and the symptoms that seem to be tied to those events often remain intact. It is only when the patient is able to articulate his history and *feel something* at the same time—some emotion or affect—that change occurs.

Representation without affect is thus sterile. This is one of the reasons for the sterility of so-called "self-analysis": you tell yourself lovely stories about the past, you analyze your dreams and fantasies to yourself or on paper, but nothing happens, nothing changes. It is all very informative and interesting; you remember all kinds of things about your past, but there is no metamorphosis. Affect is rarely brought into play without the presence of another person to whom you address all of these thoughts, dreams, and fantasies.

Lacan translates Freud's fundamental distinction between representation and affect as the distinction between language and libido, between signifier and jouissance, and his whole discussion of the subject—of who or what the subject is in psychoanalysis—has to do with this fundamental distinction or disjunction.

Freud had already grappled with where to locate representation and affect. He came up with various overlapping topographies of the mind, assigning representation to the ego and affect to the id, affect being discharged through the drives said to be part and parcel of the id. The superego did not quite fit, however, given its use of representations—imperatives, critiques, and so on—combined with a stern moral tone suggesting that the superego has a little too much fun when it berates the ego. Freud's earlier attempt to divide up the mind had left affect out of the picture altogether: the conscious-preconscious-unconscious topography suggests that representations can be found at all three levels, but what of affect? Freud is led here, inconsistently, I would argue, to suggest that affects can be unconscious, whereas most of his theoretical work goes in the direction of saying that only a representation can be unconscious.[2]

We might say that Lacan polarizes the representation/affect opposition more explicitly than Freud, though it is not always indicated as such in his work. While Lacan talks about *the* subject, we might say—following Jacques-Alain Miller's articulation in his seminar "Donc" (1993–1994)—that there are actually two subjects in Lacan's work: the subject of the signifier and the subject of jouissance.[3] Or at least two faces of the subject.

The subject of the signifier is what might be called the "Lévi-Straussian subject," in that this subject contains knowledge or acts on knowledge without having any idea that he is doing so. You ask him why he built a hut in his village in such and such a place, and the answer he gives seems to have nothing to do with the fundamental oppositions that structure his world and effectively order his village's layout. In other words, the "Lévi-Straussian subject" lives and acts on the basis of a knowledge he does not know, of which he is unaware. It lives him, in a sense. It is found in him without our having to rely on what he is consciously aware of.

This is the same kind of knowledge discovered via hypnosis, and in the end it seems not to require a subject at all, in the usual sense of the term. It is what Lacan, in "Subversion of the Subject and Dialectic of Desire" (1960), calls the subject of the combinatory: there is a combinatory of oppositions provided by the person's language, family, and society, and that combinatory functions (*Écrits*, 806).[4] In "Science and Truth" (1965), Lacan refers to this subject as the "subject of science" (ibid., 862), the subject that can be studied by science, and claims, paradoxically, that "the subject upon which we operate in psychoanalysis can only be the subject of science" (ibid., 858): the pure subject of the combinatory, the pure subject of language. (This is the strictly positional subject of game theory, the subject that falls under the "conjectural sciences.")

This claim is a bit disingenuous, for while it is true that psychoanalysis relies only on language to achieve the effects it seeks—language being its only medium—it nevertheless seeks to have an effect on affect, on the subject as affect, libido, or jouissance. One of the difficulties one encounters in reading Lacan's work is that he rarely specifies which subject he's talking about at any one time, preferring to slip surreptitiously from one meaning to the other. I would suggest that, in "Science and Truth," when Lacan talks about the "object," he is referring to the subject as affect, whereas when he talks about the "subject," he means the subject as structure, as the pure subject of the combinatory.

Thus at the outset here I want to distinguish between the subject of the signifier and the subject of the drives (or the subject as jouissance).

The first thing to be noted is that it is much easier to deal with the first than with the second. The second *n'est pas commode*, is not easy to get a handle on. This led many post–Freudian analysts to look for other ways of dealing with what we might call the J-factor, the jouissance factor. (Wilhelm Reich, at a certain stage of his work, figured, "Why not just deal with it directly, by direct contact with the patient's body? Why bother to work it out via speech?"

Contemporary cognitive-behavioral approaches to psychology can probably be understood as restricting their attention to the first as opposed to the second and, indeed, many cognitive-behavioral psychologists seem not to comprehend even intuitively that they are missing something: everything is supposed to be rational, there being no need for, and certainly no room for, anything else in their system. They seek out and "correct" or destroy "irrational beliefs." I am not saying this is true of all of them, but in my experience it is true of many cognitive-behavioral therapies.

Linguistics—that newborn science that Lacan was so infatuated with in the 1950s, thinking it could serve at the outset as a model for the kind of scientificity proper to psychoanalysis, in other words, that psychoanalysis could become a science along the lines of a science such as linguistics—restricts its attention to the subject of the signifier. The same is true of all structuralist discourses: the structuralist project, as Lacan himself shows in some of his work from the 1950s, is to draw knowledge out of the pure subject of the signifier, to elicit and map the knowledge inscribed therein.

In the early 1970s, Lacan suggests a new term for what he himself does with language, for what he does is not the same as linguistics: he calls it "linguistricks" (Seminar XX, 20/15).[5] He does not draw out the knowledge contained in language, in grammar and idioms, for example; he uses language to have effects on something other than the pure subject of the signifier.

## SPEECH

Now there must be some convergence or overlap between the subject of the signifier and the subject of jouissance if changes can be wrought in the second via the first. Lacan notices early on that the two come together in speech. Speech relies on the system of signifiers (or simply on "the signifier," as he is wont to say), borrowing its lexicon and grammar from it, and yet speech requires something else: enunciation. It has to be enunciated, and there is a bodily component that thus gets introduced: breathing and all of the movements of the jaw, tongue, and so on required for the production of speech.[6]

Linguistics can study and account for the subject of the enunciated or subject of the statement—for example, "I" in the sentence "I think so"—that is known in linguistics as the "shifter," and it notes the difference between the subject of the statement and the enunciating subject. For example, if, repeating Freud, I say, "Psychoanalysis is an impossible profession," the subject of the statement is "psychoanalysis," whereas Bruce Fink is the enunciating subject. Linguistics is forced to take cognizance of that distinction.

But linguistics does not, it seems to me, deal with the enunciating subject per se. The enunciating subject is the one who may take pleasure in speaking, or find it painful to speak, or who may make a slip while speaking. The enunciating subject is the one who may let slip something that is revealing as to his or her feelings, desires, or pleasures.

Thus speech is one of the places these two subjects collide.

I mentioned earlier that psychoanalysis shares a problem with a number of the social sciences, and before I go any further into my discussion of Lacan here, I want to suggest what I, from my own amateurish perspective, see this common ground to be. It strikes me, for example, that these same two subjects collide in economics on the stock market floor. Can we not equate the subject of the signifier with the supposedly "rational" economic subject of the market, *homo œconomicus*? Who then is the subject of jouissance? Is it not the subject who is taxed by U.S. Federal Reserve Chairman Alan Greenspan "with irrational exuberance" for bidding up stock prices "beyond all reason"? "Irrational exuberance" is an expression that has been repeated thousands of times in the media since December of 1997 when Greenspan first said it, and I would suggest that the very number of times it has been reiterated indicates that "irrational exuberance" is the very name of jouissance in the economic arena, the potlatch of our times—probably not the only potlatch, of course, but a significant one all the same.

If speech is where the two subjects collide or come together in psychoanalysis, it also is because psychoanalysis constitutes itself as a speech situation, that is, a situation in which most other forms of action are excluded at the outset. It is not a group situation, in which the mass behavior of groups might have to be taken into account—mass hysteria, rioting, pillaging, stock buying, and so on (unless waiting room behavior is, for some reason, considered part and parcel of the analytic situation itself).

## LACAN'S EARLY WORK REVISITED

In Lacan's very first model or graph of the analytic situation, the L Schema—based on a model provided in Lévi-Strauss' *Structural Anthropology*[7]—Lacan depicts the two subjects that I have been talking about as being at loggerheads (I am simplifying it here):

FIGURE 1.1
**Simplified L Schema**

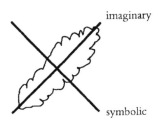

imaginary

symbolic

The imaginary register, at this point in Lacan's work, corresponds to the subject's jealous rage, envy, and rivalry. It is tantamount to what Lacan later calls the subject's "jealouissance" (Seminar XX, 91/100), combining "jealousy" and "jouissance." The idea, at that stage, was that through speech, jealouissance could be dissipated, worked through, resolved—in a word, eliminated. In the collision between the subject of the signifier and the subject of jouissance, the latter had to be gotten rid of. The latter got in the way of the former, providing a kind of interference for the former.

In 1960, in "Subversion of the Subject," Lacan provides a complex "Graph of Desire" in which we see the advent of the subject in language in the lower half of the graph and its intersection with jouissance at the top of the graph.

FIGURE 1.2
**Simplified Graph of Desire**

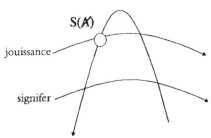

$S(\cancel{A})$

jouissance

signifer

The subject follows a pathway starting from the bottom right-hand corner and intersects first the signifying chain (bottom arrow) and then jouissance (top arrow). That second intersection is fraught with trouble, for the first thing the subject encounters there is that there is no signifier that can account for or answer for his or her jouissance: S($\not{A}$). One's jouissance is without rhyme or reason, one might say.

One finds oneself inhabited by drives with no why or wherefore. It is not my intention to go into the complexities of this encounter here, since I have done so elsewhere;[8] the important point is that the subject's predicament between the signifier (lower level) and jouissance (upper level) is no picnic, as it is depicted by Lacan: there is no sort of easy alliance between them.

I am not by any means leading up to some way in which to reconcile these two subjects, or hoping to introduce any particular formulation that shows how the two can be made to get along, so to speak. It is obvious that in psychoanalysis, we deal with the subject of jouissance through the medium of speech, and that we attempt to use speech in ways that bring about some sort of change when it comes to the jouissance of symptoms that the analysand complains of.

But since this chapter is not intended to be primarily clinical, that is not the direction I will take here. I mention it simply because it seems to me that *many* other fields in the humanities and social sciences have to come to terms with these *two* faces of the subject in theory building and praxis—no doubt in different ways than psychoanalysis, due to the different aims that inform each field.[9] Having sketched out the two different subjects at stake in much of Lacan's work, the subject of the signifier and the subject of jouissance, let me turn now to knowledge insofar as it is associated with the first of these subjects.

## KNOWLEDGE IN A PRESCIENTIFIC CONTEXT

Over the course of at least twenty years, Lacan focuses on what might be called a prescientific type of knowledge and attempts to distinguish it from knowledge in a modern scientific context. That prescientific type of knowledge is associated by Lacan with Aristotelian science, a type of science that precedes the shifts often referred to as the Copernican revolution, though they were not made by Copernicus himself.

Now why does Lacan focus on that and come back to it again and again in an almost obsessive sort of way? Is it not a moot point, of interest only to the history of science? Is Lacan a closet historian in his nonanalytic moments?

I think Lacan's motive here is that psychoanalysis has had a difficult time detaching itself from both philosophy and psychology, both in the public mind and in the minds of analysts, and it keeps slipping into all kinds of prescientific constructs, all kinds of simplistic forms of pseudo-science and age-old philosophical notions. If psychoanalysis is to be something more credible than modern psychology—which leads to a proliferation of nosological categories as glorious as "imagined ugliness disorder" (known as Body Dismorphic Disorder in the Diagnostic and Statistical Manual of Mental Disorders IV)—then it has to examine what science is all about, not simply what people think it is all about.

Modern science, for example, is ostensibly about measurement and the production of "hard facts," and thus virtually the entire American psychological establishment has enlisted itself in the production of measures and statistics of all kinds.

But is that the kind of scientificity that psychoanalysis can hope to achieve or even wish to achieve? The *APA Monitor*, the main organ of the American Psychological Association, occasionally lists which aspects of Freud's theories have been borne out by empirical research: of course, when we consider what they have reduced Freud's theories to in order to test them, and then examine the research design that they have come up with to test such watered-down theories, we may well wonder whether the supposed confirmations are of any more value than the alleged refutations!

According to Lacan, this is not at all the kind of scientificity at which psychoanalysis must aim: to his mind, psychoanalysis is not currently a science, and it is not by going in that direction that it will become one. "It is not what is measured in science that is important, contrary to what people think" (Seminar XX, 116/128). We shall see what he thinks *is* important in science in a moment.

But first let us turn to Lacan's comments about Antiquity's view of knowledge. I do not profess to be an expert on Antiquity or the history of science in any sense; I simply want to summarize what I think Lacan's main points are here and why they are pertinent to psychoanalysis.

Antiquity's view of the world is based on a fantasy, Lacan suggests, the fantasy of a preexisting harmony between mind (*nous*) and the world (Seminar XX, 116/128), between what man thinks and the world he thinks about, between the relations between the words with which he talks about the world and the relations existing in the world itself.

Modern science has rather decisively broken with this notion, presuming, if anything, the inadequacy of our preexisting language to characterize nature and the need for new concepts, new words, and new formulations. And yet, curiously enough, in the psychoanalytic journals, we find articles by the likes of Jules H. Massermann ("Language, Behaviour and Dynamic Psychiatry," *International Journal of Psycho-analysis* XXV, 1–2) [1944]: 1–8), who discovers, according to Lacan, "with an unequaled naïveté, the verbatim correspondence of the grammatical categories of his childhood to relations found in reality" (*Écrits*, 274). In other words, in the middle of the twentieth century, one finds an unquestioning approach to language and the categories and relations it provides in studies produced by analysts. This most prescientific of presumptions is still found in much of psychology today.[10]

Now the fantasy that characterized Antiquity's view of the world goes quite far, according to Lacan: it is—and I do not think he was the first to say so—all about copulation (Seminar XX, 76/82), all an elaborate metaphor for relations between the sexes. Form penetrates or inseminates matter; form is active and matter passive; there *is* a relationship, a fundamental relationship, between form and matter, active and passive, the male principle and the female principle. All knowledge at that time, participated, in Lacan's words, "in the fantasy of an inscription of the sexual link" (Seminar XX, 76/82), in the fantasy that there is such a thing as a sexual relationship, and that this link or relationship is verified all around us. The relation between knowledge and the world was consubstantial with a fantasy of copulation.

Surely no such fantasy could be at work in psychoanalysis today! But the fact is, if there is one primordial fantasy at work in psychoanalysis today it is that a harmonious relationship between the sexes *must* be possible. This view is based on what is thought to be a teleological perspective in Freud's work, a teleology that supposedly grows out of the "progression" of libidinal stages known as the oral, anal, and genital stages. Whereas in the oral and anal stages, the child relates to partial objects, not to another person as a whole, in the genital stage, post–Freudian analysts have claimed that the child relates to another person as a whole person, not as a collection of partial objects.

A thick volume was devoted to such notions in France in the mid-1950s, *La psychanalyse d'aujourd'hui* (Paris: Presses Universitaires de France, 1956), in which a whole generation of analysts put forward the idea that when one successfully reaches the genital stage, a perfectly harmonious state is reached in which one takes one's sexual partner as a subject, not an object, as a Kantian end-in-himself or herself, not as a means to an end. And the crowning achievement of this stage is that one becomes what they call "oblative"—truly altruistic, that is, capable of doing things for another person without any thought of the advantages it may bring to oneself.

Had that generation of analysts ever seen anything of the sort? It would be hard to believe. Nevertheless, those analysts did not hesitate to postulate such a perfect state of harmony between the sexes and the total elimination of narcissism and selfishness, and to push genital relations as selfless and oral and anal relations as selfish in their work with their analysands. Even though no one had ever seen such a thing, *it had to exist.*

In other words, it was yet another fantasy, distorting psychoanalytic theory and practice. (I doubt that anyone needs to be reminded that a similar fantasy is at work in contemporary psychology, at least in its most popular forms: the by-now absolute best-selling pop psychology book of all times, *Men Are from Mars, Women Are from Venus*. The title itself seems promising, suggesting that there is *nothing that predestines men and women for complementary relations*. But everything in the book after the first two chapters is designed to help the reader overcome difference and establish *the One that has to be*, the One that the age-old fantasy requires.)

Lacan's goal is to eliminate all such fantasies from psychoanalytic theory and practice. That is, of course, easier said than done, which is precisely why the study of the history of science takes on such great importance in any field that would like to become scientific at some point up the road, purging itself of unscientific elements—if one does not know the history of one's field, one is likely to repeat it.

The fantasy of harmony between the sexes has a long and distinguished lineage, insofar as we can trace it back to at least Plato's *Symposium*, where we see Aristophanes put forward the view that once we were all spherical beings lacking in nothing, but Zeus split us in two, and now we are all in search of our other half. We divided beings yearn to be grafted back together, failing which we at least find relief in each other's arms (thanks to Zeus having taken pity on us, turning our private parts around to the inside). As Aristophanes says, "Love thus seeks to refind our early estate, endeavoring to combine two into one and heal the human sore" (Loeb edition, 1967, 141). Love is what can make good the primordial split, and harmony can be achieved thereby.

A belief in a possible harmony not only at some primordially lost moment in human history (garden of Eden [phylogenesis]) or individual time (mother-child relation [ontogenesis]) but *now* can be found in contemporary Jungian psychology in the West and in certain Chinese religions in the East (e.g., in the notion of Yin and Yang).

Aristophanes' image of us as originally spherical beings also points to the sphere as the shape that was considered most perfect, most harmonious, lacking in nothing. A great deal of ancient cosmology and astronomy up until Kepler's time was based on the fantasy of the perfection of the sphere, and much "scientific" work was devoted to *saving the truth* (*salva veritate*) by showing how the noncircular phenomena could be explained on the basis of movement in accordance with that shape of shapes, the circle. Epicycles were employed even by Copernicus, and thus the Copernican revolution was not as Copernican as all that. All Copernicus said was, if we put the sun at the center of the world, we can simplify the calculations—which in that case meant something like reducing the number of epicycles from sixty to thirty.

According to Lacan, it is not such a move, which keeps entirely intact the notions of center and periphery, that can constitute a revolution: things keep revolving just as before. It is the introduction by Kepler of a not so perfect shape, the ellipse, that shakes things up a bit, problematizing the notion of the center. The still more important move after that, as Lacan sees it, is the idea that if a planet moves toward a point (a focus) that is empty, it is not so easy to describe that as turning or circling, as it had been called in the past: perhaps it is something more like falling. This is where Newton comes in. Instead of saying what everyone else had been saying for millennia—"it turns"—Newton says, "it falls."

Despite this Newtonian revolution, Lacan claims that for most of us, our "world view . . . remains perfectly spherical" (Seminar XX, 42/42). Despite the Freudian revolution that removes consciousness from the center of our view of ourselves, it ineluctably slips back to the center, or a center is ineluctably reestablished somewhere. The "decentering" psychoanalysis requires is difficult to sustain, Lacan says (Seminar XX, 42/42), and analysts keep slipping back into the old center/periphery way of thinking. Hence the need for another "subversion," the Lacanian subversion.

One of the main points of "Subversion of the Subject" is that the subject is *not* someone who knows but rather someone who does not know. Despite Freud's emphasis on the unconscious, on a knowledge known unbeknownst to the conscious, thinking subject—that is, the ego—despite Freud's emphasis on a knowledge that is inscribed, registered, recorded somewhere, but that is not, strictly speaking, known by anyone, analysts have reverted to the idea of a conscious self: an ego endowed with synthetic functions, an ego that plays an active role in "integrating reality" and mediating between the tempestuous drives of the id and the severe moral strictures of the superego—in a word, an agent imbued with intentionality and efficacy (a notion of the ego found primarily in Freud's later works).

The radicality of Freud's initial move has been lost or covered over, and it is difficult to keep such fantasies from sneaking in the back door. Lacan suggests that the importance of the unknowing subject is found virtually every step of the way in Freud's work. Why, Lacan asks, of all the ancient myths in which a man kills his father and sleeps with his mother known at Freud's time—and there were apparently quite a number of them—did Freud chose Oedipus? His answer: because *Oedipus did not know he had done those things* (Seminar VIII, 122). Oedipus was thus a perfect model for the unknowing subject, for a subject who acts without knowing why, in any conscious sense of the word "knowing." From the vantage point of psychoanalysis, "There's no such thing as a knowing subject" (Seminar XX, 114/126), says Lacan.

## KNOWLEDGE AND THE WHOLE

There seems to be something incredibly compelling to us about the visual realm and the images we encounter in that realm: the image of the circle (or at least of the egg or ellipse) returns to haunt us even in Saussure's model of the sign, to turn for a moment to other discourses than that of psychoanalysis.

**FIGURE 1.3**
**The Saussurian Sign**

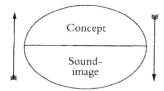

According to Saussure, the signifier and the signified, the sound-image and the concept, are indissolubly tied together. As Saussure says, "the two elements [concept (signified) and sound-image (signifier)] are *intimately united*";[11] they seem, in the image he provides for the sign, to form a whole. This is an encapsulated sign, a sign in which the signifier and signified do not diverge dangerously or uncontrollably, forming instead a Yin-Yang-like configuration. I am leaving out here the complexities that stem from the multiple relations among different signs in order to focus on this way of conceptualizing, visualizing, or representing the sign itself.

Lacan begins his forays into linguistics by subverting the Saussurian sign: there is no harmonious, totalizing relationship between signifier and signified, he says. The signifier dominates the signified, and there is a genuine barrier between the two that abolishes the reciprocal arrows that Saussure provides, suggesting a kind of mutuality or possibility that each order may have comparable effects on the other. Lacan subverts the sign in that way already in "Instance of the Letter" (1956)[12] and takes that subversion further still in the 1970s, repeatedly emphasizing the barrier or bar between the two realms and the fact that the signifier creates the signified, brings the signified into being (Seminar XX, 35/34). He strives to dissipate the hold that Saussure's image of the sign has on us.

When Lacan takes up the theme of history, it is clear that he objects to Hegel's attempt to find some sort of totalizing meaning or teleology in history. Lacan is generally suspicious of the whole and is ever pointing to the hole in every whole, to the gap in every psychoanalytic theory that attempts to account for everything, whether to explain the whole of the patient's world or to reduce all of psychoanalytic experience to, say, a relationship between two bodies (in a "two-body psychology") or to a "communication situation."

Psychoanalysts seem to have a fatal attraction to such totalizing explanations, but they are probably not alone in that regard. Even in a field as abstract and seemingly free of the seduction of images and the imaginary as modern physics, there is an increasing interest, it seems, in "theories of everything," a "unified field theory" that would take into account or account for all forces known and knowable. That strikes me as quite fanciful, as involving a view of scientific knowledge based on an image like that of the sphere—even if it is an n-dimensional sphere—as opposed to an image based on a Klein bottle, say, or a Möbius strip.

Which is, in fact, at least one of the reasons Lacan introduces such images in his work in the early 1960s: to encourage his audience to stop thinking in terms of circles and spheres, and to think instead in terms of surfaces that are less easily graspable in terms of categories such as inside and outside, front side and back side, body and orifice (see especially Seminar IX). The notion of the world as constituting a whole, Lacan says, is based on "a view, a gaze, or an imaginary hold" (Seminar XX, 43/43), a view of a sphere from the outside, as it were—as though the world were over to one side, and we were here looking at it from *some privileged outside point*. But are we on the inside or the outside of a Möbius strip? It is more difficult to situate oneself in terms of some sort of

exteriority when such surfaces are taken as models, yet even those surfaces remain images and keep psychoanalysis rooted in the imaginary. Even the knots
Lacan introduces in Seminar XX, some twelve years later, partake of the visual,
though they are perhaps still harder to picture in the mind.

Lacan, in his attempt to get us to leave behind the visual, is led to the
letter. If Kepler shook us out of our old Copernican ways of thinking by introducing the ellipse, Newton took us further still by introducing a kind of
writing:

$$F = g\,\frac{mm'}{d^2}.$$

This, according to Lacan, "is what rips us away from the imaginary function"
(Seminar XX, 43/43).

## FORMALIZATION WITHOUT MATHEMATIZATION

One way beyond fantasy is the reduction to letters. Indeed, in Seminar XX,
Lacan says, "Nothing seems to better constitute the horizon of analytic discourse than the use made of the letter by mathematics" (Seminar XX, 44/44);
note that in mathematics, many of the letters do not have the kinds of meanings they have even in physics, where $m$ stands for mass. Mathematicians such as
Bertrand Russell have been quoted as saying that the letters they use have no
meaning, and to be devoid of meaning is to be devoid of the imaginary (as
Lacan says, "meaning is imaginary," Seminar III, 65).

While Lacan ultimately concludes that, "The analytic thing will not be
mathematical" (Seminar XX, 105/117), he nevertheless spends many years
attempting to provide symbols—which he refers to as mathemes—with which
to summarize and formalize psychoanalytic theory: $, a, i(a), A, ($ ◊ a), ($ ◊ D),
S(A), Φ, and so on. It is in part an attempt to formulate certain structures in as
rigorous a manner as analysis is currently able to. The symbols he introduces
have nothing to do with measurement and thus cannot be replaced by numbers, as in Newton's formula for force and gravitation. And yet, when one is
familiar with their multiple meanings, they seem to summarize a good deal of
theorization in a very condensed form. Lacan's goal here does not seem to be
to provide a mathematization of psychoanalysis but rather a formalization. Formalization seems, at least at this stage of Lacan's work, to be a possible way of
moving toward scientificity and is what Lacan finds most important about
science—far more important than measurement.

In physics, formalization allowed theorists an independent field of specu-
lation: one could play with the formulas themselves and work out all of their
interrelations, without having the slightest idea what the new configurations
meant or implied. One could make certain assumptions not because they made
any sort of intuitive sense but simply because they simplified equations; those

assumptions could then be tested through experimentation. But the formalization itself allowed for new breakthroughs; it gave physicists *a basis for a nonintuitive, nonimage based, nonimaginary approach to their field*. Indeed, modern physics became so far removed from any intuitive understanding of the phenomena supposedly under investigation that, rather than new theoretical advances being designed to explain or account for the phenomena, often it took time to think of what never before noticed phenomena might in fact validate the theories. To give an example from my limited knowledge of the development of physics, no one had ever noticed that the sun bends the light that comes to us from Venus until modern physics posited the matter-like nature of photons and the sun's gravitational pull on them. If I am not mistaken, I believe that there are still aspects of Einstein's theories that have yet to be tested.

Obviously there is no such formalization of psychoanalysis in the offing that would allow for such an independent basis of theorization, but Lacan situates it at the horizon of a form of psychoanalysis that would like to become scientific. How such a formalization could function independently if it did not simultaneously involve mathematization is hard to say, but he seems to think that set theory provides a model for *formalization without mathematization*, set theory being a kind of logic that can be used to generate many different areas of mathematics.

One of the paradoxes of the kind of field that psychoanalysis is is that—unlike a field such as physics, in which physicists need never read the original texts written by Newton, Maxwell, Lorenz, or Einstein, learning all they need to know in order to "do" or "practice" physics by reading ordinary textbooks or simply by going to classes—in psychoanalysis, Freud's texts remain unsurpassed, indispensable reading (at least they should be!). It is not as if later work in the field could somehow subsume all of Freud's contributions and pass them on in the form of a series of formulas that anyone could learn and use.

In Lacan's work, we see a two-pronged approach: we see Lacan attempt to reduce his own work and Freud's to mathemes—indeed, he ironically claims at one point to have reduced all of psychoanalysis to set theory—and yet we see a kind of "fetishization" of the text, so to speak: on the one hand, an approach to reading Freud's and other texts (e.g., Poe's "The Purloined Letter") that has spurred great interest in the humanities and in literary criticism in particular and, on the other hand, an attention to writing that seeks to have effects on the reader that imply anything but the direct transmission of formulas and mathematically precise equations.

In Lacan's own writing, we see an explosion of polysemia, double entendres, triple entendres, equivocations, evocations, enigmas, jokes, and so on. His texts and lectures seem designed to introduce us to the very kind of work analysis itself requires, sifting through layers of meaning, deciphering the text as though it were a long series of slips of the tongue. He says at one point that his writing style is deliberately designed to contribute to the training of analysts

("All of my rhetoric aims to contribute to the effect of training," *Écrits*, 722), but it no doubt goes further than that. His writing affects us and, in certain cases, even upsets us.

If we think in terms of the distinction between the subject of the signifier—the subject of the pure combinatory or Lévi-Straussian subject—and the subject of jouissance, we might say, facetiously, that the mathemes are produced by Lacan as the subject of science, while the endless punning is produced by Lacan as the subject of jouissance, the enjoying subject. But then again, he seems to have at least as much fun with his mathemes as with his witticisms.[13]

## KNOWLEDGE BEGINS WITH A DEFICIENCY OF JOUISSANCE

Having discussed knowledge a little—above all, the attempt to eliminate the fantasies that keep creeping back into what we might call psychoanalytic knowledge—let me turn now to jouissance.

In his discussion of Aristotle, Lacan says that knowledge finds its motor force in a deficiency of jouissance (Seminar XX, 52/54–55).[14] We find the pleasures available to us in life inadequate, and it is owing to that inadequacy that we expound systems of knowledge—perhaps, first and foremost, to explain why our pleasure is inadequate and then to propose how to change things so that it will not be. You can't take the lack out of Lacan (as Shelly Silver used to say): knowledge is not motivated by some overflowing of life, some "natural exuberance." Monkeys may show signs of such exuberance at various moments, but they do not create logics, mathematical systems, philosophies, or psychologies. Knowledge, according to Lacan, is motivated by some failure of pleasure, some insufficiency of pleasure: in a word, dissatisfaction.

The French title of Seminar XX reflects this; when we say, "*encore*," we mean give us more, that is not enough, do it again (it means other things as well, but they do not concern us as directly here). It means that what we experienced was not sufficient.

Is it true that our jouissance is lesser than other people's or other animals'? Do we really see other people around us who seem to enjoy more than we do? Perhaps occasionally. The argument often has been made that racism, sexism, homophobia, and religious intolerance are based on the *belief* that some other group enjoys more than another group does, whatever that group may be. Yet that belief usually is based on next to nothing: racists have rarely, if ever, seen any such thing in the peoples they discriminate against, but that does not stop them from believing it.

It seems that we do something animals could never do—we judge our jouissance against a standard of what we think *it should be*, against an absolute standard, a norm, a benchmark. Standards and benchmarks do not exist in the animal kingdom; they are made possible only by language. In other words, language is what allows us to think that the jouissance we obtain is not up to snuff, does not cut the mustard, is not what it should be.

Language is what allows us to *say* that there is the paltry satisfaction we get in various and sundry ways, and then another satisfaction, a better satisfaction, a satisfaction that would never fail us, never come up short, never disappoint us. Have we ever experienced such a reliable satisfaction? For most of us, the answer is probably no, but that does not stop us from believing that there must be such a thing—there must be something better. Maybe we think we see some sign of it in some *other* group of people—Jews, African Americans, gays, women—and we hate and envy them for it. Maybe we project it onto some group because we want to believe it exists somewhere. (I am obviously not trying to explain all aspects of racism, sexism, and so on here with this highly simplistic formulation.)

In any case, we think that there must be something better, we say that there must be something better, we *believe* that there must be something better. By saying it over and over, whether to ourselves, to our friends, or to our analysts, we give a certain consistency to this other satisfaction, this Other jouissance. In the end, we wind up giving it so much consistency that the jouissance we do in fact obtain seems all the more inadequate. The little we had diminishes further still. It pales in comparison with the ideal we hold up for ourselves of a jouissance that we could really count on, that would never let us down.

A lot of things prop up the belief in this kind of jouissance. Hollywood certainly props it up, attempting to give it a kind of consistency few of us have probably ever known. In Hollywood's depiction of sexual relations—and sex is not the only realm in question when Lacan talks about jouissance, but it is certainly one of the more palpable ones—there is something inevitable and reliable about the satisfaction that the actors ostensibly obtain, something so reliable that one could bet the farm on it. I am not suggesting that no one ever has sexual experiences like the ones depicted on the silver screen, but that virtually no one has them with such regularity, so *infallibly*.[15]

What is the status of this unfailing jouissance that could never miss the mark? It does not exactly exist, according to Lacan, but it *insists* as an ideal, an idea, a possibility thought permits us to envision. In his vocabulary, it "ex-sists": it persists and makes its claims felt with a certain insistence from the outside, as it were. Outside in the sense that it is not the wish, "Let's do *that* again!" but, rather, "Isn't there something else you could do, something different you could try?"

When we think of the paltry jouissance we do have, this Other jouissance is the one we should have, the one that should be. Since we can conceive of its possibility, it must be. This resonates with Medieval philosophy: Anselm of Canterbury says that, "God is that than which nothing greater can be conceived." And since existence must be one of the properties of the most perfect thing going, God has to exist, otherwise He would not be the most perfect thing going. Here we see the speciousness of the ontological argument: attempting to deduce existence from essence.

The idea of an Other jouissance is thus closely related to the idea of God. There is a kind of fantasy at work here: the fantasy that we could attain such perfect, total—indeed, we might even say spherical—satisfaction. That fantasy takes on various forms in Buddhism, Zen, Catholicism, Tantrism, and Mysticism, and it goes by various names: Nirvana, Ecstasy, and so on. (By calling it fantasy, I am not saying that it is necessarily unreal.)

The fantasy is so powerful that we feel this Other jouissance has to be, has to exist. Yet if it were not for this fantasy, we might be more content with the jouissance we do actually obtain. Thus while Lacan says that, according to the fantasy, this Other jouissance should be, should exist, from the point of view of the satisfactions we actually do obtain, it should not be because it merely makes matters worse. We might say that *it never fails to make matters worse*. That is the gist of the play on words that Lacan makes over and over again in Chapter 5 of Seminar XX, "c'est la jouissance qu'il ne faudrait pas" (a play on two different verbs, *falloir*, it must be, and *faillir*, to fail, that are written and pronounced identically in certain tenses): it is the idea of a jouissance that never fails and that never fails to diminish still further the little jouissance we already have.

These two jouissances (the paltry one and the Other) are not complementary, according to Lacan, otherwise "we would fall back into the whole" (Seminar XX, 68/73), the fantasy of complementarity, Yin and Yang, one for men, say, and one for women. Instead, they form a couple, if you will, akin to that constituted by being and nonbeing—recall how worked up the Greeks got over the aporia of the being of nonbeing.

## SEXUATION

The discussion of these two jouissances brings us to the subject of what Lacan calls "sexuation." It should be recalled that sexuation is not biological sex: what Lacan calls masculine structure and feminine structure do not have to do with one's biological organs but rather with the kind of jouissance that one is able to obtain.[16] There is not, to the best of my knowledge, any easy overlap between sexuation and "gender," or between sexuation and "sexual identity," or between sexuation and what is sometimes referred to as "sexual orientation." "Gender" is a recent term in English usage and was utterly unknown in France in the early 1970s in anything other than a grammatical sense. When I refer to men, in the ensuing discussion, I mean those people who, regardless of their biological sex, fall under certain formulas—what Lacan calls the formulas of sexuation (see Figure 1.4)—the ones on the left; when I refer to women, I mean those people who, regardless of their biological sex, fall under the formulas on the right.

Lacan explicitly indicates here that he is attempting to define men and women in terms of a logic—hopefully not in terms of a fantasy (though a logic may well contain fantasy elements—Hegel's logic involves the fantasy of the whole, of totalizability), certainly not in terms of chromosomes, and not even in terms of the Oedipus complex.[17]

Now Lacan refers to the two jouissances that I have been referring to thus far as phallic jouissance and the Other jouissance (or jouissance of the Other). I have avoided saying "phallic jouissance" thus far, not wanting to put a name on it, especially such a loaded name. Why, after all, call it phallic?

There are many reasons, some of which I have talked about at great length elsewhere, but here I would like to suggest that we try to understand "phallic" as "fallible," to hear the fallibility in the phallus. Phallic jouissance is the jouissance that fails us, that disappoints us. It is susceptible to failure, and it fundamentally misses our partner. Why? Because it reduces our partner, as Other, to what Lacan refers to as object a, that partial object that serves as the cause of desire: our partner's voice or gaze that turns us on, or that body part we enjoy in our partner. It can be represented with Lacan's mathemes as $\mathcal{S} \rightarrow a$, which is, in fact, what we find under the formulas in the table that Lacan provides (Seminar XX, 73/78). As Lacan says elsewhere in this seminar, "the object is a raté," a missing, a failure: "The essence of the object is failure" (Seminar XX, 55/58).

To enjoy in this way, reducing one's partner to object a, is to enjoy like a man—that is, in the sense of someone characterized by masculine structure. Lacan even makes a pun here, saying that this kind of jouissance is "hommosexual," spelling it with two m's, homme being the term for man in French. Regardless of whether one is male or female (those are the biological terms), and regardless of whether one's partner is male or female, to enjoy in this way is to enjoy like a man.

Regarding the term phallus, note that Lacan equates the phallus with the bar between the signifier and the signified (S/s) in Seminar XX (40/39). This should give us a sense of the high degree of abstraction that Lacan brings to this highly contested Freudian concept: how we could understand the bar or barrier between the signifier and the signified as being in any way related to the biological organ associated with the male of the species is truly difficult to see.[18] Why the barrier between the signifier and the signified? That barrier is such that there is a great deal of slippage between what I say I want in words or tell myself I want and the actual object I aim at. I tell my partner I want this, she gives it to me, and I say "That's not it!" I want that. She gives me that, but that still is not it. Desire's object will not sit still; desire always sets off in search of something else. Since desire is articulated, made of the stuff of language—at least that is Lacan's contention, his certainly not being a naturalistic notion of desire—it has a very tough time designating any kind of exact signified or meaning, pinning something down. "I know that's what I said I wanted, but that's not exactly what I meant."

There is a barrier between my desire for something as formulated or articulated in signifiers (S), and what can satisfy me.[19] Thus the satisfaction I take in realizing my desire is always disappointing. This satisfaction, subject to the bar between the signifier and the signified, fails to fulfill me—it always leaves something more to be desired. That is phallic jouissance. Just as one cannot take the lack out of Lacan, one cannot take the failure out of the phallus. Phallic jouissance lets you down, comes up short. Lacan gives it a couple of other names in later seminars: he calls it "symbolic jouissance," and even "semiotic jouissance."

The Other jouissance, on the other hand, may be infallible, but it is a bit trickier: since Lacan often calls it *la jouissance de l'Autre*, it could be the jouissance that the Other gets out of us—after all, Lacan says we are duped by jouissance, *joués* (Seminar XX, 66/70), but then again it could be our enjoyment of the Other, or even our enjoyment as the Other (Seminar XX, 26/23–24). That ambiguity should be kept in mind as we turn to the formulas of sexuation themselves.

## THE FORMULAS OF SEXUATION

In the mid-1960s, Lacan borrowed a number of symbols and terms from Gottlob Frege, the logician. Frege apparently uses the term *saturated* to talk about a function that has a variable, $f(x)$. Lacan borrows and extends this terminology to talk about the subject in "Science and Truth" (*Écrits*, 863).

The subject without an object is the pure, "unsaturated" subject of the signifier, whereas the subject with an object is the "saturated" subject of jouissance. $\Phi x$, in the formulas of sexuation, is a function, even though Lacan puts a $\Phi$ in the place of the more usual $f$ in $f(x)$. It is a function with a variable, and I think we can, at least at one level, read the variable "x" here as "jouissance."

FIGURE 1.4
**The Formulas of Sexuation**

| Men | Women |
|---|---|
| $\exists x \, \overline{\Phi x}$ | $\overline{\exists x} \; \overline{\Phi x}$ |
| $\forall x \, \Phi x$ | $\overline{\forall x} \; \Phi x$ |

With this new reading, the formulas can be understood as follows, assuming we keep in mind that Lacan does not use the universal and existential quantifiers in the same way that classical logic does:

$\forall x \Phi x$:  All of man's jouissance is phallic jouissance. Every single one of his satisfactions may come up short.

$\exists x \overline{\Phi x}$:  Nevertheless, there is the belief in a jouissance that could never come up short, the belief in another jouissance.

This way of formulating things allows us to explain a number of comments that Lacan makes about Kierkegaard and Taoism. Kierkegaard, Lacan seems to claim, thinks he can accede to love only by giving up his phallic jouissance. It is only if he stops reducing Woman, the Other (the Other sex, here, as Lacan says) to object *a*—it is only by renouncing the enjoyment he gets from object *a*—that he can attain something else, something Lacan describes as "a good at one remove" or "a good to the second power," "a good that is not caused by a little *a*" (Seminar XX, 71/77). Lacan refers to that as "castrating himself," as it involves giving up the jouissance of the organ; Kierkegaard is seen to castrate himself *in order to attain the dimension of existence.* He seems to have to sacrifice one kind of love—love of object *a*—to achieve another kind of love, presumably a love that aims at something beyond object *a*.[20] (The formula in the upper left-hand corner is the only place existence comes in on the men's side of the table.)

Turning from love to certain Taoist sexual practices, Lacan says that in Taoism, "one must withhold one's cum" in order to achieve a higher or greater pleasure. In certain Tantric practices, orgasm is deferred, often for hours, and the sexual partners supposedly become surrounded by a kind of blue halo, indicative of a higher or heightened state of pleasure. Note that Lacan associates phallic jouissance with organ pleasure, the pleasure of the genitalia (Seminar XX, 13/7); the idea here would then seem to be that one must endlessly defer or altogether give up organ pleasure to obtain another kind of pleasure.

It would seem, according to these examples, that it is only through a certain kind of sacrifice that a man can attain an enjoyment beyond that of object *a*, an enjoyment that is presumably *of* the Other, of the Other sex (enjoyment of someone—usually, but not necessarily, a female—as a representative of or stand-in for the Other), and it is only by making such a sacrifice that he can truly love. Perhaps the courtly love tradition provides us with examples of this. As Lacan says, in this context, "When one loves, it has nothing to do with sex" (Seminar XX, 27/25).

Let us turn now to the formulas for women:

$\overline{\forall x}\Phi x$: Not all of her jouissance is phallic jouissance.

$\overline{\exists x\Phi x}$: There *is* not any that is not phallic jouissance—the emphasis going on the first "is." All the jouissances that *do exist* are phallic, but that does not mean there cannot be some jouissances that are not phallic—it is just that they do not exist: they ex-sist. The Other jouissance can only ex-sist, it cannot exist, for to exist it would have to be spoken.

Why can't the Other jouissance be spoken? If it were spoken, it would have to be articulated in signifiers, and if it were articulated in signifiers, it would be subject to the bar between signifier and signified. In other words, it would become fallible, capable of missing the mark. The bar brings on a disjunction between signifier and signified, the possibility—indeed, the inevitability—of slippage, noncorrespondence between signifier and signified. It brings on the whole signifying matrix, where a loss of jouissance is unavoidable (object *a*).

$$S_1 \rightarrow S_2$$
$$\frac{}{\$} \quad \frac{}{a} \leftarrow \text{loss or product}$$

This is why, Lacan seems to suggest, the Other jouissance must remain ineffable. A recurrent theme in the writings of the mystics is that what they experience in moments of rapture and ecstasy simply cannot be described: it is ineffable. No words come at that moment. That is, presumably, why Lacan says women have not told the world more about this jouissance: it is inarticulable.

Is there anything that *can* be said about it? The most concrete thing Lacan says is that it corresponds to "making love," as opposed to sexual intercourse (which is related to object *a*), "making love" being akin to poetry (Seminar XX, 68/72). He even says at one point in the seminar that it is "the satisfaction of speech" (ibid., 61/64). How that is compatible with the notion that it is an *ineffable* experience where the bar between signifier and signified does not function, I do not profess to know, though it seems to have to do with talking about love—for Lacan says, "to speak of love is in itself a jouissance" (ibid., 77/83)—instead of engaging in "the act of love," that is, in sexual intercourse. That is, after all, what the courtly love tradition was all about: talking instead of sex, which might be qualified as a kind of sublimation that provided its own pleasures ("'another satisfaction,' the satisfaction of speech" [ibid., 61/64]).

Nor can I say why Lacan associates it specifically with women, characterizing it as a specifically feminine jouissance. We need not assume that there is some sort of complete unity or consistency to his work, for he adds to and changes things as he goes along. He says, for example, in chapter 1 that, "Jouissance, qua sexual, is phallic" (ibid., 14/9) but later qualifies object *a*, the "star" of phallic jouissance, as *a*-sexual (ibid., 115/127). So is phallic jouissance asexual or sexual? Is the Other jouissance sexual or asexual? It would seem to be sexual, because it reaches the Other sex as such, not just object *a*, and yet, "When one loves, it has nothing to do with sex" (ibid., 27/25). Or is the term "*a*-sexual" simply not to be understood in the same way as "asexual," implying instead a form of sexuality that is dependent on object *a*?

Leaving these questions in abeyance, the idea here seems to be that one *can* experience this Other jouissance, though one cannot say anything about it because it is ineffable; just because it does not exist does not mean one cannot experience it: one's experience of it simply ex-sists. I do not think that Lacan is saying that everyone who has the ability to experience it actually experiences it; rather, not all women experience it. Lacan is certainly not saying that a woman *has* to experience it to obtain psychic health, and that women who do not are somehow "unhealthy" or "abnormal"—indeed, such terms are truly rare in Lacan's discourse, no matter what the context.

One crucial difference between men and women, structurally defined, then seems to be that women do not have to renounce phallic jouissance to have Other jouissance: they can have the Other jouissance without giving up their phallic jouissance. They can have *both* this hommosexual jouissance—

related to object *a*, and not to their partners as such—*and* the Other jouissance as well (Seminar XX, 78/84). For men, on the other hand, it seems to be an either/or. Does this reintroduce a fantasy dating back at least as far as Ovid, who has Tiresias say that a woman's enjoyment is greater than a man's?

In any case, this is what Lacan seems to mean by "sexuation": a man is someone who, regardless of chromosomes, can have one or the other (or at least thinks he can have the other by giving up the one), but not both; a woman is someone who, regardless of chromosomes, can potentially have both.[21]

**FIGURE 1.5**

phallic jouissance   Other jouissance

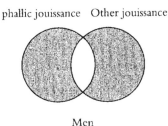

Men

phallic jouissance   Other jouissance

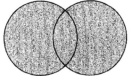

Women

Note that, since "man" and "woman" in this discussion do not correspond to male and female, Lacan's discussions about relations between men and women can apply equally well to what are more conventionally referred to as "homosexual" relations, "homosexual" without the two m's. In female homosexuality, both partners could come under feminine structure, masculine structure, or one of each; the same goes for male homosexuality. There does not seem to me to be anything specific about homosexual object choice that immediately situates someone on one side or the other of Figure 1.4.

## SUBJECT AND OTHER

For years, Lacan had been saying that the psychoanalytic subject was everything the Cartesian subject was not: if the cogito was the intersection between being and thinking,

FIGURE 1.6

Being                    Thinking

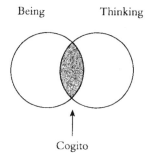

Cogito

the Lacanian subject was being in one place (imaginary or, perhaps, real), thinking in another (unconscious), with no overlap between them.

FIGURE 1.7

Being                    Thinking

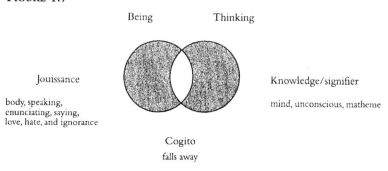

Jouissance                                              Knowledge/signifier

body, speaking,                                         mind, unconscious, matheme
enunciating, saying,
love, hate, and ignorance

Cogito
falls away

We can modify that a bit here on the basis of Lacan's formulation: "The discordance between knowledge and being is our subject" (Seminar XX, 109/120). Since he tells us, "There's no such thing as a knowing subject," I think we are justified in situating the cogito—the knowing subject *par excellence*—as what falls out between the two ("I am thinking, therefore [I *know* that] I am").

What, then, of the Other? Lacan makes it sound here like a similar disjunction is involved. There seem to be two faces of the Other: the locus of the signifier (which Lacan associates here with the father function) and "the God face . . . based on feminine jouissance" (Seminar XX, 71/77). Prior to the early 1970s, the Other is always very distinct from affect or jouissance in Lacan's work, it being the locus of the signifier, object *a* being associated with jouissance. But here the concept of the Other becomes a disjunction of these two radically opposed terms. Just as there are two faces of the subject, here there seem to be two faces of the Other. This may be where *lalangue*, whereby jouissance is "injected," so to speak, into the unconscious—that is, into the Other—comes in.

**FIGURE 1.8**

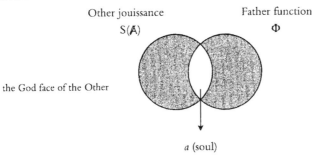

Other jouissance        Father function

S(Ⱥ)             Φ

the God face of the Other

*a* (soul)

What drops out between the two? I would suggest that it is the soul, which seems to be associated here by Lacan with object *a*. (Soulove is love, not of the Other, but of object *a*).

## CONCLUSION

Is Lacan providing something new and useful here? It is often hard to say what exactly in analysands' discourse should be characterized as indicative of the Other jouissance. On the other hand, we hear about the *idea* or *ideal* of an un-failing, infallible jouissance every day in analytic work. The gulf between the two is as palpable in clinical practice as in everyday discourse and the media. One need not endorse Lacan's account of masculine and feminine structure to agree with the idea that there are two quite different jouissances.

Has Lacan introduced all kinds of fantasies of his own in this theorization of jouissance? The same old fantasies? Perhaps *disjunction* is the most important term here.

Whatever the case may be, the fantasy of the whole that Lacan attempts to debunk is alive and well in many disciplines today. To give but one example, E. O. Wilson, the renowned sociobiologist, recently published a book, *Consilience: The Unity of Knowledge*, in which he suggests that, using methods developed in the *natural* sciences, science will eventually be able to explain everything: psychology, literature, the arts, history, sociology, and religion—the whole kit and caboodle. The theory of the whole still has a considerable hold on us!

## NOTES

1. An earlier version of this chapter was delivered as a paper on April 17, 1998, at the University of Massachusetts at Amherst, at the invitation of Professor Briankle Chang of the Department of Communications.

2. Lacan might say that affect takes refuge in the body, the body as a representational site of the unconscious.

3. The latter often goes by the name of object *a*.

4. All references to *Écrits* here are to the French edition (Paris: Seuil, 1966), the pagination of which is provided in the margins of the new translation of *Écrits: A Selection* by Bruce Fink.

5. Page references are first to the French edition of Seminar XX, *Encore* (Paris: Seuil, 1975) and then, after a slash, to the English translation, *The Seminar, Book XX, Encore, On Feminine Sexuality: The Limits of Love and Knowledge*, trans. Bruce Fink (New York: W.W. Norton & Co., 1998).

6. What are we to make, then, of machines that read aloud written texts or computer files? The absence of selective stress (other than programmed) on different words or clauses in such reading would seem to point, at the very least, to the absence of the subject of enunciation (or enunciating subject)—that is, to the absence of the subject of jouissance.

7. Claude Lévi-Strauss, *Structural Anthropology*, trans. C. Jacobson and B. G. Schoepf (New York: Basic Books, 1963), p. 125.

8. See my detailed commentary on "Subversion of the Subject" in *Lacan à la lettre: Reading* Écrits *Closely* (Minneapolis: University of Minnesota Press, forthcoming).

9. In literary theory, for example, one must take into account the structures of the text, but also what Barthes calls the "pleasure of the text" (and their interrelations). In other words, one must consider the pleasure of the reader and the writer, as well as the performative aspects of the text. We should, of course, do the same in psychoanalysis, considering that the field is defined not only by a practice that is passed on from analyst to analysand but also by a series of texts that are read and reread.

10. According to Lacan, it also is found in Jean Piaget's work on children; see his comments on Piaget in "Science and Truth" (*Écrits*, 859–60).

11. *Cours de linguistique générale* (Paris: Payot, 1972), p. 99; in English, *Course in General Linguistics* (New York: McGraw-Hill, 1959), pp. 66–67. Note that Saussure's language often is suggestive of a sexual relationship between the signifier and the signified: "they are intimately united" (*Cours*, 99); there is a "coupling of thought [the signified] with phonic matter [the signifier]" (*Cours*, 156); and "Phonic substance [the signifier] is . . . not a mold whose forms thought [the signified] must necessarily marry" (*Cours*, 155).

12. For a far more detailed account of Lacan's subversion of Saussure, see my commentary in *Lacan à la lettre: Reading* Écrits *Closely* (forthcoming).

13. The very rigidity of the distinction I have drawn between these two subjects may seem problematic and susceptible of deconstruction. Don't these two concepts themselves form a unified, unitary, binary structure, not so dissimilar to Saussure's conception of the sign? And doesn't Lacan further polarize the binary nature of the structure with his notion of the One and the Other, the Other as always and inescapably Other, in the 1970s?

This rigid binary opposition may perhaps be understood to be thrown into question by another concept that Lacan introduces in the early 1970s, *lalangue*, or llanguage—for it seems to inject jouissance into the unconscious, that is, the Other—or by writing, for "what is written are the conditions of jouissance and what is counted are the remainders" of jouissance (Seminar XX, 118/131). But as I have not introduced these concepts here, I will not attempt to resolve the opposition, confining myself to pointing out the possibility. The notion of the subject as a disjunction, to which I turn further on, may help here as well—the subject as a disjunction between signifier and affect.

14. He says the same for the Stoics regarding material implication, the deduction of the true from the false (Seminar XX, 56/60).

15. Perhaps the stereotypical cigarette smoked after sex in movies nevertheless points to a recognized lack in that jouissance, there being something more to be desired: an oral pleasure that has gone unsatisfied.

16. See, for example, my *Lacanian Subject* (Princeton: Princeton University Press, 1995), chapter 8.

17. Whether there is any point in defining men and women at all is, of course, an open question.

18. Here it would seem that the bar, rather than serving as the copula or means of copulation, as we might view it in Saussure's model of the "coupling" of the signifier and signified, serves instead as a barrier.

19. That is true of my partner as well; in my relation to my partner, "I ask [her]," as Lacan says, "to refuse what I offer [her] because that's not it" (Seminar XX, 101/111).

20. We could, perhaps, also read the upper left-hand formula as asserting that there exists something in him that wishes to make that sacrifice, to give up phallic jouissance, in the hope of finding "true love."

21. If we think of phallic jouissance as the satisfaction that corresponds to desire —and the terms $S$ and $a$ are there (in the table under the formulas of sexuation) that form fantasy that Lacan says props up desire—then a man can desire his partner, or love his partner, but not both at the same time, whereas a woman can do both. Is this a fair account of what Lacan is saying? If it is, it would seem to point to what we might call a *love beyond desire*—equivalent to what Lacan jokingly refers to here as a jouissance beyond the phallus. If so, it would seem to correspond to what Lacan qualifies in the last chapter of the seminar as a "subject-to-subject relationship" (Seminar XX, 131–32/144), in which the object drops out:

$$( \cancel{S} \Diamond a \Diamond \cancel{S} ) \quad \rightarrow \quad ( \cancel{S} \Diamond \cancel{S} )$$

[hommosexual desire]          [love]

But that might be going too far: it would, perhaps, be safer to say that a man is able to attain one kind of love *or* the other (love for the object or for the Other sex) with one and the same partner, whereas a woman is able to attain both kinds of love with the same partner (or phallic jouissance with a man and the Other jouissance with a woman or feminine instance?). I am obviously extrapolating here, since Lacan never says with one and the same partner.

# HYSTERIA IN SCIENTIFIC DISCOURSE

*Colette Soler*

The master/hysteric couple is found throughout history, but in this chapter I will try to elucidate its current configuration. That requires, first of all, something like a diagnosis of the present state of the discourses.

## HYSTORY

Hysteria bears some of the responsibility "hystorically" for this present state. Indeed, hysteria is "the unconscious in action" and did not just begin to insist in history recently, because the unconscious is based on the fact that we speak. Hysterical subjects are not the only ones to lend their voices to it, of course, but more than others they keep the leitmotif alive. The efficacy of this insistence is the origin of the desire that gave rise to science. At least, that is the thesis that Lacan develops in Seminar XVII and in "Radiophonie."[1] This thesis leaves no room for the Hegelian master/slave dialectic and makes science a pointed response to hysteria's provocation: this runs from Socrates to Newton and from Anna O. to Freud. The master's discourse "finds its reason in the hysteric's discourse," says Lacan. Antiquity's master relied on the slave's artisanal knowledge in order to produce a surplus jouissance that plugged up the sexual gap—at the cost of any and all desire to know. It took Socrates, the pure hysteric, to breathe into it the desire to know from which science issued, involving the transformation of knowledge by science from artisanal knowledge to universalizable, formalized knowledge in which mathematics dominates.

What kind of success is this for the hysteric? This resurgence of desire produces new knowledge that operates in the real, but it nevertheless leaves the subject who is confronted with the sexual impasse suffering; for, even more than Antiquity's discourse, science excludes the subject from its purview: "Science is an ideology of the suppression of the subject." It is not surprising, then, that postscientific hysteria reemerged at another point in history as a symptom against the backdrop of the failure of the Enlightenment, and that the result was the emergence of psychoanalysis by which Freud objected to medicine's foreclosure of the subject. The question, therefore, is what has become of hysteria now that psychoanalysis has emerged in science, 100 years after Freud accepted the challenge to take responsibility, both practically and theoretically, for its solicitation, having managed to inscribe the enclave of his practice in the regulation of jouissance by the dominant discourse. It is thus hysteria in science, but with psychoanalysis, that I am investigating.

## REPERCUSSIONS OF SCIENCE

Over thirty years ago, Lacan highlighted the fact that the repercussions of science in our world appear in social links due to universalization. This is now widely recognized and most often deplored. It goes hand in hand with the new supremacy of the goods produced by the modern economic system in subjects' lives, and a question arises about the extent to which it is the effect thereof. Whatever the case may be, this twofold result—universalization and the supremacy of goods—concerns the sexual couple, which is precisely what fascinates the hysteric.

The mortification that language brings with it has now shifted into reality—the reality of instruments. The latter instrumentalize us to such an extent that we are not even aware of it in our everyday lives, and it takes some accident or science fiction story to remind us of it. Our lives, which we attribute to our bodies, are now totally fitted out with gadgets. Lacan also noted at the end of his teaching that to have a body is to be able to do something with it, notably to use it for jouissance. This can take many forms: a body can be lent, sold, offered, refused, and so on. In capitalist discourse, something new has appeared: our bodies are now pledged to the enormous machine of production.

The phenomenon is not in itself new, but its mass application is, extending far beyond the proletariat to which Marx confined it. At all levels of social employment, our already instrumentalized bodies have themselves become instruments. It is obvious that we treat our bodies as we treat machines: we give them checkups, special diets, fitness training, beauty care, and so on. Not all of this can be chalked up to narcissism. In fact, we take the durability of the equipment (the body) into account—indeed, the health bulletins about our leaders have no other meaning. Why would Yeltsin, speaking on French television in the 1990s, feel compelled to tell us about his cold shower in the morning, his favorite sport, and how much sleep he gets if not to reassure us about his instrument's ability to continue to man the helm? The body is now a form of capital for all of us, and we treat it as such.

How could this not be detrimental to jouissance when the very definition of capital is that it is exempt from jouissance?[2] Love loses here, to be sure. Courtly love, for example, and *la carte du tendre*[3]—requiring patience and industry—were only for people who were idle, who had no date books or answering machines! Can you imagine a troubadour with a fax machine? While family ties have become independent from the transmission of goods, love itself is increasingly expressed in terms of having: we count its occurrences, its product, and its gains; we calculate profits and losses, and our legislation ratifies this. In this way, the capitalization of the body goes hand in hand with a widespread debasement—not merely neurotic—in the sphere of love.[4]

This new realism is accompanied by a still more remarkable effect— previously unheard of—that I will call "the unisex effect," generalizing the expression that advertisers usually apply to clothes, clothes that usually conceal rather than reveal sexual difference. It is often thought that we are moving toward a generalized transvestitism in the name of the equality of men and women. This is perhaps true, but it is an inexorable side effect of universalization: science's correlate is the Cartesian subject who knows nothing of sexual difference; science consequently adapts very easily to the reduction of every subject to a universal worker. The immediate result is especially felt by women, who for centuries have seen their jouissance confined to the perimeter of the home, whatever form that home may have taken, including husband and child. The labor market has emancipated them from this confined field, while also alienating them through the imperatives of production. Hence the hesitations of the feminist movement when it oscillates between a claim for equality and a contrary claim for difference in which the "particularity protest" is expressed.

What is clear is that there is virtually no domain to which women do not now have access. Their ingress keeps expanding, and the tide seems irreversible. Marguerite Yourcenar has succeeded where Marie Curie failed, obtaining entry into the Académie Française. The following have recently been announced: the first woman driver in a Formula One race car, the first woman to climb a difficult mountain alone, and the first girl in a chess championship. A few bastions still remain. A woman's attempt to be admitted into the French National Guard recently led to considerable protest by its members. That may still take some time! The psychoanalyst, as analyst, need not take a position on such developments. He or she cannot, however, ignore their consequences . . . on both sexes.

How can the subjective impact of these social changes be understood? They concern phallic jouissance itself, insofar as it is not only inscribed within the context of the sexual relationship, but also props up the whole relationship to reality. Phallic jouissance is jouissance that can be capitalized upon. Unisex[5] means the phallic jouissance that is available to everyone. Not that women were ever deprived of it, but they had it only within the confines of their roles as wives and mothers. It is this restriction, not to say prohibition, that has given way, allowing for widespread competition between the sexes.

The historical moment at which Freud emphasized the phallic phase—
that scandalous notion implying an inequality of the sexes in the unconscious—was not indifferent. The context of his discovery was the ideology of
human rights and the ideals of distributive justice which, in the realm of ethics,
echo the universality of the subject of science. We must agree with Freud and
everyone else around us—they are all on the same side on this point—that
boys and girls are not born "free and equal in rights." Thanks to discourse, boys
begin life with a little more capital: having the phallic signifier. It is only logical
then that girls feel poor and consequently dream—this is all that Freud discovered in exploring the feminine unconscious—of obtaining something. There
was a time when it could only be from a husband, bearer of the organ, and
then from children as substitutes. Today, alongside these engaging realities, the
whole field of what Lacan calls "the most actual realizations" is open to them:
goods, knowledge, power, and so on.

Our scientific civilization has changed women's reality. The analyst is cog-
nizant of this and observes that it does not necessarily make them any happier:
anxiety, inhibition, guilt, and feelings of failure are among its consequences. The
first psychoanalysts, Joan Riviere in particular, assumed that if, at times, women
felt precluded from phallic jouissance, it was because they feared losing their
femininity in it. But is it not true, rather, that phallic jouissance in itself engenders guilt—for men as well, although in different forms? Since it is a limited
jouissance that obeys the discrete structure of the signifier, phallic jouissance is
always at fault and prepared to entertain the superego's imperative: "always
more."

## HYSTERIA AND FEMININITY

In this context the hysteric's question about sex can but change in form, to the
point of becoming, as we know, unrecognizable to psychiatry in its current
state. But under the pretext of not overlooking hysteria, psychoanalysis should
not see it everywhere by simply confusing it with femininity. Lacan always distinguished the two positions, specifying that hysteria is not the privilege of
women alone: there also are hysterical men, and they may even be more hysterical than women! If this is the case, it is necessary to understand what causes
the confusion.

I would like to highlight a shift in the feminine problematic between
Freud and Lacan. Taking as his point of departure his discovery of the phallic
phase, which reveals the single signifier that answers for sexual difference in the
unconscious, Freud distinguished the two sexes by having: one has it, and the
other does not have it. The one that has it fears losing it, and the one that does
not have it wants to acquire it. Lacan translates this nicely when he speaks of
"the threat of or nostalgia based on not-having" (*Écrits*, 694/289).[6] Thus we
find, on the one hand, a defensive strategy of protection and, on the other
hand, several possible strategies. Freud sketched out the range of women's

different positions.[7] One position consists of completely eliding sex. A second position, a combative one, denies the phallic lack in the hope of acquiring a substitute: this is what he calls the "masculinity complex." The third position involves consent and renunciation, out of love for the father, Freud thinks, and hope for a compensatory child. It also is a position of waiting, but it requires the mediation of a man to give the phallic substitute in the form of love or the child as a gift. Thus, according to Freud, the true woman is the one who—accepting her deprivation—also is willing to say "thank you," while the other—the woman with a masculinity complex who sets out to acquire a phallic substitute by herself—refuses it with a "no thank you" that virtually rejects men as useless.

Unlike Freud, Lacan first emphasizes the dimension of being, or rather the failure to be [manque-à-être] which, as an effect of speech, is the point of departure for both men and women. In the question of sexual difference, the problematic of having is combined with that of being. We can trace the variations on these two interwoven themes through the different texts. They lead Lacan to distinguish men and women a little differently than Freud, though in the end Lacan does not contest Freud's phallocentrism. Men, if they are posited as having the phallus, make up for their failure to be by having and by the advantage [bénéfice][8] of phallic jouissance. Women, on the contrary, conjugate their failure to be at the outset with deprivation of the organ. But according to Lacan, this lack—which is, as it were, doubled—opens the way for her to a solution that consists in deriving a being-effect from her relationship with a man. Hence the possible formulation of sexual difference through the opposition between having and being: having or being the phallus in his earlier work (Écrits, 630–33/265–69), and having or being the symptom in his later work. The two formulations are not equivalent: since the phallus is a negative function of lack, and the symptom is a positive function of jouissance, they are opposed, so much so that wanting "to be the phallus," with which Lacan at one point stigmatized the hysteric, means precisely not wanting to be the symptom.

Let me simply refer here to Lacan's second 1979 lecture on Joyce;[9] there Lacan explicitly distinguishes the hysteric's position from the woman's position. A woman is specified as being a symptom. This is not the case of the hysteric, who is characterized as "being interested in the other's symptom" and is therefore not the last symptom but only "second to last." To be the unique symptom at least for One is not, strictly speaking, the hysteric's demand, as we know from Dora. We see this in analytic experience in the following way: even in private, the hysterical subject does not constitute a couple, but at least a triangle, if not a still larger configuration. The clinical difficulty is that the inverse is not true. A woman, whether she is obsessive, phobic, or even psychotic, might also have to deal with what I would call her "symptom rivals," but those rivals would not play the same role for her as that played by the other woman in hysteria. Note that an obsessive man also has his triangle when he sustains his desire through that of an alter ego.

For a hysteric, in any case, being interested in the other's symptom means not consenting to being the symptom, and it does not mean having a symptom identical to a man's symptom. Contrary to what hasty thinkers imagine, the fact that someone is not a woman does not mean that person is a man. For example, Lacan says that Socrates is not a man: instead, he occupies a third position, that of having a symptom vicariously through a man [par la procuration d'un homme], so to speak, and that, Lacan clarifies, does not imply bodily contact.

One could catalog all of the formulations in Lacan's teachings by which he progressively approached this assertion. First come the statements that indicate the hysteric's refusal or impossibility to accept herself as an object. It would be necessary to add to the list the notion of "slipping away" (Écrits, 824/321), which indicates the strategy by which the subject extricates herself from the a-sexual jouissance (Seminar XX, 13/6, 115/127) of the relationship between the sexes, as well as Lacan's formulations regarding hysterical identification with desire's lack as opposed to desire's object. It is clear, for example, that Dora is interested in Frau K. as a symptom but does not want to be Frau K.—consider the slap she gives Herr K. when he offers her the position. The butcher's wife, with her dream of defiance toward Freud (SE IV, 147), shows more clearly still—since she puts up in reality with the assiduous attentions of her husband, the man with the organ—that she dreams of nothing more than of leaving the place of the symptom and, as Lacan says in Seminar XVII (84–85), of leaving the dear butcher to another woman. As for Socrates, it is clear that he does not want to be Alcibiades' symptom, but that he is interested in Agathon insofar as Agathon occupies that place for Alcibiades.

We see here why the hysteric's position often is confused with the feminine position. To be a woman implies having a relationship with the Other, man, in order to be actualized as a symptom. Since her jouissance being involves the mediation of this Other, we understand her interest, not so much in that Other, man or God, as in his desire—the desire by means of which she comes to incarnate his jouissance. Now the hysteric submits to the same mediation by the Other but with different ends in view—not in order to be actualized as his symptom. Her desire is sustained by the Other's symptom, to the extent that one could almost say that she makes herself a cause thereof, but a cause of . . . knowledge, not because she is motivated by a desire to know, but because she would like to inspire a desire to know in the Other.

How, then, are we to situate the fact that the hysteric "plays the part of the man" [faire l'homme]?[10] This expression takes on several meanings. It designates first the hysteric's challenge: "show me if you are a man," in the sense of "stand up and fight like a man," but it also means identification with the man. However, this is not just any old identification, and this is where people often are mistaken. It can be an identification with his phallic knowledge or, on the contrary, with his lack thereof. Both can actually coexist in the same subject, but hysterical identification proper, as we find it in Dora and in the butcher's wife (as Lacan reformulates the latter's case in 1973),[11] implies identifying with a man insofar as he is not fulfilled, insofar as he too is unsatisfied, his jouissance castrated.

The clinician can easily be led astray here, for the consequences of this identification sometimes present themselves in the form of a hyper-femininity. Consider the butcher's wife: at the imaginary, visible level, she competes with her female friend in playing the part of the woman, but this masquerade results from the fact that, at the symbolic level, as a subject, she identifies with her husband insofar as he is lacking something. Another practical result is that the hysteric becomes the active agent of the Other's castration.

## TODAY AND TOMORROW

Having clarified this position, I now return to contemporary forms of hysteria. The state of our civilization is, as I said, complicit with the ever-possible identification of women with masculine having. Thanks to metonymy, a career path is open to all women, to our modern hysterics as well as to others, and they are quite talented in their pursuits. But one should nevertheless recall the clinical result that analysis attests to in all of its forms: contrary to what one often imagines, the more the hysteric succeeds in the phallic conquest, the less she can enjoy it, and the greater her sense of "disappropriation" grows. She can strive to win the different competitions open to her, but almost as soon as she has proven herself, the gain vanishes—for her real question is played out elsewhere, in the closed field, as Lacan says, of the sexual relationship. It is only there that sexual difference, repressed in all other facets of life by unisex, remains irreducible. We could perhaps say that she makes the unisex of castration rule there, too, but this is because she is only interested in the jouissance that is its correlate and that she exalts. On this point, the sexual subversion of our times owes as much to her as to science.

In this respect, psychoanalysis is really what the hysteric needed, because it agrees to recognize the enigma of sex and assumes responsibility for it. Consider the difference between psychoanalysis and Charcot's approach: Charcot thought—somewhat stupidly—that what a hysteric needed was an expert love maker. This is what is implied in the formulation that struck Freud so much, which prescribed repeated doses of the penis as a remedy for all of the ills of hysterics.[12] One hears the same thing in the lewd slang expression that a woman is "not getting the right stuff" [*mal baisée*].[13] This expression is, in fact, less shocking than simply poorly thought out. What the hysteric is seeking is not an expert love maker—someone who makes love well—but a sex connoisseur, someone who can say what jouissance it is that a woman has [*porte*] beyond that of the organ. If the one she has is not spoken, one can only mark its place by leaving the organ-related jouissance unsatisfied.

The faithlessness of the hysteric has a logic of its own (*Écrits*, 824/321). Freud accepted the challenge and invented an approach that excludes the expert love maker by forbidding bodily contact, thus obliging the subject to get the Other to respond and to produce knowledge such as that of science, in which logic plays a major role. Actually, psychoanalysis did satisfy the hysteric's request for knowledge about sex. This knowledge, however, is a surprise knowledge with respect to the aspiration that gave rise to it, for it consists only of a "structural negativity"—to use Lacan's expression—and thus leaves the hysteric's wish unsatisfied. Instead of the unconscious yielding a science of jouissance as sexual jouissance, it turns out that the unconscious is only familiar with phallic jouissance, which is a-sexual; the unconscious only approaches the other jouissance through logic and the real of that jouissance through what it is impossible to say.

It is hard to say whether hysterics would be happy with such an arid answer. Would they not rather be tempted to inspire a resurgence of religion? Lacan worried about that, but it must be said that a certain part of analytic revelation also lends itself to that, since psychoanalysis emphasizes, with respect to jouissance, that castration is not the last word for everyone; not only is there surplus jouissance that plugs it up, but there also is the Other jouissance that objects to unisex. The analysand no doubt consumes phallic jouissance, but the analyst incarnates what remains irreducible to phallic jouissance.

It is quite apparent that this irreducible element lends itself to diverse uses that are subjective. In particular, woman's supplementary jouissance, newly accredited as a limit of knowledge by Lacan and the logic he adopts, this new alliance with Tiresias, is already engendering new clinical facts in analytic discourse: a question, no doubt, but also a craving [envie]. This craving—if it is not new, then it is at least newly deployed—rivaling penis envy, is a craving for the other jouissance; it is a fear as well, or even a denunciation. We can find traces of it in both men and women and isolate its amusing use, designed to renew the resources of the masquerade that makes woman what she is. The cult of her mystery could very well make her exist, as it made God, the Father, exist.

In conclusion, our scientific civilization and the universalization it promotes engender unisex. In this context hysterics have inspired psychoanalysis, which keeps open the question of sex and provides them with a response. But in the future they might well reject its purely logical response and prefer instead the religion of woman. That will depend on whether or not hysterical discourse yields to analytic discourse.

Translated by François Raffoul and David Pettigrew,<br>
revised and edited by Bruce Fink.

## NOTES

1. *Le Séminaire, Livre XVII, L'envers de la psychanalyse* (1969–1970), ed. J.-A. Miller (Paris: Seuil, 1991); "Radiophonie," *Scilicet* 2/3 (1970): 55–99. All footnotes as well as references in the text have been added by the editor.

2. The French here plays on the contrast in French economic terminology between capital (fixed assets) and the usufruct (the enjoyment or jouissance) of that capital.

3. A sort of map of the landscape of love (the "tender" feelings), described by Madelaine de Scudéry.

4. Cf. Sigmund Freud, *The Standard Edition of the Complete Psychological Works of Sigmund Freud*, 24 vols., trans. J. Strachey (London: Hogarth Press), vol. XI, "On the Universal Tendency to Debasement in the Sphere of Love," 179–90. Hereafter, all references to the *Standard Edition* will be given as SE, followed by volume and page numbers.

5. "Unisex" is used here and elsewhere in this chapter as a noun, such as "masculinity" or "femininity."

6. All references to *Écrits* here are first to the French edition (Paris: Seuil, 1966) and then to English translation, trans. Alan Sheridan (New York: Norton, 1977), although all translations have been modified.

7. See "Female Sexuality," SE XXI, 229–30 and "Femininity," SE XXII, 126–30.

8. The French here also means gain or profit.

9. "Joyce le symptôme II," in *Joyce avec Lacan*, eds. J. Aubert & M. Jolas (Paris: Navarin, 1987).

10. The French here can also mean to make a man, that is, to make a man of someone.

11. "Introduction à l'édition allemande d'un premier volume des *Écrits* (Walter Verlag)," *Scilicet* 5 (1975): 11–17.

12. Cf. "Rx Penis normalis dosim repetatur," in SE XIV, 15, where the "prescription" is attributed to Chrobak.

13. American English does not seem to have any exact equivalent for this French expression, which literally means "badly laid."

# THE REAL OF SEXUAL DIFFERENCE

☯

*Slavoj Zizek*

## THE "FORMULAS OF SEXUATION"

Roger Ebert's *The Little Book of Hollywood Clichés*[1] contains hundreds of stereo-
types and obligatory scenes—from the famous "Fruit Cart!" rule (during any
chase scene involving a foreign or an ethnic locale, a fruit cart will be over-
turned and an angry peddler will run into the middle of the street to shake his
fist at the hero's departing vehicle) or the more refined "Thanks, but no thanks"
rule (when two people have just had a heart-to-heart conversation, as Person A
starts to leave room, Person B tentatively says "Bob [or whatever A's name is]?"
and Person A pauses, turns, and says "Yes?" and then Person B says, "Thanks")
to the "Grocery Bag" rule (whenever a scared, cynical woman who does not
want to fall in love again is pursued by a suitor who wants to tear down her
wall of loneliness, she goes grocery shopping; her grocery bags then break,
and the fruits and vegetables fall, either to symbolize the mess her life is in or so
the suitor can help her pick up the pieces of her life, or both). This is what
the "big Other," the symbolic substance of our lives, is: a set of unwritten rules
that effectively regulate our speech and acts, the ultimate guarantee of Truth
to which we have to refer even when lying or trying to deceive our partners
in communication, precisely in order to be successful in our deceit.

We should bear in mind, however, that in the last decades of his teaching,
Lacan twice severely qualified the status of the big Other:

- first in the late 1950s, when he emphasized the fact that the "quilting
  point" (or "button tie")—the quasi-transcendental master signifier that
  guarantees the consistency of the big Other—is ultimately a fake, an

empty signifier without a signified. Suffice it to recall how a community functions: the master signifier that guarantees the community's consistency is a signifier whose signified is an enigma for the members themselves—nobody really knows what it means, but each of them somehow presupposes that others know it, that it has to mean "the real thing," and so they use it all the time. This logic is at work not only in politico-ideological links (with different terms for the cosa nostra: our nation, revolution, and so on), but even in some Lacanian communities, where the group recognizes itself through the common use of some jargon-laden expressions whose meaning is not clear to anyone, be it "symbolic castration" or "divided subject"—everyone refers to them, and what binds the group together is ultimately their shared *ignorance*. Lacan's point, of course, is that psychoanalysis should enable the subject to *break* with this safe reliance on the enigmatic master signifier.

• and second, and even more radically, in Seminar XX, when Lacan developed the logic of the "not-all" (or "not-whole") and of the exception constitutive of the universal. The paradox of the relationship between the series (of elements belonging to the universal) and its exception does not reside merely in the fact that "the exception grounds the [universal] rule," that is, that every universal series involves the exclusion of an exception (all men have inalienable rights, with the exception of madmen, criminals, primitives, the uneducated, children, etc.). The properly dialectical point resides, rather, in the way a series and exceptions directly coincide: the series is always the series of "exceptions," that is, of entities that display a certain exceptional quality that qualifies them to belong to the series (of heroes, members of our community, true citizens, and so on). Recall the standard male seducer's list of female conquests: each is "an exception," each was seduced for a particular *je ne sais quoi*, and the series is precisely the series of these exceptional figures.[2]

The same matrix is at work in the shifts in the Lacanian notion of the symptom. What distinguishes the last stage of Lacan's teaching from the previous ones is best approached through the changed status of this notion. Previously a symptom was a pathological formation to be (ideally, at least) dissolved in and through analytic interpretation, an index that the subject had somehow and somewhere compromised his desire, or an index of the deficiency or malfunctioning of the symbolic Law that guarantees the subject's capacity to desire. In short, symptoms were the series of exceptions, disturbances, and malfunctionings, measured by the ideal of full integration into the symbolic Law (the Other). Later, however, with his notion of the universalized symptom, Lacan accomplished a paradoxical shift from the "masculine" logic of Law and its constitutive exception to the "feminine" logic, in which there is *no* exception to the series of symptoms—that is, in which there are *only* symptoms, and the symbolic Law (the paternal Name) is ultimately just one (the most efficient or established) in the series of symptoms.

This is, according to Jacques-Alain Miller, Lacan's universe in Seminar XX: a universe of radical split (between signifier and signified, between jouissance of the drives and jouissance of the Other, between masculine and feminine), in which no a priori Law guarantees the connection or overlapping between the two sides, so that only partial and contingent knots-symptoms (quilting points, points of gravitation) can generate a limited and fragile coordination between the two domains. In this perspective, the "dissolution of a symptom," far from bringing about a nonpathological state of full desiring capacity, leads instead to a total psychotic catastrophe, to the dissolution of the subject's entire universe. There is no "big Other" guaranteeing the consistency of the symbolic space within which we dwell: there are just contingent, punctual, and fragile points of stability.[3]

One is tempted to claim that the very passage from Judaism to Christianity ultimately obeys the matrix of the passage from the "masculine" to the "feminine" formulas of sexuation. Let us clarify this passage apropos of the opposition between the jouissance of the drives and the jouissance of the Other, elaborated by Lacan in Seminar XX, which also is sexualized according to the same matrix. On the one hand, we have the closed, ultimately solipsistic circuit of drives that find their satisfaction in idiotic masturbatory (auto-erotic) activity, in the perverse circulating around object *a* as the object of a drive. On the other hand, there are subjects for whom access to jouissance is much more closely linked to the domain of the Other's discourse, to how they not so much talk as are talked about: erotic pleasure hinges, for example, on the seductive talk of the lover, on the satisfaction provided by speech itself, not just on the act in its stupidity. Does this contrast not explain the long-observed difference in how the two sexes relate to cybersex? Men are much more prone to use cyberspace as a masturbatory device for their lone playing, immersed in stupid, repetitive pleasure, while women are more prone to participate in chat rooms, using cyberspace for seductive exchanges of speech.

Do we not encounter a clear case of this opposition between masculine phallic-masturbatory jouissance of the drive and feminine jouissance of the Other in Lars von Trier's *Breaking the Waves*? Confined to his hospital bed, Jan tells Bess that she must make love to other men and describe her experiences to him in detail—this way, she will keep awake his will to live. Although she will be physically involved with other men, the true sex will occur in their conversation. Jan's jouissance is clearly phallic/masturbatory: he uses Bess to provide him with the fantasmatic screen that he needs in order to be able to indulge in solipsistic, masturbatory jouissance, while Bess finds jouissance at the level of the Other (symbolic order), that is, in her words. The ultimate source of satisfaction for her is not the sexual act itself (she engages in such acts in a purely mechanical way, as a necessary sacrifice) but the way she *reports* on it to the crippled Jan.

Bess' jouissance is a jouissance "of the Other" in more than one way: it is not only enjoyment in words but also (and this is ultimately just another aspect of the same thing) in the sense of utter alienation—her enjoyment is totally alienated/externalized in Jan as her Other. That is, it resides entirely in her awareness that she is enabling the Other to enjoy. (This example is crucial insofar as it enables us to dispense with the standard misreading of Lacan, according to which jouissance feminine is a mystical beatitude beyond speech, exempted from the symbolic order—on the contrary, it is women who are immersed in the order of speech *without exception*.)[4]

How does this allow us to shed new light on the tension between Judaism and Christianity? The first paradox to take note of is that the vicious dialectic of Law and its transgression elaborated by Saint Paul is the invisible third term, the "vanishing mediator" between Judaism and Christianity. Its specter haunts both of them, although neither of the two religious positions effectively occupies its place: on the one hand, Jews are *not yet* there, that is, they treat the Law as the written Real, which does not engage them in the vicious, superego cycle of guilt; on the other hand, as Saint Paul makes clear, the basic point of Christianity proper is to *break out* of the vicious superego cycle of the Law and its transgression via Love. In Seminar VII, Lacan discusses the Paulinian dialectic of the Law and its transgression at length. Perhaps we should thus read this Paulinian dialectic along with its corollary, the *other* paradigmatic passage by Saint Paul, the one on love from Corinthians 13:

> If I speak in the tongues of mortals and of angels, but do not have love, I am a noisy gong or a clanging cymbal. And if I have prophetic powers, and understand all mysteries and all knowledge, and if I have all faith, so as to remove mountains, but do not have love, I am nothing. If I give away all my possessions, and if I hand over my body so that I may boast [alternative translation: "may be burned"], but do not have love, I gain nothing. [. . .]
>
> Love never ends. But as for prophecies, they will come to an end; as for tongues, they will cease; as for knowledge, it will come to an end. For we know only in part, and we prophesy only in part; but when the complete comes, the partial will come to an end [. . .] For now we see in a mirror, dimly, but then we will see face to face. Now I know only in part; then I will know fully, even as I have been fully known. And now faith, hope, and love abide, these three; and the greatest of these is love.

Crucial here is the clearly paradoxical place of Love with regard to All (to the completed series of knowledge or prophesies). First, Saint Paul claims that there is love, even if we possess *all* knowledge—then, in the second paragraph, he claims that there is love only for *incomplete* beings, that is, beings possessing incomplete knowledge. When I will "know fully [. . .] as I have been fully known," will there still be love? Although, unlike knowledge, "love never ends," it is clearly only "now" (while I am still incomplete) that "faith, hope, and love abide."

The only way out of this deadlock is to read the two inconsistent claims according to Lacan's feminine formulas of sexuation: even when it is "all" (complete, with no exception), the field of knowledge remains in a way not-all, incomplete. Love is not an exception to the All of knowledge but rather a "nothing" that renders incomplete even the complete series or field of knowledge. In other words, the point of the claim that, even if I were to possess all knowledge, without love, I would be nothing, is not simply that *with* love, I am "something." For in love, *I also am nothing*, but as it were a Nothing humbly aware of itself, a Nothing paradoxically made rich through the very awareness of its lack. Only a lacking, vulnerable being is capable of love: the ultimate mystery of love is therefore that incompleteness is in a way higher than completion.

On the one hand, only an imperfect, lacking being loves: we love because we do *not* know everything. On the other hand, even if we were to know everything, love would inexplicably still be higher than complete knowledge. Perhaps the true achievement of Christianity is to elevate a loving (imperfect) Being to the place of God, that is, the place of ultimate perfection. Lacan's extensive discussion of love in Seminar XX is thus to be read in the Paulinian sense, as opposed to the dialectic of the Law and its transgression. This latter dialectic is clearly "masculine" or phallic: it involves the tension between the All (the universal Law) and its constitutive exception. Love, on the other hand, is "feminine": it involves the paradoxes of the non-All.

## SEXUAL DIFFERENCE AS A ZERO-INSTITUTION

The notion of sexual difference that underlies the formulas of sexuation in Seminar XX is strictly synonymous with Lacan's proposition that "there's no such thing as a sexual relationship." Sexual difference is not a firm set of "static" symbolic oppositions and inclusions/exclusions (heterosexual normativity that relegates homosexuality and other "perversions" to some secondary role) but the name of a deadlock, a trauma, an open question—something that *resists* every attempt at its symbolization. Every translation of sexual difference into a set of symbolic opposition(s) is doomed to fail, and it is this very "impossibility" that opens up the terrain of the hegemonic struggle for what "sexual difference" will mean. What is barred is *not* what is excluded under the present hegemonic regime.[5]

How, then, are we to understand the "a-historical" status of sexual difference? Perhaps an analogy to Claude Lévi-Strauss' notion of the "zero-institution" might be of some help here. I am referring to Lévi-Strauss' exemplary analysis, in *Structural Anthropology*, of the spatial disposition of buildings among the Winnebago, one of the Great Lakes tribes. The tribe is divided into two subgroups ("moieties"), "those who are from above" and "those who are from below." When we ask an individual to draw the ground plan of his or her village (the spatial disposition of cottages), we obtain two quite different answers, depending on which subgroup he or she belongs to. Both groups perceive the village as a circle. For one subgroup, however, there is within this circle another circle of central houses, so that we have two concentric circles, while for the other subgroup, the circle is split into two by a clear dividing line.

In other words, a member of the first subgroup (let us call it "conservative-corporatist") perceives the ground plan of the village as a ring of houses more or less symmetrically disposed around the central temple, whereas a member of the second ("revolutionary-antagonistic") subgroup perceives his or her village as two distinct heaps of houses, separated by an invisible frontier.[6]

Lévi-Strauss' central point here is that this example should in no way entice us into cultural relativism, according to which the perception of social space depends on which group the observer belongs to: the very splitting into the two "relative" perceptions implies a hidden reference to a constant. This constant is not the objective, "actual" disposition of buildings but rather a traumatic kernel, a fundamental antagonism the inhabitants of the village were unable to symbolize, account for, "internalize," or come to terms with: an imbalance in social relations that prevented the community from stabilizing in a harmonious whole. The two perceptions of the ground plan are simply two mutually exclusive endeavors to cope with this traumatic antagonism, to heal its wound via the imposition of a balanced symbolic structure.

Is it necessary to add that things are exactly the same with respect to sexual difference? "Masculine" and "feminine" are like the two configurations of houses in the Lévi-Straussian village. In order to dispel the illusion that our "developed" universe is not dominated by the same logic, suffice it to recall the splitting of our political space into Left and Right: a leftist and a rightist behave exactly like members of the opposite subgroups of the Lévi-Straussian village. They not only occupy different places within the political space, each of them perceives differently the very disposition of the political space—a leftist as the field that is inherently split by some fundamental antagonism, a rightist as the organic unity of a Community disturbed only by foreign intruders.

However, Lévi-Strauss makes a further crucial point here: since the two subgroups nonetheless form one and the same tribe, living in the same village, this identity has to be symbolically inscribed somehow. Now how is that possible, if none of the tribe's symbolic articulations—none of its social institutions—are neutral, but are instead overdetermined by the fundamental and constitutive antagonistic split? It is possible through what Lévi-Strauss ingeniously calls the "zero-institution"—a kind of institutional counterpart to "mana," the empty signifier with no determinate meaning, since it signifies only the presence of meaning as such, in opposition to its absence. This zero-institution has no positive, determinate function—its only function is the purely negative one of signaling the presence and actuality of social institution as such in opposition to its absence, that is, in opposition to presocial chaos. It is the reference to such a zero-institution that enables all members of the tribe to experience themselves as members of the same tribe.

Is not this zero-institution ideology at its purest, that is, the direct embodiment of the ideological function of providing a neutral, all-encompassing space in which social antagonism is obliterated and all members of society can recognize themselves? And is not the struggle for hegemony precisely the struggle

over how this zero-institution will be overdetermined, colored by some particular signification? To provide a concrete example: is not the modern notion of
the nation a zero-institution that emerged with the dissolution of social links
grounded in direct family or traditional symbolic matrixes—that is, when, with
the onslaught of modernization, social institutions were less and less grounded
in naturalized tradition and more and more experienced as a matter of "con-
tract"?[7] Of special importance here is the fact that national identity is experienced as at least minimally "natural," as a belonging grounded in "blood and
soil" and, as such, opposed to the "artificial" belonging to social institutions
proper (state, profession, and so on). Premodern institutions functioned as "naturalized" symbolic entities (as institutions grounded in unquestionable tradi-
tions), and the moment institutions were conceived of as social artifacts, the
need arose for a "naturalized" zero-institution that would serve as their neutral
common ground.

Returning to sexual difference, I am tempted to risk the hypothesis that
the same zero-institution logic should perhaps be applied not only to the unity
of a society, but also to its antagonistic split. What if sexual difference is ultimately a kind of zero-institution of the social split of humankind, the naturalized, minimal zero-difference, a split that, prior to signaling any determinate
social difference, signals this difference as such? The struggle for hegemony
would then, once again, be the struggle for how this zero-difference is overdetermined by other particular social differences.

It is against this background that one should read an important, although
usually overlooked, feature of Lacan's schema of the signifier. Lacan replaces the
standard Saussurian scheme (above the bar the word "arbre," and beneath it the
drawing of a tree) with the two words "gentlemen" and "ladies" next to each
other above the bar and two identical drawings of a door below the bar. In
order to emphasize the differential character of the signifier, Lacan first replaces
Saussure's single signifier schema with a pair of signifiers: the opposition gen-
tlemen/ladies—that is, sexual difference. But the true surprise resides in the
fact that, at the level of the imaginary referent, *there is no difference*: Lacan does
not provide some graphic index of sexual difference, such as the simplified
drawings of a man and a woman, as are usually found on the doors of most
contemporary restrooms, but rather *the same* door reproduced twice. Is it possible to state in clearer terms that sexual difference does not designate any
biological opposition grounded in "real" properties but a purely symbolic opposition to which nothing corresponds in the designated objects—nothing but
the Real of some undefined $x$ that cannot ever be captured by the image of the
signified?

Returning to Lévi-Strauss' example of the two drawings of the village, let
us note that it is here that we can see in what precise sense the Real intervenes
through anamorphosis. We have first the "actual," "objective" arrangement of
the houses and then the two different symbolizations that both distort the
actual arrangement anamorphically. However, the "real" here is not the actual

arrangement but the traumatic core of the social antagonism that distorts the tribe members' view of the actual antagonism. The Real is thus the disavowed *x* on account of which our vision of reality is anamorphically distorted. (Incidentally, this three-level apparatus is strictly homologous to Freud's three-level apparatus for the interpretation of dreams: the real kernel of the dream is not the dream's latent thought, which is displaced onto or translated into the explicit texture of the dream, but the unconscious desire which inscribes itself through the very distortion of the latent thought into the explicit texture.)

The same is true of today's art scene: in it, the Real does *not* return primarily in the guise of the shocking brutal intrusion of excremental objects, mutilated corpses, shit, and so on. These objects are, for sure, out of place—but in order for them to be out of place, the (empty) place must already be there, and this place is rendered by "minimalist" art, starting with Malevitch. Therein resides the complicity between the two opposed icons of high modernism, Kazimir Malevitch's "The Black Square on the White Surface" and Marcel Duchamp's display of ready-made objects as works of art. The underlying notion of Duchamp's elevation of an everyday common object into a work of art is that being a work of art is not an inherent property of the object. It is the artist himself who, by preempting the (or, rather, *any*) object and locating it at a certain place, makes it a work of art—being a work of art is not a question of "why" but "where." What Malevitch's minimalist disposition does is simply render—or isolate—this place as such, an empty place (or frame) with the proto-magic property of transforming any object that finds itself within its scope into a work of art. In short, there is no Duchamp without Malevitch: only after art practice isolates the frame/place as such, emptied of all of its content, can one indulge in the ready-made procedure. Before Malevitch, a urinal would have remained just a urinal, even if it was displayed in the most distinguished gallery.

The emergence of excremental objects that are out of place is thus strictly correlative to the emergence of the place without any object in it, of the empty frame as such. Consequently, the Real in contemporary art has three dimensions, which somehow repeat the Imaginary-Symbolic-Real triad within the Real. The Real is first there as the anamorphic stain, the anamorphic distortion of the direct image of reality—as a distorted image, a pure semblance that "subjectivizes" objective reality. Then the Real is there as the empty place, as a structure, a construction that is never actual or experienced as such but can only be retroactively constructed and has to be presupposed as such—the Real as symbolic construction. Finally, the Real is the obscene, excremental Object out of place, the Real "itself." This last Real, if isolated, is a mere fetish whose fascinating/captivating presence masks the structural Real, in the same way that, in Nazi anti-Semitism, the Jew as an excremental Object is the Real that masks the unbearable "structural" Real of social antagonism. These three dimensions of the Real result from the three modes by which one can distance oneself from "ordinary" reality: one submits this reality to anamorphic distortion; one introduces an object that has no place in it; and one subtracts or erases all content (objects) of reality, so that all that remains is the very empty place that these objects were filling.

## "POST-SECULAR THOUGHT"? NO, THANKS!

In Seminar XX, Lacan massively rehabilitates the religious problematic (Woman as one of the names of God, etc.). However, against the background of the properly Lacanian notion of the Real, it is easy to see why the so-called "post-secular" turn of deconstruction, which finds its ultimate expression in a certain kind of Derridean appropriation of Levinas, is totally incompatible with Lacan, although some of its proponents try to link the Levinasian Other to the Lacanian Thing. This post-secular thought fully concedes that modernist critique undermined the foundations of onto-theology, the notion of God as the supreme Entity, and so on. Its point is that the ultimate outcome of this deconstructive gesture is to clear the slate for a new, undeconstructable form of spirituality, for the relationship to an unconditional Otherness that precedes ontology. What if the fundamental experience of the human subject is not that of self-presence, of the force of dialectical mediation-appropriation of all Otherness, but of a primordial passivity, sentiency, of responding, of being infinitely indebted to and responsible for the call of an Otherness that never acquires positive features but always remains withdrawn, the trace of its own absence? One is tempted to evoke here Marx's famous quip about Proudhon's *Poverty of Philosophy* (instead of actual people in their actual circumstances, Proudhon's pseudo-Hegelian social theory gives these circumstances themselves, deprived of the people who bring them to life): instead of the religious matrix with God at its heart, post-secular deconstruction gives us this matrix itself, deprived of the positive figure of God that sustains it.

The same configuration is repeated in Derrida's "fidelity" to the spirit of Marxism: "Deconstruction has never had any sense or interest, in my view at least, except as a radicalization, which is also to say in the tradition of a certain Marxism, in a certain spirit of Marxism."[8] The first thing to note here (and of which Derrida is undoubtedly aware) is how this "radicalization" relies on the traditional opposition between Letter and Spirit: reasserting the authentic spirit of the Marxist tradition means to leave behind its letter (Marx's particular analyses and proposed revolutionary measures, which are irreducibly tainted by the tradition of ontology) in order to save from the ashes the authentic messianic promise of emancipatory liberation. What cannot but strike the eye is the uncanny proximity of such "radicalization" to (a certain common understanding of) Hegelian sublation (*Aufhebung*): in the messianic promise, the Marxian heritage is "sublated," that is, its essential core is redeemed through the very gesture of overcoming/renouncing its particular historical shape. And—herein resides the crux of the matter, that is, of Derrida's operation—the point is not simply that Marx's particular formulation and proposed measures are to be left behind and replaced by other, more adequate formulations and measures but rather that the messianic promise that constitutes the "spirit" of Marxism is betrayed by *any* particular formulation, by *any* translation into determinate economico-political measures. The underlying premise of Derrida's "radicalization" of Marx is that the more "radical" these determinate economico-political measures are (up to the Khmer Rouge or Sendero Luminoso killing fields), the less they are effectively radical and the more they remain caught in the metaphysical ethico-political horizon. In other words, what Derrida's "radicalization" means is in a way (more precisely, practically speaking) its exact opposite: the renunciation of any actual radical political measures.

The "radicality" of Derridean politics involves the irreducible gap between the messianic promise of the "democracy to come" and all of its positive incarnations: on account of its very radicality, the messianic promise forever remains a promise—it cannot ever be translated into a set of determinate, economico-political measures. The inadequacy between the abyss of the undecidable Thing and any particular decision is irreducible: our debt to the Other can never be reimbursed, our response to the Other's call never fully adequate. This position should be opposed to the twin temptations of unprincipled pragmatism and totalitarianism, which both suspend the gap: while pragmatism simply reduces political activity to opportunistic maneuvering, to limited strategic interventions into contextualized situations, dispensing with any reference to transcendent Otherness, totalitarianism identifies the unconditional Otherness with a particular historical figure (the Party *is* historical Reason embodied directly).

In short, we see here the problematic of totalitarianism in its specific deconstructionist twist: at its most elementary—one is almost tempted to say ontological—level, "totalitarianism" is not simply a political force that aims at total control over social life, at rendering society totally transparent, but a short-circuit between messianic Otherness and a determinate political agent. The "to come [*à venir*]" is thus not simply an additional qualification of democracy but its innermost kernel, what makes democracy a democracy: the moment democracy is no longer "to come" but pretends to be actual—fully actualized—we enter totalitarianism.

To avoid a misunderstanding: this "democracy to come" is, of course, not simply a democracy that promises to arrive in the future, but all arrival is forever postponed. Derrida is well aware of the "urgency," of the "now-ness," of the need for justice. If anything is foreign to him, it is the complacent postponement of democracy to a later stage in evolution, as in the proverbial Stalinist distinction between the present "dictatorship of the proletariat" and the future "full" democracy, legitimizing the present terror as creating the necessary conditions for the later freedom. Such a "two stage" strategy is for him the very worst form of ontology; in contrast to such strategic economy of the proper dose of (un)freedom, "democracy to come" refers to the unforeseeable emergencies/outbursts of ethical responsibility, when I am suddenly confronted with an urgency to answer the call, to intervene in a situation that I experience as intolerably unjust. However, it is symptomatic that Derrida nonetheless retains the irreducible opposition between such a spectral experience of the messianic call of justice and its "ontologization," its transposition into a set of positive legal and political measures. Or, to put it in terms of the opposition between ethics and politics, what Derrida mobilizes here is the gap between ethics and politics:

> On the one hand, ethics is left defined as the infinite responsibility of uncon-
> ditional hospitality. Whilst, on the other hand, the political can be defined as
> the taking of a decision without any determinate transcendental guarantees.
> Thus, the hiatus in Levinas allows Derrida both to affirm the primacy of an
> ethics of hospitality, whilst leaving open the sphere of the political as a realm
> of risk and danger.[9]

The ethical is thus the (back)ground of undecidability, while the political is the domain of decision(s), of taking the full risk of crossing the hiatus and translating this impossible ethical request of messianic justice into a particular intervention that never lives up to this request, that is always unjust toward (some) others. The ethical domain proper, the unconditional spectral request that makes us absolutely responsible and cannot ever be translated into a positive measure/intervention, is thus perhaps not so much a formal a priori background/frame of political decisions but rather their inherent, indefinite *differance*, signaling that no determinate decision can fully "hit its mark."

This fragile, temporary unity of unconditional, ethical injunction and pragmatic, political interventions can best be rendered by paraphrasing Kant's famous formulation of the relationship between reason and experience: "If ethics without politics is empty, then politics without ethics is blind."[10] Elegant as this solution is (ethics is here the condition of possibility *and* the condition of impossibility of the political, for it simultaneously opens up the space for political decision as an act without a guarantee in the big Other and condemns it to ultimate failure), it is to be opposed to the act in the Lacanian sense, in which the distance between the ethical and the political collapses.

Consider the case of Antigone. She can be said to exemplify the unconditional fidelity to the Otherness of the Thing that disrupts the entire social edifice. From the standpoint of the ethics of *Sittlichkeit*, of the mores that regulate the intersubjective collective of the polis, her insistence is effectively "mad," disruptive, evil. In other words, is not Antigone—in the terms of the deconstructionist notion of the messianic promise that is forever "to come"— a proto-totalitarian figure? With regard to the tension (which provides the ultimate coordinates of ethical space) between the Other qua Thing, the abyssal Otherness that addresses us with an unconditional injunction, and the Other qua Third, the agency that mediates my encounter with others (other "normal" humans)—where this Third can be the figure of symbolic authority but also the "impersonal" set of rules that regulate my exchanges with others—does not Antigone stand for the exclusive and uncompromising attachment to the

Other qua Thing, eclipsing the Other qua Third, the agency of symbolic medi-
ation/reconciliation? Or, to put it in slightly ironic terms, is not Antigone the
anti-Habermas par excellence? No dialogue, no attempt to convince Creon
of the good reasons for her acts through rational argumentation, but just the
blind insistence on her right. If anything, the so-called "arguments" are on
Creon's side (the burial of Polyneices would stir up public unrest, etc.), while
Antigone's counterpoint is ultimately the tautological insistence: "Okay, you
can say whatever you like, it will not change anything—I stick to my decision!"

This is no fancy hypothesis: some of those who read Lacan as a proto-
Kantian effectively (mis)read Lacan's interpretation of Antigone, claiming that
he condemns her unconditional insistence, rejecting it as the tragic, suicidal
example of losing the proper distance from the lethal Thing, of directly
immersing oneself in the Thing.[11] From this perspective, the opposition
between Creon and Antigone is one between unprincipled pragmatism and
totalitarianism: far from being a totalitarian, Creon acts like a pragmatic state
politician, mercilessly crushing any activity that would destabilize the smooth
functioning of the state and civil peace. Moreover, is not the very elementary
gesture of sublimation "totalitarian," insofar as it consists in elevating an object
into the Thing (in sublimation, something—an object that is part of our ordinary reality—is elevated into the unconditional object that the subject values
more than life itself)? And is not this short-circuit between a determinate
object and the Thing the minimal condition of "ontological totalitarianism"?
Is not, as against this short-circuit, the ultimate ethical lesson of deconstruction
the notion that the gap that separates the Thing from any determinate object is
irreducible?

## THE OTHER: IMAGINARY, SYMBOLIC, AND REAL

The question here is whether Lacan's "ethics of the Real"—the ethics that
focuses neither on some imaginary Good nor on the pure symbolic form of
a universal Duty—is ultimately just another version of this deconstructive-
Levinasian ethics of the traumatic encounter with a radical Otherness to which
the subject is infinitely indebted. Is not the ultimate reference point of what
Lacan himself calls the ethical Thing the neighbor, *der Nebenmensch*, in his or
her abyssal dimension of irreducible Otherness that can never be reduced to
the symmetry of the mutual recognition of the Subject and his Other, in which
the Hegelian–Christian dialectic of intersubjective struggle finds its resolution,
that is, in which the two poles are successfully mediated?

Although the temptation to concede this point is great, it is *here* that one
should insist on how Lacan accomplishes the passage from the Law to Love, in
short, from Judaism to Christianity. For Lacan, the ultimate horizon of ethics is
*not* the infinite debt toward an abyssal Otherness. The act is for him strictly
correlative to the suspension of the "big Other," not only in the sense of the
symbolic network that forms the "substance" of the subject's existence but also

in the sense of the absent originator of the ethical Call, of the one who addresses us and to whom we are irreducibly indebted and/or responsible, since (to put it in Levinasian terms) our very existence is "responsive"—that is, we emerge as subjects in response to the Other's Call. The (ethical) act proper is *neither* a response to the compassionate plea of my neighborly semblable (the stuff of sentimental humanism) *nor* a response to the unfathomable Other's call.

Here, perhaps, we should risk reading Derrida against Derrida himself. In *Adieu à Emmanuel Levinas*, Derrida tries to dissociate decision from its usual metaphysical predicates (autonomy, consciousness, activity, sovereignty, and so on) and think it as the "other's decision in me": "The passive decision, condition of the event, is always in me, structurally, an other decision, a rending decision as the decision of the other. Of the absolutely other in me, of the other as the absolute who decides of me in me."[12] When Simon Critchley tries to explicate this Derridean notion of "the other's decision in me" with regard to its political consequences, his formulation displays a radical ambiguity:

> [. . .] political decision is made *ex nihilo*, and is not deduced or read off from a pre-given conception of justice or the moral law, as in Habermas, say, and yet it is not arbitrary. It is the demand provoked by the other's decision in me that calls forth political invention, that provokes me into inventing a norm and taking a decision.[13]

If we read these lines closely, we notice that we suddenly have *two* levels of decision: the gap is not only between the abyssal ethical Call of the Other and my (ultimately always inadequate, pragmatic, calculated, contingent, unfounded) decision how to translate this Call into a concrete intervention. Decision itself is split into the "other's decision in me," and my decision to accomplish some pragmatic political intervention as my answer to this other's decision in me. In short, the first decision is identified with/as the injunction of the Thing in me to decide; it is a *decision to decide*, and it still remains my (the subject's) responsibility to translate this decision to decide into a concrete actual intervention—that is, to "invent a new rule" out of a singular situation where this intervention has to obey pragmatic/strategic considerations and is never at the level of decision itself.

Does this distinction of the two levels apply to Antigone's act? Is it not rather that her decision (to insist unconditionally that her brother have a proper funeral) is precisely an *absolute* one in which the two dimensions of decision *overlap?* This is the Lacanian act in which the abyss of absolute freedom, autonomy, and responsibility coincides with an unconditional necessity: I feel obliged to perform the act as an automaton, without reflection (I simply *have* to do it, it is not a matter of strategic deliberation). To put it in more "Lacanian" terms, the "other's decision in me" does *not* refer to the old structuralist jargon-laden phrases on how "it is not I, the subject, who is speaking, it is the Other, the symbolic order itself, which speaks through me, so that I am spoken by it," and other similar babble. It refers to something much more radical and unheard of: what gives Antigone such unshakable, uncompromising fortitude to persist in her decision is precisely the *direct* identification of her particular/determinate decision with the Other's (Thing's) injunction/call. Therein lies Antigone's monstrosity, the Kierkegaardian "madness" of decision evoked by Derrida: Antigone does not merely relate to the Other-Thing; for a brief, passing moment of decision, she *is* the Thing directly, thus excluding herself from the community regulated by the intermediate agency of symbolic regulations.

The topic of the "other" must be submitted to a kind of spectral analysis that renders visible its imaginary, symbolic, and real aspects. It perhaps provides the ultimate case of the Lacanian notion of the "Borromean knot" that unites these three dimensions. First there is the imaginary other—other people "like me," my fellow human beings with whom I am engaged in the mirrorlike relationships of competition, mutual recognition, and so on. Then there is the symbolic "big Other"—the "substance" of our social existence, the impersonal set of rules that coordinate our coexistence. Finally there is the Other qua Real, the impossible Thing, the "inhuman partner," the Other with whom no symmetrical dialogue, mediated by the symbolic Order, is possible. It is crucial to perceive how these three dimensions are linked. The neighbor (*Nebenmensch*) as the Thing means that, beneath the neighbor as my semblable, my mirror image, there always lurks the unfathomable abyss of radical Otherness, a monstrous Thing that cannot be "gentrified." Lacan indicates this dimension already in Seminar III:

> And why [the Other] with a capital O? No doubt for a delusional reason, as is the case whenever one is obliged to provide signs that are supplementary to what language offers. That delusional reason is the following. "You are my wife"—after all, what do you know about it? "You are my master"—in point of fact, are you so sure? Precisely what constitutes the foundational value of this speech is that what is aimed at in the message, as well as what is apparent in the feint, is that the other is there as absolute Other. Absolute, that is to say that he is recognized but that he isn't known. Similarly, what constitutes the feint is that ultimately you do not know whether it's a feint or not. It's essentially this unknown in the otherness of the Other that characterizes the speech relation at the level at which speech is spoken to the other. (Seminar III, 48/37–38)

Lacan's early 1950's notion of the "founding word," of the statement that confers on you a symbolic title and thus makes you what you are (wife or master), usually is perceived as an echo of the theory of performatives (the link between Lacan and Austin was Emile Benveniste, the author of the notion of performatives). However, it is clear from the above quote that Lacan is aiming at something more: we need to resort to performativity, to symbolic engagement, precisely and only insofar as the other whom we encounter is not only the imaginary semblable but also the elusive absolute Other of the Real Thing with whom no reciprocal exchange is possible. In order to render our coexistence with the Thing minimally bearable, the symbolic order qua Third, the pacifying mediator, has to intervene: the "gentrification" of the homely Other-Thing into a "normal fellow human" cannot occur through our direct interaction but presupposes the third agency to which we both submit—there is no intersubjectivity (no symmetrical, shared, relation between humans) without the impersonal symbolic Order. So no axis between the two terms can subsist without the third one: if the functioning of the big Other is suspended, the friendly neighbor coincides with the monstrous Thing (Antigone); if there is no neighbor to whom I can relate as a human partner, the symbolic Order itself turns into the monstrous Thing that directly parasitizes upon me (like Daniel Paul Schreber's God, who directly controls me, penetrating me with the rays of jouissance); if there is no Thing to underpin our everyday, symbolically regulated exchange with others, we find ourselves in a "flat," aseptic, Habermasian universe in which subjects are deprived of their hubris of excessive passion, reduced to lifeless pawns in the regulated game of communication. Antigone–Schreber–Habermas: a truly uncanny ménage à trois.

## HISTORICISM AND THE REAL

How, then, can we answer Judith Butler's well-known objection that the Lacanian Real involves the opposition between the (hypostasized, proto-transcendental, prehistorical, and presocial) "symbolic order," that is, the "big Other," and "society" as the field of contingent socio-symbolic struggles? Her main arguments against Lacan can be reduced to the basic reproach that Lacan hypostasizes some historically contingent formation (even if it is Lack itself) into a proto-transcendental presocial formal a priori. However, this critical line of reasoning only works if the (Lacanian) Real is silently reduced to a prehistorical a priori symbolic norm: only in this case can Lacanian sexual difference be conceived of as an ideal prescriptive norm, and all concrete variations of sexual life be conceived of as constrained by this nonthematizable, normative condition. Butler is, of course, aware that Lacan's "il n'y a pas de rapport sexuel" means that any "actual" sexual relationship is always tainted by failure. However, she interprets this failure as the failure of the contingent historical reality of sexual life to fully actualize the symbolic norm: the ideal is still there, even when the bodies in question—contingent and historically formed—do not conform to the ideal.

I am tempted to say that, in order to get at what Lacan is aiming at with his "il n'y a pas de rapport sexuel," one should begin by emphasizing that, far from serving as an implicit symbolic norm that reality can never reach, sexual difference as real/impossible means precisely that there is no such norm: sexual difference is that "bedrock of impossibility" on account of which every "formalization" of sexual difference fails. In the sense in which Butler speaks of "competing universalities," one can thus speak of competing symbolizations/normativizations of sexual difference: if sexual difference may be said to be "formal," it is certainly a strange form—a form whose main result is precisely that it undermines every universal form that aims at capturing it.

If one insists on referring to the opposition between the universal and the particular, between the transcendental and the contingent/pathological, then one could say that sexual difference is the paradox of the particular that is more universal than universality itself—a contingent difference, an indivisible remainder of the "pathological" sphere (in the Kantian sense of the term), that always somehow derails or destabilizes normative ideality itself. Far from being normative, sexual difference is thus pathological in the most radical sense of the term: a contingent stain that all symbolic fictions of symmetrical kinship positions try in vain to obliterate. Far from constraining in advance the variety of sexual arrangements, the Real of sexual difference is the traumatic cause that sets in motion their contingent proliferation.[14]

This notion of the Real also enables me to answer Butler's reproach that Lacan hypostasizes the "big Other" into a kind of prehistorical transcendental a priori. For as we have already seen, when Lacan emphatically asserts that "there is no big Other," his point is precisely that there is no a priori formal structural scheme exempted from historical contingencies—there are only contingent, fragile, inconsistent configurations. (Furthermore, far from clinging to the paternal symbolic authority, the "Name-of-the-Father" is for Lacan a fake, a semblance that conceals this structural inconsistency.) In other words, the claim that the Real is inherent to the Symbolic is strictly equivalent to the claim that "there is no big Other": the Lacanian Real is that traumatic "bone in the throat" that contaminates every ideality of the symbolic, rendering it contingent and inconsistent.

For this reason, far from being opposed to historicity, the Real is its very "ahistorical" ground, the a priori of historicity itself. We can thus see how the entire topology changes from Butler's description of the Real and the "big Other" as the prehistorical a priori to their actual functioning in Lacan's edifice. In her critical portrait, Butler describes an ideal "big Other" that persists as a norm, although it is never fully actualized, the contingencies of history thwarting its full imposition, while Lacan's edifice is instead centered on the tension between some traumatic "particular absolute," some kernel resisting symbolization, and the "competing universalities" (to use Butler's appropriate term) that endeavor in vain to symbolize/normalize it. The gap between the symbolic a priori Form and history/sociality is utterly foreign to Lacan. The "duality" with which Lacan operates is not the duality of the a priori form/norm, the symbolic Order, and its imperfect historical realization: for Lacan, as well as for Butler, there is *nothing* outside of contingent, partial, inconsistent symbolic practices, no "big Other" that guarantees their ultimate consistency. However, in contrast to Butler and historicism, Lacan grounds historicity in a different way: not in the simple empirical excess of "society" over symbolic schemas but in the resisting kernel *within* the symbolic process itself.

The Lacanian Real is thus not simply a technical term for the neutral limit of conceptualization. We should be as precise as possible here with regard to the relationship between trauma as real and the domain of socio-symbolic historical practices: the Real is neither presocial nor a social effect. Rather, the point is that the Social itself is *constituted* by the exclusion of some traumatic Real. What is "outside the Social" is not some positive a priori symbolic form/norm but merely its negative founding gesture itself.

In conclusion, how are we to counter the standard postmodern rejection of sexual difference as a "binary" opposition? One is tempted to draw a parallel to the postmodern rejection of the relevance of class antagonism: class antagonism should not, according to this view, be "essentialized" into the ultimate, hermeneutic point of reference to whose "expression" all other antagonisms can be reduced, for today we are witnessing the thriving of new, multiple political (class, ethnic, gay, ecological, feminist, religious) subjectivities, and the alliance between them is the outcome of the open, thoroughly contingent, hegemonic struggle. However, philosophers as different as Alain Badiou and Fredric Jameson have pointed out, regarding today's multiculturalist celebration of the diversity of lifestyles, how this thriving of differences relies on an underlying One, that is, on the radical obliteration of Difference, of the antagonistic gap.[15] The same goes for the standard postmodern critique of sexual difference as a "binary opposition" to be deconstructed: "there are not only two sexes, but a multitude of sexes and sexual identities." In all of these cases, the moment we introduce "thriving multitude," what we effectively assert is the exact opposite: underlying all-pervasive Sameness. In other words, the notion of a radical, antagonistic gap that affects the entire social body is obliterated. The nonantagonistic Society is here the very global "container" in which there is enough room for all of the multitudes of cultural communities, lifestyles, religions, and sexual orientations.[16]

## NOTES

1. See Roger Ebert, *The Little Book of Hollywood Clichés* (London: Virgin Books, 1995).

2. I owe this point to a conversation with Alenka Zupancic. To give another example: therein also resides the deadlock of the "open marriage" relationship between Jean-Paul Sartre and Simone de Beauvoir: it is clear, from reading their letters, that their "pact" was effectively asymmetrical and did not work, causing de Beauvoir many traumas. She expected that, although Sartre had a series of other lovers, she was nonetheless the Exception, the one true love connection, while to Sartre, it was not that she was just one in the series but that she was precisely *one of the exceptions*—his series was a series of women, each of whom was "something exceptional" to him.

3. The difference between these two notions of the symptom, the particular distortion and the universalized symptom ("sinthome"), accounts for the two opposed readings of the last shot of Hitchcock's *Vertigo* (Scottie standing at the precipice of the

church tower, staring into the abyss in which Judy-Madeleine, his absolute love, vanished seconds ago): some interpreters see in it the indication of a happy ending (Scottie finally got rid of his agoraphobia and is able fully to confront life), while others see in it utter despair (if Scottie will survive the second loss of Judy-Madeleine, he will stay alive as one of the living dead). It all hinges upon how we read Lacan's statement that "woman is a symptom of man." If we use the term *symptom* in its traditional sense (a pathological formation that bears witness to the fact that the subject betrayed his desire), then the final shot effectively points toward a happy ending: Scottie's obsession with Judy-Madeleine was his "symptom," the sign of his ethical weakness, so his rectitude is restored when he gets rid of her. However, if we use the term *symptom* in its more radical sense, that is, if Judy-Madeleine is his sinthome, then the final shot points toward a catastrophic ending: when Scottie is deprived of his sinthome, his entire universe falls apart, losing its minimal consistency.

4. For a closer reading of *Breaking the Waves*, see Slavoj Zizek, "Death and the Maiden," in E. Wright (ed.), *The Zizek Reader*, ed. (Oxford: Blackwell, 1998), pp. 206–221.

5. The gap that forever separates the Real of an antagonism from (its translation into) a symbolic opposition becomes palpable in a surplus that emerges apropos of every such translation. Say the moment we translate class antagonism into the opposition of classes qua positive, existing social groups (bourgeoisie versus working class), there is always, for structural reasons, a surplus, a third element that does not "fit" this opposition (e.g., lumpenproletariat). And, of course, it is the same with sexual difference qua real: this means that there is always, for structural reasons, a surplus of "perverse" excesses over "masculine" and "feminine" as two opposed symbolic identities. One is even tempted to say that the symbolic/structural articulation of the Real of an antagonism is always a triad; today, for example, class antagonism appears, within the edifice of social difference, as the triad of "top class" (the managerial, political, and intellectual elite), "middle class," and the nonintegrated "lower class" (immigrant workers, the homeless, etc.).

6. Claude Lévi-Strauss, "Do Dual Organizations Exist?" in *Structural Anthropology* (New York: Basic Books, 1963), pp. 131–63; the drawings are found on pp. 133–34.

7. See Rastko Mocnik, "Das 'Subjekt, dem unterstellt wird zu glauben' und die Nation als eine Null-Institution," in *Denk-Prozesse nach Althusser*, ed. H. Boke (Hamburg: Argument Verlag, 1994), pp. 87–99.

8. Jacques Derrida, *Spectres of Marx* (New York: Routledge, 1994), p. 92.

9. Simon Critchley, *Ethics-Politics-Subjectivity* (London: Verso Books, 1999), p. 275.

10. Ibid., p. 283.

11. See Rudolf Bernet, "Subjekt und Gesetz in der Ethik von Kant und Lacan," in *Kant und Psychoanalyse*, ed. Hans-Dieter Gondek and Peter Widmer (Frankfurt: Fischer Verlag, 1994), pp. 15–27.

12. Jacques Derrida, *Adieu à Emmanuel Levinas* (Paris: Galilée, 1997), p. 87.

13. Critchley, op. cit., p. 277.

14. I rely here, of course, on Joan Copjec's pathbreaking "Sex and the Euthanasia of Reason," in *Read My Desire* (Cambridge: MIT Press, 1995), pp. 201–236. It is symptomatic how this essay on the philosophical foundations and consequences of the Lacanian notion of sexual difference is silently passed over in numerous feminist attacks on Lacan.

15. Alain Badiou, in his *Deleuze* (Paris: PUF, 1998), fully emphasizes how Deleuze, the philosopher of the thriving rhizomatic multitude, is at the same time the most radical monist in modern philosophy, the philosopher of Sameness, of the One that pervades all differences—not only at the level of the content of his writings but already at the level of his formal procedure. Is not Deleuze's style characterized by an obsessive compulsion to assert the same notional pattern or matrix in all the phenomena he is analyzing, from philosophical systems to literature and cinema?

16. There is already a precise *philosophical* reason the antagonism has to be a dyad, that is, why the "multiplication" of differences amounts to the reassertion of the underlying One. As Hegel emphasized, each genus has ultimately only two species, that is, the specific difference is ultimately the difference between the genus itself and its species "as such." Say in our universe sexual difference is not simply the difference between the two species of the human genus but the difference between one term (man) that stands for the genus as such and the other term (woman) that stands for the Difference within the genus as such, for its specifying, particular moment. So in a dialectical analysis, even when we have the appearance of multiple species, we always have to look for the exceptional species that directly gives body to the genus as such: the true Difference is the "impossible" difference between this species and all others.

# "FEMININE CONDITIONS OF JOUISSANCE"

*Geneviève Morel*

There are feminine conditions of jouissance, if only that of the Proustian ho-mosexual, Mademoiselle Vinteuil, who could only experience jouissance [*jouir*] with her partner in front of the portrait of her dead father (who was thereby ridiculed)—a condition that Ernest Jones encountered in his clinical work and that Lacan defined as "the fantasy of man, the invisible witness."[1] Psychoanaly-sis, which for structural reasons cannot tell us much about women's "supple-mentary jouissance," tells us more about the ways a neurotic woman experi-ences jouissance with a man, and why the phallic function and castration are, in theory, required. When it comes to conditions of jouissance, each woman cer-tainly has her own, and it would be futile to try to classify them or undertake an inventory—that would amount to treating women the way zoology treats a species: as a totality.

Having encountered it repeatedly in clinical experience, I confine my attention here to the figure of the "castrated lover" or "dead man" (*Écrits*, 733/95), which Lacan, in his 1958 text, "Guiding Remarks for a Convention on Feminine Sexuality," understands as a nonanatomical condition of the kind of jouissance that has been trivially and falsely called vaginal (ibid., 727/89). I examine the part of this text devoted to "Frigidity and Subjective Structure" in relation to "The Taboo of Virginity," where Freud discusses frigidity.[2]

## IMMATURE SEXUALITY

In his text, Freud examines the fear of deflowering virgins among "primitives." He is quite categorical about the fact that this fear is not a masculine fantasy but is, rather, based on a real danger. What proves it to him is his analysis of modern women. He begins from the following paradox: the sexual act, and not only the first one, which should tie a woman to a man and inspire tenderness and recognition, even sexual "bondage," instead sometimes inspires frigidity—a frigidity that is enigmatic when the man is not impotent. There is nevertheless a phenomenologically "contradictory" case that allows Freud to resolve the paradox and the enigma. The case is that of a woman whom he was "able to submit to a thorough analysis," in which her own hostility, going as far as insults and blows, served as the conclusion of the "great satisfaction" she experienced during the sexual act with her beloved husband (SE XI, 201). In this way, frigidity is clarified by its apparent opposite—"the greatest jouissance"—a situation that the Lacan of Seminar XX would not disavow, for there he sees frigidity as a problem that is less physical than epistemic: a woman can experience jouissance—here that of the Other—without knowing it. Freud infers its existence from a hostile feminine impulse that expresses itself either in such a way that it is "united [with jouissance] to produce an inhibiting effect" (ibid., 202), going as far as frigidity, or in a way that is separated from jouissance by the staging of murder or castration fantasies that follow jouissance, fantasies that might even be acted upon.

What then is the etiology of this feminine hostility? Let us dispense with the anthropological and psychological explanations that Freud considers inessential. His conclusion is as follows: responsibility for the paradoxical reaction to satisfaction or frigidity must be attributed to penis envy, linked to a woman's pathological stasis at the virile phase. As Freud says, "a woman's *immature sexuality* [*die unfertige Sexualität*] is discharged on to the man" (ibid., 206) out of bitterness and especially vengeance, hence, the obvious interest in marrying a widow, who is perhaps inoffensive.

## FRIGIDITY AND SUBJECTIVE STRUCTURE

Freed from the notion of development that hindered Freud, Lacan takes an entirely different approach in 1958.[3] He does not stress feminine envy and hostility, which certainly exist, but rather the conditions of possibility for a woman to recognize a man as such, and to experience jouissance with his penis. Lacan's theoretical reference for this is symbolic castration, but it remains to be seen how it comes into play in the feminine unconscious and how it intervenes in sexual jouissance. Indeed, it is almost as if, responding to Freud's comment that a widow would perhaps be "no longer dangerous" (SE XI, 206), Lacan had said, "Yes, I would say that only widows experience jouissance. . . . Your patient does not experience jouissance in spite of her castrating fantasies but rather thanks to them, except that her pantomime proves that they are not sufficiently symbolized." The Freudian opposition between feminine satisfaction and castration fantasies is resolved here in a causal relationship.

In "Guiding Remarks," Lacan clarifies what he put forward the same year in "The Signification of the Phallus." Frigidity was defined there as "a lack of satisfaction of sexual needs," and it was assumed to be "relatively well tolerated"

(*Écrits*, 694/290) because of the convergence of feminine love and desire on the same object. Lacan now answers three questions:

1. How can we "mobilize" and gain access to frigidity?
2. What are the causes of frigidity?
3. Under what conditions can a woman experience sexual jouissance and therefore not be frigid?

Lacan infers the answer to the first and second questions from the answer to the third.

## The "Fetishistic Form of Love"
### Characteristic of Men

Lacan begins by defining the fetishistic form of masculine love in order to distinguish it from the erotomaniacal form of feminine love. The masculine subject loves his partner "inasmuch as the phallic signifier clearly constitutes her as giving in love what she does not have" (*Écrits*, 695/290). However, he desires "beyond" his partner, in a *Venusberg* where "phallus-girls" proliferate (ibid., 733/94). The phallus that thus makes the latter desirable depends, in the subject's unconscious, on the mother's desire that formerly acquired phallic signification due to the paternal metaphor. He desires them therefore *quoad matrem*, that is, qua mother (Seminar XX, 36/35), hence, the divergence between love and desire in relation to the object, a divergence treated by Freud as a debasement in the sphere of love.[4] If one can speak of the "fetishistic form of love" (*Écrits*, 733/94) in men, it is in the sense that the phallic brilliance that issues from this "beyond" of the loved partner reflects on her as a phallic veil, masking the unbearable character of castration. This is what makes him desire her nonetheless and enjoy her. At this stage in his teaching, Lacan does not yet situate object *a* as the cause of desire in this dialectic. The "centrifugal tendency of the genital drive in the sphere of love" (ibid., 695/290) results from the splitting of love and desire in men.

## The "Erotomaniacal Form of Love"
### Characteristic of Women

For women, on the contrary, there is an apparent convergence of love and desire onto one and the same object. Indeed, a woman finds the signifier of her desire in her partner's organ which, being endowed with this signifying function, "takes on the value of a fetish" (*Écrits*, 694/290). She also can choose the same man as the "Other involved in Love," who is "deprived of what he gives" (ibid., 695/290). However, already in "Signification of the Phallus," Lacan noted that this Other is "difficult to see." In the section on frigidity, he therefore specifies its structure as that which "hides behind the veil" (ibid., 733/95) and establishes how this apparent unity masks a real "duplicity of the subject" (ibid., 734/95) that cannot be reduced to the conservation of the

Oedipal link to the father. Recall that Freud says that a girl can enter "the Oedipus situation as though into a haven of refuge" (SE XXII, 129) and never leave her father.

The following schema will guide my reading of Lacan's construction of a kind of fantasy that links the feminine subject, through a "going and coming" [aller-retour] (I justify this expression on the basis of Lacan's section title "Frigidity and Subjective Structure"), to the Other, the Other of the unconscious.

**FIGURE 4.1**

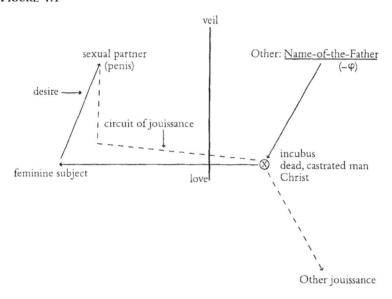

First, the "going": in order to accede to the Other, a woman requires a male partner as a "relay." This can be seen in Lacan's comment in Seminar XX: "It is only from where the dear woman is whole, in other words, from the place from which man sees her, that the dear woman can have an unconscious" (90/98–99). But as a subject, it is because of her defense—masquerade—that she can maintain a veil between herself as subject and the Other. The Other here is thus the Other of the unconscious, the locus of the law, and what "brings symbolic castration into play" (*Écrits*, 732/93). Lacan bases himself here on the axiom that "there is no virility that castration does not consecrate" (ibid., 733/95), which anticipates the formulas of sexuation for men (Seminar XX, 73/78). There is no "whole man" ($\forall x \Phi x$) without the law of castration made possible by the father as an exception ($\exists x \overline{\Phi x}$). According to this axiom, a woman can only recognize the virility of her partner by marking it with symbolic castration. But unlike Freud, Lacan does not localize this castration in a more or less staged castrating fantasy; on the contrary, he localizes it in the fem-

inine unconscious and in connection to love. If, therefore, feminine desire aims
at the sexual partner in front of the veil, it is from a point "behind the veil"
(*Écrits*, 733/95) that her love is called forth in the erotomaniacal form that
presupposes that the initiative comes from the Other. Here it is an entirely
Other partner who calls "her adoration to it," "a castrated lover or a dead man
(or the two in one)" (ibid.), collected under the term *ideal incubus.* An incubus
is a demon who visits women in the middle of the night, in a nightmare; this
also is the literal meaning of the Latin *incubare*, which reminds us of the un-
wished for dimension, beyond the pleasure principle, of jouissance.

Note the central place of symbolic castration in Lacan's elegant construction here. Behind the equivocal figure of the incubus, is it not in fact the
Name-of-the-Father that we find in the "locus beyond the maternal semblable
from which the threat came to [the woman] of a castration that does not really
concern her" (ibid.). And should we not seek the secret of this incubus in the
dead father, who is both the guardian of jouissance and the principle of castration?[5] The imaginary representation of the "dead man" or the "castrated lover"
takes on its symbolic and real weight by emanating from the point at which the
law is enunciated.

The fact that feminine jouissance has the virile organ as a condition lies
then in a return of love to desire in a circuit of jouissance that begins from the
point behind the veil and ends at the desired organ: "Thus it is because of this
ideal incubus that an embrace-like receptivity must be displaced in a sheath-
like sensitivity onto the penis" (ibid.). Lacan, who in section V of "Guiding Remarks" rejects the anatomical theories of so-called vaginal jouissance, succeeds
here in locating jouissance not in the feminine body but rather in the surrealis-
tic trajectory in which we have followed it, from the incubus to the fetishized
penis. The importance given to this point behind the veil underlines the clinically undeniable proximity of jouissance to love in women and explains what
is, at times, their overestimation of love that can almost be absolute. This is
noted by Lacan in the curious "ideal" that he relates to the "incubus." This trajectory illustrates the formulation that Lacan introduces in Seminar X, *Anxiety*:
"Only love allows jouissance to condescend to desire" (March 13, 1963).

A WOMAN'S "TRUE" PARTNER

Let us focus now on some consequences that Lacan draws from the construction of this point "behind the veil." First of all, his reference to Christ as
"a broader instance than the subject's religious allegiance involves" (*Écrits*,
733–34/95) points toward his subsequent work in which the Other jouissance,
"beyond the phallus" in S(A/), is viewed as a prop for the existence of God:
". . . the God face, as based on feminine jouissance" (Seminar XX, 71/77).
Léon Bloy's novel, *La femme pauvre*, cited by Lacan in Seminar VIII, *Transference*,
also indicates the shift from phallic jouissance related to the figure of Christ,
the dead man, to a jouissance in God where Woman would exist. Indeed, the

"duplicity" of the feminine subject in 1958 between love and desire is rewritten by Lacan in the 1970s in terms of a "splitting" [*dédoublement*], with respect to the jouissance of Woman who does not exist, between $\Phi$ and $S(\cancel{A})$: "Woman has a relation with $S(\cancel{A})$, and it is already in that respect that she is split, that she is not-whole, since she can also have a relation with $\Phi$" (Seminar XX, 75/81). If she wants to have a sexual partner, she must accept this relation to the phallic function, $\Phi$, on the basis of which she has an unconscious that makes her a "divided subject," $\cancel{S}$, and has a fantasy ($\cancel{S} \lozenge a$) that allows her, if she is lucky, to meet a "man who speaks to her according to her fundamental fantasy."[6] $S(\cancel{A})$, the signifier of the lack in the Other, is that by which she makes up for the sexual relationship that does not exist: it is her relationship to the Other, a "supplementary" jouissance, that is experienced without her knowing how to speak it. The difficulty here is to line up the following nonoverlapping sets of terms: the "duplicity" between love and desire; the "splitting" of jouissance between $\Phi$ and $S(\cancel{A})$; and the "division" of the subject of the unconscious. If desire, for example, is to be situated on the side of $\Phi$, love can be distributed between $\Phi$ and $S(\cancel{A})$, as the mystics prove. We will return later to the "division" of the subject and the "splitting" of the not-whole when we turn to hysteria.

With his 1958 formulation, Lacan explains other points as well. First the claim that "the duplicity of the subject is masked in women, all the more so in that the partner's servitude makes him especially apt to represent the victim of castration" (*Écrits*, 734/95), shows the danger for the sexual partner of wanting to be everything for a woman, or of having all of her for himself. Thus the maladroit man[7] who tries to play the part of the Other is ineluctably pushed —by she who Lacan refers to in "L'Étourdit" as his "over half" [*surmoitié*][8]— into the place of the dead or castrated man.

Next we can deduce the "true reason why the demand that the Other be faithful takes on its particular character in women" (ibid.). We might have thought that it was in order to keep her partner's penis for herself alone, but what is far more important is to have exclusive rights to that which in him reevokes for her the point of adoration "behind the veil," from whence she loves and enjoys: that is her "true" partner. Later Lacan takes up this "demand that the Other be faithful" with another formulation: "[I]t is as his one and only that she wants to be recognized by him" ("L'Étourdit," 23). This "one and only" also refers to feminine jouissance insofar as, like in Ovid's account of the myth of Tiresias, that jouissance exceeds what man experiences in coitus.[9]

Lastly, "the fact that she justifies this demand all the more readily with the supposed argument of her own faithfulness" (*Écrits*, 734/95) results from the subjective structure deployed by Lacan. A woman is in fact fundamentally unfaithful to her partner, however unique he may be, since she cheats on him with the ideal incubus harbored in her own unconscious. This is literally repre-

sented in the film *Dracula* by Francis Ford Coppola, in which we see what
happens when the partner is abandoned for the ideal incubus.

FRIGIDITY AS AN OBSTACLE

Let us turn now to the second question raised in this section of "Guiding
Remarks": frigidity—its nature, its causes, and its modalities.

Frigidity is not necessarily a symptom, that is, the subject does not always
complain about it. According to Lacan in "Signification of the Phallus," it often
is "relatively well-tolerated" because of the apparent convergence of love and
desire on the same object. In Seminar XX (69/74), he calls into question the
very existence of frigidity, noting instead a jouissance that is experienced by
a woman with her partner without her knowing it, and that is therefore in the
register of the Other jouissance, a jouissance that cannot be said. But Lacan
obviously does not refer to it as an "extra" jouissance in section VIII of
"Guiding Remarks"; there it is understood, on the contrary, as a deficiency
of satisfaction. Even apart from the "context of symptoms," it "presupposes
the entire unconscious structure that determines neurosis" (*Écrits*, 731/93) and
is a "symbolically commanded defense" (ibid., 732/93). The "nature" of frigidity is thus that of a defense by the subject against a jouissance that presents itself, as we saw, at the border between adoration and anxiety. Its final cause is
thus a refusal of feminine jouissance, due to the risk it implies of going beyond
and submersion for she who experiences it.[10]

The subject's defense against jouissance here must be understood within
the "dimension of masquerade" (ibid.). Now in 1958 Lacan gives a prominent
place to the masquerade, since it is the way a woman lends herself to a man's
desire: "[I]t is in order to be the phallus—that is, the signifier of the Other's
desire—that a woman rejects an essential part of femininity, namely, all its
attributes, in the masquerade" (ibid., 694/290). This masquerade, a feminine
seeming [*paraître*] or "para-being" [*par-être*] (Seminar XX, 44/44), metamorphoses a "not-having" (the phallus) into a "being" (the phallus). Like a veil
dissimulating the feminine subject's deprivation, the phallic masquerade also
provokes a "veiling effect" (*Écrits*, 732/94) with respect to the feminine unconscious as Other.

Once he constructs his subtle dialectic between desire, love, and jouissance, Lacan tells us what acts as an obstacle to it, namely, the material and formal cause of frigidity: "any imaginary identification a woman may have (in her
stature as an object offered up to desire) with the phallic standard that props up
fantasy" (ibid., 733/95). Hence, a difficulty: a woman must engage in the masquerade, which is phallic by its very nature, in order to be desired by a man,
yet, if she alienates herself excessively in it, wanting too much to be a "phallus-
girl," she risks losing all of her sexual satisfaction. Are we to understand that
by adhering too closely to this phallic para-being, she risks believing herself to

be in it [*s'y croire*] and imaginarily saturating the lack that it covers over—thus becoming deaf to the call to adore the ideal incubus?

## MODALITIES OF FRIGIDITY

Let us try to deduce, obviously not exhaustively, the different ways in which one can refuse the dialectic of desire, love, and jouissance, isolating the points at which it can break down. Frigidity is obviously not the necessary consequence of these breaks, since it also requires imaginary identification with the phallus.

*The Adulterous Woman*   The adulterous woman loves and desires, but not the same partner. There are two possible cases. The first resembles the classic form of debasement in the sphere of love in men: in love, she is faithful to her companion, but frigid. She seeks jouissance in liaisons with one or more other men she desires but does not love (see Figure 4.2).

**FIGURE 4.2**

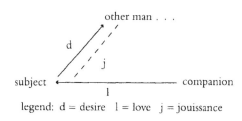

legend: d = desire   l = love   j = jouissance

   The second is a more enigmatic model also encountered in psychoanalysis: an adulterous woman who loves her companion—it is even only with him that she experiences sexual satisfaction—and yet cannot help desiring other men, one after another. In her relations with these other men, however, she remains frigid (see Figure 4.3).

**FIGURE 4.3**

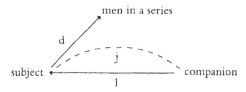

*The Collector of Men*   In this case, the woman is desirous but refuses or never feels love. She pursues jouissance with a series of men whom she desires (see Figure 4.4).

**FIGURE 4.4**

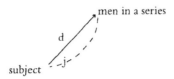

*The Disgusted Woman*   In this case, the woman overestimates love but neither desires nor experiences jouissance (see Figure 4.5). This is a form that one often finds in hysteria, when the penis is refused out of disgust.

**FIGURE 4.5**

I present here a few elements from the beginning of an analysis that brings to light the "narcissism" that creates an obstacle to the "embrace-like receptivity."

### The Perfume Bottle

A young woman came to see me to begin an analysis because of her professional difficulties. Working in the movie industry, she felt "undressed" and "unveiled" in her relations with others, which was unbearable to her. Regarding a symptom that took the form of an obsession [*idée fixe*], she complained, in passing, of frigidity. For some time, she had been waking up at night because her upstairs neighbors made love noisily. At work she was obsessed with noises and interpreted them with her sleepless nights in the back of her mind. This made work difficult, because she was "a sound engineer" and had to edit sounds. The expression she used to characterize her obsession was "the cries of a woman who is coming [*jouit*]." She also told me then that she had been refusing to have sexual relations with her companion, whom she loved but who had begun to lose patience with her. She responded by saying to him, "Tenderness, but nothing more."

Certain elements from childhood allowed her to identify what had sustained her professional "vocation." Up until age five, she lived with her maternal grandparents, across the street from her parents' house. Every evening she hoped her mother would pay her a visit, a visit announced by the sound of her car, but her car did not always stop. Once her mother had left, or gone by without visiting, the child would keep an eye on the window of her parents' bedroom, watching the light go on and then off, the curtains being drawn and reopened, and so on. The cuts of the sound and the image were thus associ-

ated—in the phrase "the cries of a woman who is coming"—with
"the sound of her mother," who comes and goes and perhaps joins
the father in the bedroom: a primal scene, therefore, or even a staging
of the paternal metaphor.

In another vein, she related the fact that she was disgusted by
penises to the fact that she was also disgusted by meat, which was indicative of the desexualization of the organ when not endowed with
the phallic signifier. This brought to mind her disgust for her father
who, mortally ill at the moment of her puberty, displayed his suffering
"in his flesh," which horrified her. She let her mother care for him.
I relate here a sequence of dreams she had around the time of the discovery in analysis of her frigidity.

In the first dream, a man cut another man into pieces in front of
her and her mother. The dreamer jumped on him and castrated him.
In the second dream, her mother was beside the dead father when the
dreamer entered their bedroom, where she had heard noises. These
dreams brought out the theme of the castrated man and its link to the
figure of the dead father. They highlighted the mother's ambiguous
and baleful role.

After having "tried" a sexual relationship that once again proved
to be unsatisfactory, she dreamed that her legs turned into meat, and
that her mother cut her ears off. This brought to mind her sick and
impotent father. The dream allows us to glimpse the fragmented body
of the mirror stage, becoming rotten after being cut up, rather than
any phallic signification. The mother here is castrating and prohibiting.

But another sequence brought out her "imaginary identification
with the phallus." Her companion had offered her a bottle of perfume, but instead of appreciating it she was haunted by the idea of
breaking it and losing the precious liquid it contained. That reminded
her of an earlier dream in which her mother broke one of the daughter's perfume bottles. Mad with rage, the daughter grabbed one of the
mother's bottles and smashed it on the ground. Alas, the perfume that
the second bottle contained turned out to be the daughter's, the
mother having poured the contents of the first bottle into the second
before breaking the first. In this way, the woman's vengeance against
her mother turned back against herself; in the end, it was her own
fault that she lost the precious perfume.

It appears in this little anecdote that what is important to her is
not only the bottle (cf. Dora's jewel-case, SE VII, 64, 69–70) but also
what it contains: the phallic *agalma* constituted by the precious perfume. Thus it is not only the phallic seeming that must be saved, for
the inside is even more valuable. Indeed, the patient had fantasies of a
closed body that could only be opened through breaking and enter-

ing. In addition to the masquerade and phallic seeming, her very being was identified with the phallus. Even in love she could not accept herself as lacking. To desire's lack, which would imply endowing her partner's penis with the phallic signifier, she preferred to keep this signifier for herself, rendering her invulnerable, even if her dreams showed that she had a little Achilles' heel. The metaphors of her dreams evoked "feminine sexuality [ . . . ] as the effort of a jouissance enveloped in its own contiguity" (Écrits, 735/97) and fear mingled with envy of a "symbolic break" that would free her from her precious but weighty phallic ego.

## THE "TREATMENT" OF FRIGIDITY: "AN UNVEILING OF THE OTHER"

This case will help us interpret Lacan's answer to his third question: How can frigidity be "mobilized"? He means in analysis, of course, somatic treatments being ruled out due to the fact that analysis has nothing to do with anatomy. Any hope of a cure through lovemaking, which would imply that frigidity can be reduced to sexual frustration, would be equally futile ("the usual failure of the dedicated efforts of the most desired partner," Écrits, 731/93). How can frigidity be mobilized in analysis, then, and more precisely, "in a transference [ . . . ] that brings symbolic castration into play" (ibid., 732/93)? The goal is to bring about an "unveiling of the Other involved in the transference [that] can modify a symbolically commanded defense" (ibid.). Now is not this Other involved in the transference the very Other of love sustained by the subject-supposed-to-know? The analyst attempts, by means of the transference, to get the subject to glimpse that point "behind the veil" that her excessive masquerade masks: the ideal incubus which causes love, though not without anxiety that must be overcome, and which is linked to the Name-of-the-Father and to the origin of the law in the unconscious.

This also reveals that there is a certain implicit analogy here between the feminine position and the analyst's position. Indeed, if the "unveiling of the most hidden signifier, that of the Mysteries, was reserved for women" (Écrits, 734/95), it is the analyst who has to unveil for the frigid subject the Other who is the receiver [receleur][11] of feminine jouissance.

## HYSTERIA AND FEMININITY

In the two texts we have studied by Freud and Lacan, frigidity is understood in terms of the castration complex, albeit in different ways. What is at stake for Freud is *Penisneid* (penis envy or envy of the penis), that is, the very modality of desire as lack, whereas for Lacan it is imaginary identification with the phallus—thus, rather, something that plugs up desire, creating an obstacle to the circuit of jouissance.

Neither of the two speaks of hysteria in the passages we have examined. We could, however, "reconcile" their conceptions of frigidity by noting that the virile phase of the frigid woman in Freud's thought refers to "playing the part of the man" in hysteria, whereas "final identification with the signifier of desire" (*Écrits*, 627/262)—the phallus—specifies hysteria for the Lacan of the 1960s. This leads us to the distinction between hysteria and femininity.

It would be tempting to draw the dividing line between the man who has to be killed and the man who is already dead, that is, to situate hysteria in terms of the castrating fantasy of the Freudian neurotic and femininity in terms of the woman who welcomes [*reçoit*] the dead or castrated lover. Why not, as long as we do not conclude that there are women on the one side and hysterics on the other—in other words, as long as we realize that, while femininity and hysteria are conceptually distinct, the extensions of these concepts intersect significantly.

Earlier I enumerated three oppositions or divisions: the duplicity in women between desire and love, the splitting of the not-whole that characterizes her jouissance between $\Phi$ and $S(\cancel{A})$, and the division of the subject of the unconscious, $\cancel{S}$. Let us begin then with a speaking being who is inscribed under "women" in the formulas of sexuation (Seminar XX, 73/78). That speaking being "grounds itself as being not-whole in situating itself in the phallic function" (ibid., 68/72). If, however, the said woman wants "to be joined with what plays the part of man" ("L'Étourdit," 23),[12] it is suggested that she use the "shoe horn" of the phallic function (ibid., 21). She would then have a relation—albeit contingent, that is, dependent on her encounters—with the phallic function, $\Phi$. She would then also be a subject of the unconscious, divided by the signifier and related to object $a$ as the cause of desire in accordance with her own fantasy. She would have symptoms and would therefore be neurotic, that is, obsessive or hysteric (but obsession presupposes a hysterical core, according to Freud).

If we consider, on the contrary, that there is an incompatibility between "being a woman" and "being a hysteric," where, then, are the women? Must they be reduced to several mythical or literary figures? Must we say that they are precisely where the analyst does not meet them? That they are crazy or psychotic? In that case, the analyst would see only men, many of whom have female anatomy. Such a rarity of women would seem clinically unsustainable and would contradict Lacan's statement: "How can we conceive of the fact that the Other can be, in some sense, that to which half [ . . . ] of all speaking beings refer" (Seminar XX, 75/81)?

I will thus take the position of asserting that hysteria and femininity can coexist in the same woman who is said to have a hysterical structure, and, furthermore, that hysteria is thus always partial, and that a woman goes beyond or exceeds her hysteria. We can sketch this simply by representing a not-whole woman as an open set that excludes its own limit, something Lacan suggests in Seminar XX (15/9). Hysteria can then be represented as a closed "whole," containing its own limit, that is situated inside the aforementioned open set: it is the whole constituted by "playing the part of a man" that does not coincide with "being a man" (see Figure 4.6).

FIGURE 4.6

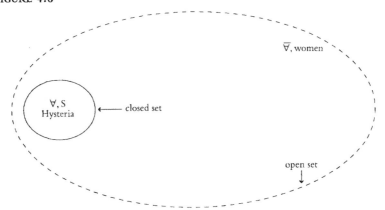

You can expand hysteria within the not-whole (or open set) as much as you like, and you will still have an infinite remainder between the two, between the hysterical limit and the missing boundary of femininity. You will still have a not-whole between the two. This shows that a not-whole cannot be saturated by any whole, indeed, not even by several "wholes." In this sense, the concept of the not-whole, which defines Woman as an indeterminate existence (Seminar XX, 68, 93/72, 102), takes us beyond the metaphor of the hole and the cork that is all too easily used to characterize women.

Nevertheless, the analyst first encounters the hysteric in the closed set and only has "sporadic" (Seminar XX, 75/81) and contingent access to Woman's fundamental relation to the Other in the "infinite" open set that contains the closed set. The analyst must not forget, however, that a not-whole woman's jouissance is related to the Other in such a way that, at any moment, it can give rise to manifestations that are as unpredictable as they are unexpected.

Lacan's work allows us to differentiate and link hysteria and femininity in several respects. With respect to jouissance we can discern, on the one hand, the jouissance tied to hysterical symptoms, especially conversion symptoms, which incarnate the master's castration (Seminar XVII, 99) within a discourse that constitutes a social link—that is the meaning of such symptoms; on the other hand, we can discern a woman's sexual jouissance with a man, that jouissance which, even with phallic mediation, is not inscribed in any discourse. Whereas symptoms are necessary and based on the subject's fundamental fantasy, sexual jouissance is contingent and linked to one or more feminine conditions of jouissance. We have considered one modality of this, the dead or castrated man.

THREE TYPES OF JOUISSANCE

I now briefly discuss one of the clinical cases that has underpinned this chapter. We can differentiate the loci of three jouissances: hysterical symptoms, sexual jouissance, based here on the figure of the dead man, and the Other jouissance.

> Mrs. A. came to see me due to a series of symptoms triggered by her husband's heart problems. She saw him fall, and ever since then she has been falling, twisting her arms and legs, wearing herself out, and becoming spasmophilic. In classic style, her symptoms defied medical science, and her doctors eventually encouraged her to see an analyst. During the preliminary meetings, she quickly mentioned a "trauma" that had occurred when she was nine. Her father had had a serious motorcycle accident in front of the house. She can still hear the horrible sound of her father falling. It happened at a crucial moment for her: she could not stand her parents, especially her mother, and she had obtained their permission to go to boarding school. Her father's fall, and his resulting physical and mental deterioration, prevented her much-needed departure. She became slightly depressed and herself fell off her bicycle.
>
> Mrs. A. is the fourth child in her family. Her oldest siblings died young. The first was a sister, who was said to be beautiful and blonde like her mother. The second was a brother, who was supposedly poisoned by his mother's milk. After their death, a third child was born—the spitting image of the dead sister—who was adored by her mother in place of the first. Mrs. A. was born last, unattractive and "swarthy" like her father, the "opposite of a 'top model,'" as she put it. The "top model" was her sister, who shielded her from her mother by attracting the latter's anxiety-ridden mothering. "Very early on," Mrs. A. told me, "I decided to escape my mother's deadly surveillance. I associated myself with the living, like my father."
>
> At the time of her falling symptoms, she described a haunting fear that her husband, her child, or someone else close to her would die. During her sessions, she elaborated on her sad thoughts in detail, alternating them with narratives and fantasies of giving birth. One day, wanting to get her to feel the weight of the fantasy that could be deciphered in her statements and symptoms, which I will characterize as "the living being who falls," I said to her, "But this is terrible, you spend all your time imagining the death of your fellow man." She responded, "No, not all my time, just most of my time, except when I have ecstasies." I asked her about what she called "ecstasies." She explained, essentially, that it was what happened when she was alone in her garden, empty of thoughts and images. Although she was a believer, the ecstasies were not related to God. All she could say was that she experienced them as something unique, different from sexual jouissance. I did not learn any more about them, even though she had seemed to want to speak about them.
>
> Her sexual jouissance had always been intense with her husband, whom she loved and to whom she generally had been faithful. She regretted the recent cessation of their sexual relations following his coronary illness and her

own hysterical pains. As a backdrop to this, she immediately mentioned the distant figure of a lover from before her marriage who died tragically and whose memory still haunted her. She then associated this dead lover with her brother, who died before she was born, telling me, "He was the only man my mother ever cherished."

Not wanting to be her mother's dead son, she had thus chosen to be the "living being who falls" by identifying with her father. But in her relations with her husband, she got off on [jouissait] the dead man, who she was not, but who she forever possessed. Behind the figure of the dead lover lurked for her the unnameable point—the son who died a martyr—from which the following order had been given to her: "You will not be the dead son, your mother's fetish object." Here we have the Name-of-the-Father, which names and forbids maternal jouissance.

This case allows us to distinguish the following: (1) the jouissance tied to her hysterical symptoms, sustained by the fantasy of "the living being who falls"; (2) the barely sketched out place of the Other jouissance in the form of her ecstasies; and (3) her sexual jouissance with her husband—but not without the dead man—to which hysteria is an obstacle but which it does not cover over.

The fact that a woman is more than or exceeds her hysteria, and that sexual jouissance must be situated where she is not-whole but not unrelated to the unconscious (Seminar XX, 73/78)[13]—as Lacan's notation ($\overline{\text{Woman}} \rightarrow \Phi$) indicates—is also proven by the different ways analysis ends. We see some duly analyzed women whose hysteria and relation to symbolic castration have been decisively modified. Among these, some continue to experience jouissance on the basis of representations such as those of the dead or castrated lover, representations that have not changed but became conscious at one point due to analysis. Does a hysterical remainder point to a failure of the analysis? It does not, because we have seen that it is not a question of imaginary fantasies that are reducible to the hysterical subject's fundamental fantasy but rather of a direct emanation of the origin of the law in a not-whole woman, the condition of her recognition and enjoyment of a man.

Translated by François Raffoul and David Pettigrew,
revised and edited by Bruce Fink.

## NOTES

1. See Marcel Proust, *Remembrance of Things Past*, trans. C.K.S. Mongrieff (New York: Random House, 1934), p. 210; E. Jones, "The Early Development of Female Sexuality," *Papers on Psychoanalysis* (Boston: Beacon Press, 1961); J. Lacan, "Guiding Remarks for a Convention on Feminine Sexuality," *Feminine Sexuality: Jacques Lacan and the École Freudienne*, trans. J. Rose (New York: W. W. Norton & Co., 1982), p. 97 (735). Hereafter, all references to "Guiding Remarks" and other texts from Lacan's *Écrits* (Paris: Seuil, 1966) will simply be indicated in the text as *Écrits*, followed first by the French page number and then by the page number in the corresponding English translation: either

*Feminine Sexuality* or *Écrits: A Selection*, trans. Alan Sheridan (New York: W. W. Norton & Co., 1977). All translations have been modified, often significantly, to reflect the new forthcoming translation of *Écrits* by Bruce Fink.

2. Sigmund Freud, *The Standard Edition of the Complete Psychological Works of Sigmund Freud*, 24 vols., trans. J. Strachey (London: Hogarth Press), vol. XI, "The Taboo of Virginity," pp. 193–208. Hereafter, all references to the *Standard Edition* will be provided in the text as SE, followed by the volume and page numbers.

3. "Guiding Remarks," section VIII, "Frigidity and Subjective Structure," *Écrits*, 731/93. Lacan disengaged himself from Freud's developmental approach, particularly in section VI of the same text ("The Imaginary Complex and Questions of Development"), where he constructs the "sexual metaphor" (*Écrits*, 730/91), which substitutes the subject's "not-being" for its "not-having," symbolized from then on by the phallus. On this basis, he concludes: "This remark assigns a limit to questions about development, requiring that they be subordinated to a fundamental synchrony" (730/91). This can be noted as follows:

$$\frac{-\varphi}{\text{development}}$$

4. See Freud's "On the Universal Tendency to Debasement in the Sphere of Love," SE XI, 179–90.

5. Lacan, *Le Séminaire, Livre XVII, L'envers de la psychanalyse* (1969–1970), ed. J.-A. Miller (Paris: Seuil, 1991), p. 143.

6. Lacan, "D'Écolage" (March 11, 1980), *Annuaire et textes statutaires* (Paris: ECF, 1982), p. 87.

7. Cf. "Les solitudes," Philippe La Sagna, Fall Meeting of the ECF, 1992, with a commentary by Carmen Gallano in the *Lettre Mensuelle* of the ECF, no. 114, 5 "Maladroit!"

8. Lacan, "L'Étourdit," *Scilicet* 4 (1973): 25. The translation given here, "over half," plays off the expression "better half."

9. Ovid, *Metamorphoses*, trans. F. J. Miller (Cambridge: Harvard University Press, 1984), p. 147.

10. See J.-A. Miller, "L'homologue de Malaga," *La Cause freudienne* 26 (1994): 7–16.

11. A *receleur* is a receiver of stolen goods, also known as a "fence."

12. The French here, "se conjoindre à ce qui fait thomme," is rather more complicated, since it indicates a neologism, *thomme*, which includes *homme* (man) and evokes Thomas d'Aquin (Saint Thomas Aquinas).

13. In this sense, we must not confuse the concept of the "not-whole" with that of S(Ⱥ)—they are not isomorphic. A woman is not-whole, even in her relation to the phallus, as Lacan shows in the first class of Seminar XX. Lacan takes up the not-whole there, in its relation to man, in terms of what he calls the hypothesis of "compactness" (Seminar XX, 14/9) for sexual jouissance. He illustrates it by the "feminine myth of Don Juan" (ibid. 15/10), which concerns the not-whole in relation to man, a relation contaminated by the Other, without it being a question there either of supplementary jouissance or of the hysteric's relation to the other woman.

# LOVE ANXIETIES

*Renata Salecl*

In Seminar XX, Lacan makes the puzzling statement that "there's no such thing as a sexual relationship" (12/17). He also views love as the subject's attempt to cover up the impossibility of this relationship. To understand the subject's love relationships, it is crucial to focus on the schema found below Lacan's formulas of sexuation, where on the male side one finds the split subject and the phallus (ibid., 73/78). There is no direct link between the phallus and the split subject: the subject has a relationship only with object *a* on the female side of the schema. On the female side, one finds three elements: a barred Woman, who has a relationship with the phallus on the side of man and with a barred Other, while she has no relationship with object *a*, which is on her side of the schema.

The major problem of male and female subjects is that they do not relate to what their partners relate to in them. The phallus that we find on the side of the man is not something a man can be happy about. Although a woman relates precisely to this phallus, the man is not at all in control of it. A man thus constantly tries to take on his symbolic function, since he knows that the symbolic function is what the woman sees in him. However, he necessarily fails in this attempt, which causes him anxiety and inhibits him. As Lacan points out: "The fact that the phallus is not found where we expect it to be, where we require it to be—namely, at the level of genital mediation—is what explains the fact that anxiety is the truth of sexuality [ . . . ]. The phallus, where it is expected as sexual, never appears except as lack, and this is its link with anxiety" (Seminar X, *Anxiety*, June 5, 1963, unpublished seminar). For men, the way they desire (which also is crucial for the relationship they form with object *a* on the side of their partners) is conditioned by the fact that castration has marked them by a lack, which also means that their phallic function has been negated. As a result of this negation, men are constantly anxious that they

93

might not be able to do it: that their organ might disappoint them when they need it most, that others might find them powerless, and so on.

Lacan points out that it is because of this anxiety that men created the myth of Eve being made out of Adam's rib. This myth allows a man to think that if just a rib was taken from him, then he is essentially not missing anything, that is, there is no lost object and woman is, therefore, just an object made from man. Although this myth tries to assure men of their wholeness, it nonetheless does not alleviate their anxiety. Anxiety often arises precisely when a man encounters a woman who becomes an object of his desire.

For Lacan, it is crucial that a man give up as lost the hope of finding in his partner his own lack $(-\varphi)$, that is, his fundamental castration. If this happens, everything works out well for a man: he enters into the Oedipal comedy, thinking it is Daddy who took the phallus from him—that is, that he is castrated because of the law. This comedy helps a man in his relationships; otherwise, the man takes all guilt onto himself and thinks that he is "a sinner beyond all measure" (Seminar X, March 26, 1963).

What about a woman's problem with castration? A woman also is a split subject and is thus concerned with finding the object she does not have; she also is caught up in the mechanism of desire. However, for Lacan, the fundamental dissatisfaction involved in the structure of desire in a woman is "pre-castrational": a woman "knows that in the Oedipus complex what is involved is not to be stronger or more desirable than her mother [ . . . ] but to have the object" (Seminar X, March 26, 1963). Thus object $a$ is, for a woman, constituted in her relationship with her mother. Lacan also claims that if a woman becomes interested in castration $(-\varphi)$, it is insofar as she enters into men's problems, which means that castration is secondary for a woman. As a result, "For a woman, it is initially what she doesn't have as such that becomes the object of her desire, while at the beginning, for the man it is what he is not, it is where he fails" (Seminar X, March 26, 1963). A woman is concerned that she does not possess the object that a man sees in her, and thus she constantly wonders what is in her more than herself; because of this uncertainty, she endlessly questions the Other's desire.

In short, a man is traumatized by not being able to assume his symbolic role and a woman by not possessing the object of the Other's desire. This explains why some men are so concerned with keeping intact their well-organized life, dreading encounters with women who incite their desire. Clinging to self-imposed rules gives a man at least temporary assurance that the symbolic order is whole, and that it might have endowed him with phallic power. But coming close to the object of desire opens up the possibility that this fantasy will collapse, and that the man will then be stripped naked, exposed in his essential impotence and powerlessness.

If men often respond to their love troubles by clinging tightly to obsessive rituals and self-imposed rules that are supposed to prevent them from becoming overly consumed by the object of desire, women's dilemma concerning what kind of an object they are for men might result in the fact that they somehow give up on love and immerse themselves in melancholic indifference. How can we understand such gestures of resignation by women who, for example, realize that they were not loved in the ways they hoped to be, or who acknowledge that they have ceased to be the object *a* around which a man's love fantasy used to revolve?

When the subject somehow "gives up" and becomes indifferent to the outside world, it is not that he or she reaches "the zero level of desire, but its more or less complete reduction to the foundation of the $-\Phi$ of castration. The subject in this state definitely takes pleasure in something [ . . . ]. In effect, doesn't it let the subject take pleasure in the a-corporeal consistency of castration as formulated ($-\varphi = a$)?"[1] The subject thus takes pleasure precisely in the lack introduced by castration, but this symbolic lack ($-\Phi$) often gets an imaginary inscription in terms of $-\varphi$. Colette Soler points out that there are various ways in which the subject rejects the gifts of life and detaches himself or herself from the world: "From conquering desire to melancholy's abolished desire— the problematic or dubious desire of neurosis lying somewhere in-between —love of the object, self-hatred, and narcissistic investment of the self are arranged in this order. The connection between desire and jouissance is obviously crucial here: since desire is itself a defense, jouissance arises where desire diminishes. It is clear, therefore, that a depressive state is also a mode of jouissance, but this formulation is serviceable only if we manage to give it particular coordinates in each case."[2]

In a woman, melancholy is especially linked to feminine jouissance. When Lacan tries to decipher this jouissance, he usually invokes the example of the mystics—women (and men) who find enjoyment in a total devotion to God, who immerse themselves in an ascetic stance and detach themselves from the world. This feminine jouissance, which language cannot decipher, is thus usually perceived as the highest "happiness" that the subject can experience. However, because this jouissance is foreclosed from language, it also is something that the unconscious does not know and thus cannot assimilate. If we invoke Lacan's thesis that the remedy for sadness is for the subject to find itself in the unconscious, then the question becomes, how is this indecipherable feminine jouissance related to female melancholy?

One possible answer might be that the enjoyment a woman finds in melancholic seclusion from the world is precisely a form of feminine jouissance. In this case, an ecstatic mystic and a melancholic woman would not be very different in terms of their jouissance. However, feminine melancholy also can be a result of the fact that the woman does not find herself in feminine jouissance. Since this jouissance does not pass through the unconscious, it passes beyond the woman, which is why in women one often finds "a plus of sadness": "The delusion of melancholic indignity [ . . . ] is revealing here: moving to extremes it shows that the decay of the foreclosed jouissance into self-insult is the ultimate verbal rampart before that same jouissance is expulsed

through an acting out that takes the form of a suicidal gesture. More commonly, I mean when we are not talking about cases of psychosis, the throwback
into injury is like the first degree of paradoxical sublimation, having come to
this place from jouissance where 'the universe is a flaw in the purity of Non-
Being is vociferated.'"[3]

This immersion into sadness or even self-injury often happens when the
woman loses love. But why would this loss incite such desperate reactions in
women? Following Lacan, Soler claims that it is because of the nature of feminine jouissance that one finds in women a specific call to an elective love,
which cannot resolve the discord between phallic and feminine jouissance. In
the love relationship she establishes, a woman will always be Other, that is,
Other to herself: "Love will leave her, then, alone with her otherness, but at
least the Other that love erects can label her with her lover's name, as Juliette
is eternalized by Romeo, Iseult by Tristram, and Beatrice by Dante. We can
deduce from this the fact that, for a woman, the loss of love exceeds the phallic
dimension to which Freud reduced it. For what she loses in losing love is herself, but as an Other."[4]

If feminine jouissance brings women much closer to the real, specifically
to the lack in the symbolic, which might result in either their mystical or depressive states, women nonetheless are also concerned with the question of
what their place is in the Other's desire, and it is in order to reassure themselves
about this desire that women engage in redoubling their partners. But such
women often seek out men who themselves cannot commit to just one
woman. Why does this happen?

A woman who constantly questions whether or not she is the object of a
man's love also tries to present herself as the phallus that the man lacks. Paradoxically, a woman finds an answer to her concerns about men's desire and
their phallic power in the fantasy of Don Juan which, as Lacan points out, is essentially a feminine fantasy (Seminar X, March 26, 1963; Seminar XX, 15/10).
For women, this fantasy proves that there is at least one man who has it from
the outset, who always has it and cannot lose it, meaning that no woman can
take it from him. Since women often are concerned that a man may completely lose himself when he is with another woman, the fantasy of Don Juan
reassures women that there is at least one man who never loses himself in a relationship. The fantasy of Don Juan thus assures women that the object of male
desire is what belongs to them essentially, and that it is thus something that
cannot be lost. Women and Don Juan thus have something in common here:
no one can take the object away from women or from Don Juan, since none of
them ever had it in the first place (Seminar X, March 26, 1963).

In order to deal with their love problems, men and women often redouble
their partners into the figure of a stable partner and an inaccessible lover; however, this redoubling serves different purposes in the two sexes. Men often redouble their partners because the object of their desire is something they are
essentially horrified by. That is why men cling so tightly to the self-imposed

prohibitions and rituals that govern their daily lives. Women redouble their partners because they can never be sure what kind of an object they are in the Other's desire. Thus for a woman it is better to fantasize that there is more than one man who is emotionally interested in her. But, paradoxically, a woman might get the most reassurance about her own value as object $a$ in fantasizing about a man (e.g., Don Juan) who never actually desires her in the first place.[5]

## NOTES

1. See Colette Soler, "A 'Plus' of Melancholy," in *Almanac of Psychoanalysis: Psychoanalytic Stories after Freud and Lacan*, eds. R. Golan, G. Dahan, S. Lieber, and R. Warshawsky (Jaffa: G.I.E.P., 1998), p. 101 [text modified].

2. Ibid.

3. Ibid., pp. 106–7 [text modified]. Soler quotes here from Lacan's "Subversion of the Subject and the Dialectic of Desire in the Freudian Unconscious," *Écrits* (Paris: Seuil, 1966), p. 819. Trans. by Alan Sheridan (New York: Norton, 1977), p. 317.

4. Soler, "A 'Plus' of Melancholy," p. 107 [text modified].

5. This theme is further elaborated on in Renata Salecl, "Love and Sexual Difference: Doubled Partners in Men and Women," in *Sexuation*, ed. Renata Salecl (Durham: Duke University Press, 2000), pp. 297–316.

# WHAT DOES THE UNCONSCIOUS
# KNOW ABOUT WOMEN?

*Colette Soler*

The title chosen for this chapter, "What does the unconscious know about women?" makes sense to the extent that the unconscious is a kind of knowledge. It is a kind of knowledge once it is deciphered and interpreted on the basis of what the analysand (male or female) says.

I could answer the question this title asks immediately, but that would not reduce the suspense: the unconscious does not know everything, but what it knows is sufficient for us to analyze women.

## FREUD AND FEMININITY

Freud's discoveries regarding sexuality were not welcomed in the culture at large. We might wonder why this was so. People usually refer to the customs of the time, but that is not necessarily the only reason. In any case, it is well known that Freud was accused of pansexualism, of finding sex everywhere. It is a curious pansexualism because, in fact, it does not involve the fairer sex, French designating the latter as *le sexe*—that is, as Sex itself. In deciphering the unconscious, Freud never found a term with which to inscribe feminine difference. This is quite striking. Instead, he put forward three major categories with which to situate sexuality.

As early as 1905, he discovered the drives, but in the form of partial drives, hence, the idea of "polymorphous perversion," which means that there is no genital drive in the unconscious. Children certainly construct sexual theories— namely, theories of the relationship between the sexes—but they invent them on the basis of the partial drives with which they are familiar. These partial drives have nothing to do with the difference between men and women; they exist in the little boy as well as in the little girl and leave unanswered the question of what distinguishes the essence of women.

Freud next noted the prevalence of a single formulation of sexual difference in anatomical terms, a formulation he consistently maintained: having or not having a penis. This led him to advance his main thesis, a scandalous one, stating that the subject's sexual identity forms on the basis of the fear of losing it for the one who has it, and the desire to have it for the one who is deprived of it. Making male and female development hinge upon the castration complex, Freud introduced, implicitly at least, the idea of a denaturing of sex in human beings. There is certainly a sexual being of the organism that cannot be reduced to anatomy, but it is nevertheless insufficient to constitute the sexual being of the subject. As proof of this, we have the fact that people constantly and quite openly worry about their degree of sexual conformity. Thus there is hardly a woman who is not preoccupied, at least periodically, with her true femininity and hardly a man who is not insecure about his virility.

Freud's third category explaining male and female development is the Oedipus complex, which he advances as a myth in order to account for both sexual taboos and ideals.

What then, according to Freud, is a woman? We know that he distinguishes three possible paths that have penis envy as their point of departure, only one of which he characterizes as truly feminine.[1] From this we can conclude the following: not all women are women. The word "women" obviously does not mean the same thing in its two different occurrences in this formulation. When we say "all women," it is the civil status definition that prevails. The latter is determined by one's anatomy at birth: if a child has a penis, we say "boy"; if not, we say "girl." But when we say "they are not all women," we are implicitly referring to an essence of femininity that escapes both one's anatomy and one's civil status, an essence whose origin remains to be determined. Freud's definition of this essence is clear; it derives from "being castrated": a woman is someone whose phallic lack causes her to turn to love for a man. The man here is at first the father, who himself inherits her love through a transfer of love that was originally addressed to the mother. In short, discovering that she is deprived of a penis, a little girl becomes a woman if she expects or waits [attend] to receive the phallus from the person who has it.

A woman is thus defined here solely by her partnership with a man, and the question is to determine what unconscious conditions permit a subject to consent or not consent to that partnership. This is where feminists protest, rejecting what they perceive to be a sexual hierarchy. The feminist objection did not begin with the contemporary women's liberation movement. It arose within Freud's own circle and was taken up by Ernest Jones. It was made in the name of a priori equality and denounced the injustice that would be committed if the absence of a penis were to be made the core of feminine being, thereby granting that being inferior status. To Freud's way of thinking, this objection clearly falls under the heading of what he calls the phallic protest. That does not, however, tell us whether or not it is valid.

## LACAN AND FEMININITY

When Lacan reconsiders the problem some years later, after the debate pursued by Jones and others over the prevalence of the phallus in the unconscious aborted, he does not take the same position as Freud on femininity.

He nevertheless claims to embrace Freud's thesis wholeheartedly. If we read the first page of "The Signification of the Phallus," we see that Lacan vigorously reaffirms Freud's thesis about the importance of the castration complex in the unconscious and in sexual development. "We know," he says "that the unconscious castration complex functions as a knot, first in the dynamic structuring of symptoms [ . . . ], and second in regulating the development that gives its *ratio* to this first role: namely, the instating in the subject of an unconscious position without which he could not identify with the ideal type of his sex or even answer the needs of his partner in sexual relations without grave risk—much less appropriately meet the needs of the child who may be produced thereby" (*Écrits*, 685/281).[2] This is a categorically Freudian ideal: identification, the possibility of a heterosexual couple, and happy maternity are governed by the castration complex.

Lacan not only adopts Freud's thesis, he also justifies it. He makes a wager, a wager on Freud's position (*Écrits*, 688/284). He says that Freud's theses are so surprising and paradoxical that we must assume they forced themselves on he who alone was able to discover the unconscious, through the unique access he had to that unconscious. Lacan takes up, condenses, and clarifies Freud's thesis, striving all the while to grasp its intelligibility. It is not the penis that is involved, he says, but rather the phallus—that is, a signifier that, like any signifier, has its locus in the Other's discourse. Except for this change, which in certain respects changes everything in what he himself called "the debate over the phallus" (*Écrits*, 689/284), Freud and Lacan both affirm the "phallocentrism" of the unconscious. Lacan, however, goes further than Freud in his definition of feminine desire.

There are in fact two stages to his teachings on femininity. The first—a more Freudian stage—takes place in 1958, the year he writes "The Signification of the Phallus" (1958) and "Guiding Remarks for a Convention on Feminine Sexuality" (1960). His more innovative theses follow in 1972–1973 with "L'Étourdit"[3] and Seminar XX, *Encore*.

In "The Signification of the Phallus," although he professes his Freudian allegiance, Lacan already begins to rework Freud's terms—as, for example, when he states that the relations between the sexes "revolve around a being and a having" . . . the phallus (*Écrits*, 694/289). "Being the phallus" is an expression not found in Freud's work. It obviously transforms the binary opposition of "having or not having" to which Freud confined himself, although it does not contradict it. Lacan's argument emphasizes rather that, in relations between the sexes, having or not having the *penis* only constitutes man or woman through a convention that amounts to having or being the *phallus*. This does not occur without the intervention of a seeming [*paraître*] animated by sexual ideals, and it has the contrasting function, on the one hand, of protecting the having and, on the other hand, of masking the lack thereof (ibid.). Freud emphasized the demand for love as characteristically feminine. Lacan, with a slight shift, suggests that in the relation of sexual desires, a woman's phallic lack is converted into a benefit of being . . . the phallus.

There is an implicit response to the feminist critique in these texts. More than a response, they situate the logic of that critique. But would feminists be satisfied to be given this phallic being? It is not clear, for if it is justified to affirm that a woman *is* the phallus, it is only at the level of her relation to man. The phallus, or being, is always for another, never in itself; this brings us back to her partnership with man, which Freud had stressed. Of course, Lacan emphasizes the relation to her desire rather than the demand she addresses to a man, but he maintains a definition of feminine being that involves the obligatory mediation of the opposite sex. If we ask what condemns her to this "relative" being, the answer can be found simply enough: in a heterosexual couple, the man's desire, indicated by his erection, is a necessary condition. The so-called sexual relationship puts masculine desire in a primary position. This is so true that without it there can be many kinds of erotic encounters, but not what we commonly call "making love." Accordingly, a woman, if she wants to inscribe herself in such a relationship, can only be called to the place of the correlate of his desire.

All of the formulations that Lacan provided to specify the place of "woman" make her a partner of the masculine subject: (1) being the phallus, that is, the representative of what man is missing; (2) being the object that serves as the cause of his desire; and (3) being his symptom upon which his jouissance is fixated. All of these define woman relative to man and say nothing of her own being but only of her being for the Other. This gap implicitly underpins Lacan's discussion in "Guiding Remarks," including his discussion of frigidity. One of the subjective conditions of frigidity seems to be imaginary identification with the "phallic standard" (*Écrits*, 733/95). One must conclude from this that if she is the phallus for the Other in a sexual relationship, she must not be it for herself through identification if she is to have her own jouissance.

The result is that everything that can be said about women is said from the point of view of the Other and only concerns semblance, their own being remaining, according to Lacan's expression, foreclosed from discourse.

## PLAYING THE PART . . .

Let us examine the function of "seeming" that I mentioned earlier and that instates the masquerade between the sexes. It constrains each of the partners to put on an act, either to "play the part of the woman" or to "play the part of the man" (Seminar XX, 79/85). This dimension, which is quite obvious in every-day life, appears very early on in the education of young children, but in this respect, there is no symmetry between the sexes. Lacan also says about women, however, that we should "recall that images and symbols *in* women cannot be isolated from images and symbols *of* women" (*Écrits*, 728/90). We see that these "images and symbols" are early place holders for the term *semblance* [*semblant*] that Lacan introduced much later. But why say it of women rather than of men, for whom the Other's verdicts also are quite important? Can we not ob-ject, without contradicting ourselves, that there also is a virile masquerade, a necessity, as I just said, to "play the part of a man"? This masquerade is present right from early childhood, because mothers, concerned about the future of their little cherubs, already judge them in relation to their ideal man and push them in general to incarnate the masculine standard. I say "in general" because there are exceptions, not to say anomalies. We come across mothers who push their boys to act like girls, to play the part of the "girl," but this is not what is most frequent, and it is a function of the mother's own pathology.

Lacan does not overlook this dimension in men. He even calls it "virile display" (*Écrits*, 695/291). It is not symmetrical to the feminine masquerade, however. In women, the agency of semblance is accentuated and even doubled insofar as their place in the sexual couple structurally requires them, in order to be the phallus, to don the colors—flaunted colors, I would be tempted to say—of the Other's desire. Lacan even notes that virile display itself feminizes by revealing the regency of the Other's desire (ibid.). The phallus is in fact a term that is always veiled, which means concretely that the conditions of desire are unconscious for each of us. An entire industry endeavors, in order to sustain the sexual market, to standardize the imaginary conditions of masculine desire's fantasy. It succeeds in part, but the fact remains—and this is what psychoanaly-sis reveals—that for each person, there are particular conditions set by the unconscious. The result is that seduction is not a technique but perhaps an art, because it never concerns merely the automatic functions that the collective imaginary programs. The ability to "make [the Other] desire" that is character-istic of women does not escape interference by the unconscious, the latter not being collective. Their response is thus the masquerade that adjusts to the Other's demands in order to captivate that unknown named desire.

I could mention here numerous clinical facts that are quite precise in terms of what women say—notably, a major complaint against the mother that consists in reproaching her for not having transmitted any feminine *savoir-faire* to her daughter. This complaint is not always direct, of course. It most often takes metonymic detours, which substitute one reproach for another. In the case of one particular woman, the complaint of not having learned the secrets of good cooking meant that the "trick" to attracting men had not been passed down to her. I also could refer to the hysteric's frequent protest against her sub-jection to the Other, her dream of autonomy being nothing but the counter-part at the level of the ego of the alienation that results from her demand to be.

It also is at the level of the woman's phallic metaphor that we find what is most persuasive in the feminist objection. When such an objection emphasizes the early constraints that the culture's images and symbols foist upon women—in order to denounce them, no doubt—that objection is not wrong, and it was to Lacan's credit that he admitted this, something Freud never did. However, it must not be forgotten that this subjection is a function of demand. A logic is at work here that can be found in certain positions adopted by the most extreme contemporary American feminists. The September issue of the *Times Literary Supplement* presented a ferociously ironic review of a book by Marianne Hexter. Her thesis is quite extreme, indeed, since on the questions of rape and sexual harassment she intends to do away with the limit that most of her feminist sisters think define sexual abuse—namely, nonconsensual sex. She sees that as an arbitrary dividing line and criticizes the sexual relationship itself—whether consensual or not—as the fundamental cause of feminine alienation. To be sure, this extremism might seem ridiculous, but it is not without its logic, since the alienation in question is a function of sexual demand.

What are Freud's and Lacan's positions on this point? They diverge. Freud was not exposed to the hard-core feminists of our time. This is unfortunate, because it is rather amusing to imagine his reaction. What is certain is that when he constructed his "masculinity complex," he did not do so without a certain contempt, and he betrays a note of clear reprobation. In his eyes, the only suitable destiny for a woman—namely, the assumption of castration—is to be a man's wife.

On the contrary, Lacan always endeavored to distinguish the psychoanalyst from the master and to remove from psychoanalysis any and every normative exigency, leaving only the sole constraints imposed by structure. This orientation prevails with respect to women when he affirms in "L'Étourdit" that he does not make the relation to castration that conditions the sexual link to man an "obligation." This can be stated in the following way: in the eyes of the analyst, the only thing that is obligatory is what it is impossible to avoid. This is not true of the relationship between the sexes, for this relationship is merely possible. The mistake in Freud's position becomes evident when he tries to measure women, as Lacan says, with the same "yardstick" [*la toise*][4] as men. He notes that the 1970s' women's liberation movement bears witness to this, "although sporadically, I'm afraid," he adds ("L'Étourdit," 21).

We might well wonder about the origin of this divergence between Freud and Lacan. Is it simply a question of taste, or even bias, Lacan's greater liberalism being a function of the change in mentality since Freud's time? I think not. Why would we assume that one had less prejudices than the other? Nothing indicates anything of the sort. Nevertheless, by taking structural terms further than Freud did, Lacan succeeded more than Freud in isolating the logical constraints of structure and their difference from ideal norms.

This does not mean that no objection can be made to the feminist argument. The main one, which deprives their militant position of its meaning, seems to me that they are certainly free to reject the company of men—this is a question of taste—but they will not free themselves from the problematic of the phallus for all that, because this problematic is tied to speech itself. Once the signifier is in the Other of discourse, it plays a role in even the slightest demand made to any other, whether man or woman, beginning especially with the mother—who, as Freud saw, is central here.

### "FEMININE DESIRE"

If a woman "is the phallus," her position in the sexual couple—where she is inscribed only by "allowing herself to be desired," according to an expression that Lacan uses at times—her position as the partner of masculine desire, leaves the question of her own desire unanswered. Hence, Freud's conundrum when, after so many years spent saying "They want the phallus," he finally asked his famous question: "What does a woman want?"[5]

The expression of feminine desire is problematic. Freud's doctrine at least had the merit of distinguishing between all of the desires that women can possibly have and what would constitute a feminine desire, strictly speaking. Desire as such is a phenomenon of the subject, related to castration; hence, its essential correlation with not having [manque à avoir], which is not specifically feminine. This is why, moreover, the notion of the "masculinity complex" is not only tainted with prejudice but conceptually confused. There is nothing specifically feminine about the desire to acquire or appropriate, which also is found in men as a metonymy of their having the penis, but it need not be forbidden to women, whether wealth, power, or influence is at stake—in short, the phallic quests of everyday life. On this point, the difference between Freud and Lacan is quite apparent. Lacan was not hostile to women, either in his texts or in the analyses he conducted, and he was hardly inclined, it seems, to discourage them from acquiring whatever they wanted, as long as it was possible.

Nevertheless, for a desire to be properly feminine, if there is any sense in using such a term, would be an entirely different matter. Freud only understands it as a variation on the desire to have—in the form of having a man's love or a male child. Beyond that, he throws in the towel. Lacan, on the other hand, tries to answer the question, even before Seminar XX, in which he addresses it explicitly. In "Guiding Remarks," he attempts a sort of deduction of that desire. Curiously, even paradoxically—and I am surprised it is not emphasized more often—it is in the course of his considerations on feminine homosexuality that he introduces it.

His presentation takes place in several steps. Far from attributing to a homosexual woman a supposed renunciation of femininity, he emphasizes on the contrary that femininity is her primary interest, evoking the facts brought to light by Jones who "clearly detected the link here between the fantasy of man, the invisible witness, and the care taken by the subject in giving her partner jouissance" (Écrits, 735/97). This means that, if a female homosexual competes as a subject with a man, it is with the intention of exalting femininity—with the proviso that she locates femininity in her partner. Lacan next remarks on the "natural ease with which such women claim to be men," and then adds: "Perhaps we see thereby the doorway that leads from feminine sexuality to desire itself" (ibid.). (This is a remarkable sentence that would be inapplicable to men, since their path leads from desire to the sexual act itself and not the other way around.) Lacan thus moves from women's "playing the part of the man," in sexual activity itself or elsewhere, to the affirmation of the erotic desire that identifies them, as though in their "playing the part of the man" they reveal what a woman as such expects from her partner.

This desire manifests itself as "the effort of a jouissance enveloped in its own contiguity [ . . . ] in order to be *realized in competition* with the desire that castration liberates in the male" (ibid.). This is Lacan's answer, at the time, to the famous question, "What does a woman want?": she has a desire that is quite foreign to any interest in having but is not a demand for being either. It is defined as equivalent, if not to a will, at least to an aim of jouissance [*une visée de jouissance*].[6] But it is a specific jouissance that is excepted from the "discrete" and thus limited character of phallic jouissance proper. It is more than a simple wish, application, or "effort" that competes. I would willingly risk formulating it as follows: "enjoying [*jouir*] as much as he desires." Note, moreover, that the expression "in competition with" [*à l'envi*], which connotes emulation, is redoubled on the following page when Lacan observes that, in the sexual relationship, the "appellants of the fairer sex," and "desire's supporters"—that is, women and men respectively—"act [ . . . ] as rivals" (*Écrits*, 736/97).

## THE UNCONSCIOUS AND FEMININE JOUISSANCE

This answer to the question of desire still does not address the question of what the unconscious knows of feminine jouissance. Lacan provided three terms that, in the unconscious, have jouissance as their referent. The first term is obviously the Phallus, written here with a capital *P*. The unconscious knows something about phallic jouissance, which is a signifier-syntonic[7] jouissance. Like the signifier, phallic jouissance is discrete and fragmented; it allows of greater and lesser amounts and can be appropriated by men or women, even though there is certainly a dissymmetry between the sexes when it comes to phallic jouissance. The second term is "surplus jouissance" or object *a*, which is not the partner in the couple but the object as cause of desire. This object, which is concealed within the partner, was first formulated by psychoanalytic theory as a partial object. This object as cause is not independent of the phallic problematic, since it intervenes as a complement that compensates for the phallic lack resulting from castration—this is inscribed in the structure of fantasy. This is why, when Lacan evokes feminine jouissance, he indicates that it is not caused by an object *a*. Lacan's third term is S(Ⱥ), and he teaches us to read it as "the signifier of a lack in the Other" (*Écrits*, 818/316). It is a signifier, but one that paradoxically is not in the Other. We can equally say that it is the signifier of the jouissance of the Other, insofar as that jouissance is foreclosed from the Other of the signifier, which only inscribes the phallic signifier.

We can situate women quite easily in relation to these three terms. Phallic jouissance is certainly accessible to women—Freud noted that long ago, and Lacan does not contradict him. With respect to object *a*, it is the child who eminently incarnates it for them. Lastly, there is what Lacan in Seminar XX calls other jouissance foreclosed from the symbolic, a jouissance that can be qualified as "outside the unconscious." The unconscious knows nothing of this jouissance. It is manifest in the experience of the sexual relationship and also in mystical love, but it cannot be translated in terms of unconscious knowledge. Unlike phallic jouissance, it is not caused by an object correlated with castration and in this sense cannot be measured. This is why Lacan says in "L'Étourdit" that it is "beyond" the subject [*le sujet en est dépassé*]. In contrast, phallic jouissance is not beyond the subject. I will not claim that phallic jouissance is homeostatic, because it can be disturbing and rise to the level of pathos, as we know, but it remains proportionate to the subject [*à la mesure du sujet*], just like object *a*, which certainly divides the subject but is adjusted to his gap.

What use can the analyst make of these indications? Can the foreclosed other jouissance be analyzed? I would say that, although the unconscious knows nothing of this jouissance, this is not an objection to analysis—for one analyzes the subject and not jouissance itself. It is no accident that analysis has led to an emphasis on phallic jouissance, for its practice is only concerned with jouissance that is filtered through the signifier [*passée au signifiant*].[8] On that basis, analysis reveals that there is a remainder, and that the whole of jouissance can never be said. I would conclude, then, that it is not necessary that the unconscious know more, for this more—a quantity—merely makes all the more tormenting what is Other, which the Other does not know.

Translated by François Raffoul and David Pettigrew,
revised and edited by Bruce Fink.

## NOTES

1. See Sigmund Freud, *The Standard Edition of the Complete Psychological Works of Sigmund Freud*, 24 vols., trans. J. Strachey (London: Hogarth Press), "Female Sexuality," vol. XXI, 229–30 and "Femininity," vol. XXII, 126–30. All notes here are editor's or translator's notes.

2. All references to *Écrits* (Paris: Seuil, 1966) will be simply indicated in the text as *Écrits*, followed first by the French page number and then by the page number in the corresponding English translation: either *Feminine Sexuality: Jacques Lacan and the École Freudienne*, trans. J. Rose (New York: W. W. Norton & Co., 1982), or *Écrits: A Selection*, trans. A. Sheridan (New York: W. W. Norton & Co., 1977). All translations have been modified, often significantly, to reflect the new forthcoming translation of *Écrits* by Bruce Fink.

3. Lacan, "L'Étourdit," *Scilicet* 4 (1973): 5–52.

4. The French here refers to an instrument for measuring height. Figuratively, it suggests holding someone to one's own standards or measuring someone up against oneself and one's own conceptions.

5. From a letter to Princess Marie Bonaparte.

6. Note that *visée* (aim) is one of the four components of the drive, according to Freud. The French here also might be translated as "an aiming at jouissance," or "a jouissance aim."

7. In the sense that one says "ego-syntonic."

8. Or, "that has been signifierized."

# LACAN'S ANSWER TO THE CLASSICAL MIND/BODY DEADLOCK: RETRACING FREUD'S *BEYOND*

☙

*Paul Verhaeghe*

Seminar XX is Lacan's obstinate, almost heroic fight to leave behind the deadlock of the classical binary oppositions: body/mind, nature/nurture, sex/gender, and finally man/woman. It is a fight that continues Freud's original attempts, Freud who produced an alternative to this classical opposition without intending to or even knowing it. Indeed, in his theory, the split is an internal one, and the idea of an external agency is drastically reconsidered, hence, his ever-insistent internal topologies: conscious/unconscious, ego/id/superego, and the split in the ego itself. Both Freud and Lacan demonstrate that a binary opposition fails to get it right. Descartes' ideas about *res cogitans* and *res extensa* are too poor to get hold of the complex dialectics of the human condition.

The danger of this chapter lies in its interpretative aspect. Interpretation always belongs to the realm of secondary revision, the mania to understand, of which all analysts should be wary. It will become clear that secondary revision is especially germane to the subject of this chapter. It also will become clear that we cannot do without it: it does not stop not being written—that is one of Lacan's conclusions. This is all the more true because Lacan's seminars are "works in progress"—belonging to an oral tradition of teaching and thinking at the same time—which cannot be adequately rendered by any written transcription. The latter will always be "not-whole," compared to the original that has disappeared, hence, the inevitability of interpretation. In my interpretation—there are others—I follow the basic, analytic rule: consider the text as part of a larger text; all meaning has to do with the larger part. Seminar XX cannot be read and studied in an isolated fashion—it is one of the highlights of a larger series of seminars. And, as Lacan considered himself a Freudian, Seminar XX cannot be studied in isolation from the texts of Lacan's Other: Freud.

I address three questions in this chapter: (1) What does Lacan's theory have to say about the age-old body/mind deadlock? (2) What does this teach us about knowledge? (3) What relation does this have to jouissance?

In answering the first question, I argue that Lacan ultimately leaves the binary deadlock of the first question behind. For him, the "mind" and "body" are not in opposition but are instead in an open-ended dialectical relationship. This suggests that the "essentialism" versus "constructivism" debate is all too naïve. The body we "have" exists only through the mind; it is the Other that constructs the body. But in and through this construction, the shape of something else becomes clearer and clearer, something that is contained in the constructed body while simultaneously foreign to it. This idea of "something else" is not new: it has been studied for a long time, in a very typical manner—that is, in such a way that this something else is a mirror image of ourselves, a Being under our being, different but alike at the same time. Such an underlying Being must necessarily be supported by yet a further underlying Supreme Being, as a necessary ground and final point. Lacan denounces the deadlocks of this kind of reasoning. He presents us instead with what he calls a circular but nonreciprocal relationship that keeps going between two terms that contain but do not hold each other—from object *a* to body, to ego, to subject, to gender. Albeit in reversed order: the so-called "previous" comes into existence retroactively, starting from the "next" in which it ex-sists.

The second question arises insofar as reconsidering this binary deadlock is impossible without rethinking knowledge about it and, hence, rethinking knowledge as such. Lacan opposed a familiar form of knowledge to another form. The former belongs to the Other of the signifier and is monotonous, completely determined by what he coins the "phallic One." Traditionally the latter is situated in an outside, again in a mirror image, the supreme Other of the Other who keeps final Knowledge. Again, Lacan leaves behind this binary system: this unknown form of knowledge is not a separate something; it belongs to the Other as well, except it belongs to that part of the Other that is the "not-whole" part, the gap in the Other in which something else of this Other makes its appearance.

For Lacan, this also is a form of knowledge, albeit of a different kind, a knowledge of the Other of the body. The next question concerns the relationship between these two forms of knowledge. But the most important question for Lacan involves the way in which this other form of knowledge is inscribed. Indeed, if this other knowledge does not belong to the Other of the signifier, its inscription presents us with a serious problem. The answer to this question entails a rethinking of the theory of the unconscious.

Last but not least is the third question, first seen from a clinical standpoint: the deadlocks of pleasure. The pleasure principle fails, as Freud discovered soon enough. Lacan describes another form of pleasure, operating from *within* phallic pleasure. This other jouissance stands outside of the signifier, outside of the phallic symbolic order, albeit from the inside. It is by no means a coincidence that Lacan needed the help of topology in order to demonstrate how "inside" and "outside" are continually part of each other. The Freudian idea of drive fusion (*Triebmischung*) receives a new illustration here. This other form of jouissance belongs to the "not-whole" part of the Other of the signifier. This means that this other form of jouissance can only be made clear through this Other of the signifier, albeit at the point at which this Other meets its limit.

These three subjects are not easy ones and cannot be treated in an exhaustive manner—indeed, from the very nature of the subjects, any form of exhaustiveness is impossible. It is no coincidence that Lacan evokes the idea of "infinity" several times in Seminar XX, and it is obvious that the three subjects are not in any way separate subjects. Isolating them is just another illustration of the way in which our symbolic cognitive system functions, that is, through the signifier.

## ENCORE: *"VINGT FOIS SUR LE METIER, REMETTEZ VOTRE OUVRAGE"*

### JOUISSANCE

In Seminar XX, Lacan is concerned with a jouissance beyond the phallic pleasure principle, that is, the typical remainder after the failure of the sexual relationship. Notably, even the psychopathology of everyday life demonstrates the necessity of an "encore,"[1] which is sufficient proof in itself of the unattainability of its goal. On top of that, it seems that the two forms of pleasure Lacan articulates stand in opposition to each other, which is by itself sufficient for us to question the very nature of "pleasure." Finally, the association he makes between the male and the phallic pleasure principle seems to raise the idea that the other form of pleasure belongs to woman.

The *familiar* pleasure, familiar also meaning "well known," is phallic pleasure, to be expected on the masculine side. It must be noted that "masculine" implies the psychosexual position, not biological sex as such. Phallic pleasure is first of all pleasure through the signifier and, therefore, the sole pleasure attainable for the subject. The fact that this phallic pleasure is never enough is not caused by castration—here Lacan corrects Freud, for indeed it is symbolic castration that creates its very possibility. The not enough has to do with the jouissance that is supposed to lie beyond this phallic pleasure. The other jouissance may have to do with woman, but Lacan specifies that it is an asexual jouissance, hence, the relationship between subject and other jouissance is to be situated outside of the Other of the signifier and more precisely in that part where the Other is not-whole.

At this point, several basic questions arise, including who or what enjoys this other jouissance? And how and where is this other jouissance inscribed, if it does not belong to the Other of the signifier?

*Lacan* Lacan begins with a question: "Jouissance—jouissance of the Other's body—remains a question" (Seminar XX, 11),[2] and he makes sure that it re-mains a question, avoiding the all-too-easy answers and making it clear to us why it has to remain a question. Indeed, his first answer brings yet another question: where does this jouissance of the body of the Other, as an answer to the Other of the signifier, come from? He offers us the idea of traces on the body, coming from a beyond that must have to do with life, death, and repro-duction (ibid., 11–12, 32–33). He does not further elaborate on this (see Semi-nar XI), but stresses the fact that these traces are originally not sexual ones, their sexual character being secondary: "The body's being is of course sexed, but it is secondary, as they say" (ibid., 11–12). Asexual in this context means not-phallic, hence, not signified by the symbolic.

This other form of jouissance has nothing to do with sexual pleasure, meaning phallic pleasure. It originates elsewhere and has to be understood as belonging to Being, except that the term *being* is redefined in a very serious way in Seminar XX. Lacan announces this at the very beginning of the Semi-nar, where he defines being as follows: "Where there is being, infinity is re-quired." This is understood as the opposite of the Other, where one finds the requirement of the One (ibid., 15).

Other jouissance concerns the "enjoying substance" ("the substance of the body") (ibid., 26), which is confirmed, says Lacan, by analytic experience.[3] In this experience, jouissance appears as the correlate of the failure in matters of the sexual relationship (ibid., 55), meaning the failure of the fantasy as the sub-stitution for the nonexistent sexual relationship. The idea of "correlate" is im-portant. It does not imply independent of or opposite to; on the contrary, it evokes the idea of a kind of implication.[4] Seminar XX is one long elaboration of this implied otherness, each time in opposition to what it is *not*. Lacan thereby introduces an opposition that never becomes a real binary opposition. On the one hand, there is the jouissance through the signifier (i.e., through the pleasure principle—phallic pleasure). On the other hand, something has to be situated beyond this, *but at the same time incorporated into it*, something providing jouissance to the Other.

But the hard question concerns the status of this Other. It is impossible to place the Other of the signifier here, because this Other belongs to phallic pleasure. Lacan specifies: the part that enjoys involves the not-whole part, some-thing that he still has to elaborate on at this (early) time of the Seminar, the not-whole *within* the Other, meaning that part of the Other that is other, that is not completely covered by the Other of the signifier. It is in that part that the traces, coming from an elsewhere, are operative.

Of course, it is very tempting to situate woman at this place, woman as the materialization of jouissance. It is the very same temptation in which courtly love found its origin, just like its counterpart—that is, the rejection of femin-inity by the Church, defamation ("diffâme"—defame; "dit-femme"—called woman, ibid., 79). Both reactions amount to the same thing: an attempt to recuperate something by articulation, something that ultimately cannot be recuperated by the signifier. The first one resides with love, and the latter one sleeps with hate (ibid., 64). For Lacan, men, women, and children are nothing more than signifiers, there being no prediscursive reality in these matters (ibid., 34).[5]

Insofar as woman has something to do with this otherness, it lies beyond her subjectivity and thus beyond her possibility of saying anything about it. The post–Lacanian hype about "feminine jouissance" is nothing more than a hysterical attempt to recuperate something that cannot be recuperated, owing to its very nature. Lacan presents us with only one clear statement, although made almost casually, about the occurrence of this other jouissance in women. With this statement, he implicitly takes up anew his comments on that elsewhere, life in combination with death through reproduction. Insofar as this other jouissance appears with women, it has to do with her child: "She finds the cork for this jouissance [ . . . ] in the *a* constituted by her child" (ibid., 35). This seems to me to be a clear hint to rethink female perversion beyond the myth of maternal love.

This other jouissance, in its relation to the beyond, might very well be understood as an original one, a primary one within a linear perspective, followed by a later, second one. Lacan corrects this in a very explicit way. Primary does not mean "first" (ibid., 52–53). The not-whole is an aftereffect, *nachträglich*, only to be delineated by the impact of the Other of the signifier, which tries to establish a totalizing effect through the One of the phallic signifier.[6] As a result, this Other is condemned to a kind of double vision. Indeed, it wants to see by and through the signifier something that is precisely defined by this signifier as being something beyond itself, hence, its "cross-sightedness" (ibid., 71).

This reasoning leads us back to a central line of thought in Seminar XX: "'The Other' here is more than ever thrown into question" (39). Indeed, through the different classes of the Seminar, the status of the Other changes (ibid., 21). As this happens during the Seminar itself, as a result of Lacan's work in progress, to study it becomes even more difficult. The main shift takes place in chapter VI, starting with the idea of "another satisfaction, the satisfaction of speech" (ibid., 61). This is then reversed, and by the end of the chapter, we read that the reason for "the being of signifierness" (beautiful paradox!) has to be identified in the "jouissance of the body" (ibid., 67). The Other, as the Other of the signifier, does not fill the scene anymore. It is the body, the "being of the body," that enjoys, not the "signified body."[7]

In the meantime, this other jouissance has changed sides. It does not belong to the "familiar" Other any more, the Other of the signifier. From now on, it belongs to the other Other, the Other of the body, albeit not the body of the mirror image. It seems that we are faced with an opposition between the Other of the signifier, on the one hand, and the Other of the body, on the other hand, which of course is not so new. The innovation resides in their redefinition beyond the Platonic binary psyche/soma schema. This jouissance of the body may very well lie beyond the phallus; it nevertheless ex-sists within this phallic jouissance, and this has to do with *a*-natomy (ibid., 87).

This *a*-natomy demonstrates, again, that this jouissance is related to these traces, which attest to a corporeal contingency (ibid., 86). This demonstration takes place in a retroactive manner; it is only when these traces have become (secondarily) sexualized (i.e., phallicized) that they also become visible, along with the *a*-sexual remainder that ex-sists in them. This is the transition from (a) to (*a*)/-phi. Phallic pleasure, and especially the insufficiency of phallic pleasure, makes this remainder obvious. In clinical terms, beyond the truth (the failure of the sexual relationship), the Real makes its appearance. This remainder— "enjoying substance"—resides with the objects *a* (oral, anal, scopic, invocative), which are indeed by their use value not so much known as they are enjoyed but which garner exchange value during the nurturing process and hence become phallicized.[8] It is this exchange that introduces them into the dialectic between subject and (m)Other and in its wake into phallic exchange, but even in this exchange, they ex-sist as foreign bodies, Freud's *Fremdkörper*.

Who or what enjoys? By the end of the Seminar, it becomes clear that it is not being that enjoys—being as the mirror image of the subject—but something else, something infinite, for which (*a*) is the ever-failing denomination. Object (*a*) is only a semblance of being (ibid., 87). Even more so: "It (object *a*) only dissolves, in the final analysis, owing to its failure, unable as it is to sustain itself in approaching the real," and that is the truth (ibid., 87–88).

The riddle that remains, says Lacan, involves the economy of jouissance. Who or what enjoys? The answer never concerns a "who" but focuses on a "what." The other jouissance can only be defined in a negative way: it neither concerns gender, nor the Other of the signifier, nor being. Each time it has to be understood, not so much in a beyond but in the fact that all of the previous ones are not-whole; it is within this whole not-whole that it flourishes. Coming from a beyond (ibid., 101), it has to do with the combination of life and death within sexual reproduction. Its elaboration takes place within the dialectics of corporeal contingency ("to stop not being written"), necessity ("it doesn't stop being written"), and impossibility ("it doesn't stop not being written").

How is this jouissance inscribed? The inscription takes place on the body in a contingent way, coming from this beyond. The body is not the body of the mirror stage; it concerns the interaction gates of this body with the outside (see the particularity of the four objects *a*).[9] This contingent inscription on the body (Freud's "somatic compliance") must necessarily be taken up anew, by the speaking subject, in and through the articulation of the signifier, where it becomes impossible. Instead of a binary opposition, we meet with an open-ended dialectic. We shall re-encounter this dialectic later in this chapter.

*Freudian Antecedents* In Freud's work, we find the same clinical experience, although with a different elaboration. In his initial search for the truth with his hysterical patients, he encountered the Real beyond the reality of trauma. At that time (letter to Fliess, September 21, 1897), Freud stopped and concentrated on the part that is the mere envelope of this Real, that is, patients' fantasies and their symptoms. Nevertheless, Freud already had a clear insight into the fact that something was wrong within the pleasure economy itself, independent of social and cultural inhibitions: "In my opinion there must be an independent source for the release of unpleasure in sexual life" (Draft K to Fliess, *Standard Edition*, Vol. I, 222). But he did not develop this insight any further at the time.

Twenty years later, after all possible elaborations and analyses of fantasies and symptoms (i.e., elaborations of the pathology of desire), Freud again encounters the Real. This time he grasps it much better: he reads it as something that lies beyond the pleasure principle. The failure of the pleasure principle is his formulation of what Lacan, half a century later, calls the failure of the sexual relationship.

In his elaboration, Freud hesitates to consider this factor as something that belongs to the economy of pleasure. He hesitates, because from his point of view, it is precisely something that works against the pleasure of the pleasure principle, thus presenting him with a major obstacle to therapeutic success. For him, it is first and foremost something traumatic. Indeed, it is the traumatic factor par excellence, a structural trauma in the sense that the ego can never get hold of it via word presentations.[10] Lacan echoes this idea when he talks about the "bad encounter" in Seminar XI. Strangely enough, in Seminar XX, he speaks about an encounter with love in a more optimistic way, although he adds that this requires courage (Seminar XI, 64; Seminar XX, 87, 132) and leads to a form of ethics beyond sex (Seminar XX, 78).

For Freud, this structural trauma gives rise to repetition compulsion and traumatic dreams, which are nothing more than endlessly repeated attempts to introduce the traumatic Real into the word representation, to articulate this Real inside the secondary process and its bound energy.[11] But these attempts fail, and finally he formulates his theory of the life and death drives as an attempt to articulate something coming from a beyond.

This further elaboration can be studied in Freud's metapsychology. The similarities to Lacan's issues are striking. To summarize them: (1) The pleasure beyond the pleasure principle is, for Freud, impossible to articulate; indeed, outside of the pleasure principle also means outside of the secondary process and the binding to word presentations, which makes it an unbound primary process of energy. As a result, it cannot be discharged through the use of words. This evokes Lacan's idea of infinity. (2) In Freud's work, there is no linear sequence or binary opposition; on the contrary, Freud describes a fusion, which he tries to understand with his last drive theory: the fusion between Eros and Thanatos. The other jouissance ex-sists within phallic jouissance. (3) The consequence of the impossibility to signify this traumatic jouissance nevertheless entails an endless attempt to signify it (repetition compulsion), but the impossibility to interpret it (for lack of a signifier), and hence to analyze it, remains. As a result, analysis becomes interminable, because analysis as such cannot gain access to this problem. The endless phallic interpretations circle around the not-whole of the phallic order, delineating it without signifying it.

For Freud, the jouissance beyond the pleasure principle is first of all related to trauma. It is interesting to note that this also was Lacan's first approach to the Real. His conceptualization in Seminar XI is so crucial with respect to Seminar XX that we must consider it here. It will permit us to bridge the distance between Freud and Lacan and provide us with a better understanding of Seminar XX as well.

At the time of Seminar XI (1964), the Lacanian audience is under the spell of the signifier, the opposition between the imaginary and the symbolic, between empty speech and full speech. But they are in for something new, something real.[12] Right from the beginning of the Seminar, Lacan introduces them to another kind of unconscious, the unconscious of the *Unbegriff*, the not-understandable, the nonconceptual (Seminar XI, 26), represented by the cut or gap and operating in a causal manner (ibid., 21–22). Lacan's elaboration introduces an interaction between the automaton (the network of signifiers) and the tuché (the real). In the terms of Seminar XX, the network of signifiers is the Other of the signifier, and the tuché or real is the other jouissance. The automaton is organized, contains verbal thoughts, and illustrates the function of recollection. Owing to its organization, recollection works perfectly, automatically, although only up to a certain point (Seminar XI, 49). This is best illustrated by the productions of the unconscious, which always demonstrate a failure, an impediment at that particular point (ibid., 25). This point is not so much a point but should rather be considered a discontinuity (ibid.), that is, the causal gap of the unconscious as such. Lacan describes this unconscious as unborn and unrealized (ibid., 23), hence, pre-ontological: "It does not lend itself to ontology." "Manque-à-être," lack of being, is the word for it (ibid., 29).

At this gap, where recollection fails, something else enters the scene, something that repeats through the repetition compulsion. This something else is the real "which always comes back to the same place" (ibid., 49). This meeting between the network of signifiers (the Other) and the real (the other jouissance) is always a failed meeting. It is the failed meeting between reality and the real, on very particular points. Indeed, reality (constructed by the symbolic, by the Other), is *unterlegt, untertragen* (supported, sustained) by radical points in the real, which is thereby condemned to painful pending ("en souffrance," Seminar XI, 55). These radical points are the asexual traces from Seminar XX, with which the network (the Other) fails to meet. Insofar as the subject thinks (in signifiers), he or she does not meet the real (of the other jouissance).

This was already made clear by Freud's study of traumatic neurosis, to which Lacan refers. But in Lacan's conceptualization, this impossible although necessary relationship between tuché and automaton attests to the very nature of the unconscious. This is the unconscious as causal gap, *obliging* the Other to the automaton of articulated thinking in order to master something beyond this kind of thinking as such. Automaton and tuché are two sides of the same coin that can never meet but are bound to try. Automaton is the not-whole, the not-enough of the network. Tuché is the real as the "unassimilable" (Seminar XI, 55), but Lacan specifies it. It is the Real of the drive, "the drive to come" (ibid., 60). Indeed, dream analysis demonstrates that the most important characteristic of the drive is its lack of representation; we meet only with a substitutional representative, a replacement representative ("un tenant-lieu de la représentation," my translation, Seminar XI, 60), through which the failure, the impediment of every production of the unconscious, becomes obvious. Lacan concludes that the question of the real and reality must be studied anew (Seminar XI, 55). Seminar XX is one of the major results.

*Conclusion* The other jouissance ex-sists within phallic jouissance, functioning as a foreign body. It causes an inner split in the subject. If there is any opposition with something external, it concerns a vague "beyond." Freud's theory on Eros and Thanatos reappears in Lacan's attempt to differentiate between "the advent of living" and "the advent of the subject," especially in his attempt to study the dialectic between the two forms of jouissance and their relation to the signifier.

In view of the close relationship between phallic pleasure, the pleasure principle, and the signifier, it is obvious that knowledge is patent in these matters. The subject knows "everything" about this. The question that remains involves the relationship between the other jouissance and knowledge. Is there something to know about this other jouissance and, if so, who knows it? This last question necessarily implies a reconsideration of the relationship between the unconscious and knowledge as such.

KNOWLEDGE

The subject's "wish to know" (Foucault's *volonté de savoir*) is always suspicious. The subject knows everything it has to know and assumes the existence of the same knowledge in the Other. Based on this mirroring, it provides itself and the Other with being, with a substantial identity. The crack in such a mirror was made clear earlier—in spite of this supposedly whole knowledge, there is a form of jouissance that escapes from this totality. The subject produces in this respect a mere *mi-dire*, a half-telling of the truth, thus meeting with a not-whole in truth itself. The not-whole of the Other is here displaced to a not-whole in articulated knowledge.

This leaves us with the following questions: What is the status of the Other in this other knowledge? How does this other knowledge become inscribed if it stands outside of articulated, signified knowledge? What is the relationship to the unconscious?

*Lacan* Lacan reads the history of knowledge as a history of an increasing decentering and desexualization. The Copernican revolution is not a genuine revolution, he says, because it keeps the idea of a center intact. The genuine revolution comes with Kepler, more particularly with the shift from the circle (with a center) to the ellipse (hence, without a center) (Seminar XX, 42–43).

The idea of this center in traditional (pre-)science always comes down to the assumption of being-in-the-world as a One—as a One that can have knowledge of this world through a mirroring process. Lacan denounces this reasoning in Aristotle's work. Indeed, Aristotle's assumption of such a being led necessarily to the assumption of a "supreme sphere" (ibid., 77). In Lacan's reading, this supreme sphere is nothing but an imaginary implementation of the jouissance of the Other, where woman would be situated if she existed (ibid.). In the Catholic interpretation of Aristotle, God took the place of this supreme sphere as the supreme Being. God became the center of all love and knowledge, to which all of the little beings belong in one way or another and to which they long to return. In this way, the Church saved both God and the father—and Freud produced the same salvation operation with his myth of the primal father (ibid., 99).

Such reasoning entails an endless mirroring process. It also produces the illusion of the existence of an underlying being that is supposed to possess the same knowledge as our own being. Beyond the thinking of the thinker lies the thinking of a hidden Thinker who keeps the reins in hand (ibid., 96–97). To Lacan, this is more a matter of tinkering, the brutal reduction of the Real to the One. Moreover, it is a reduction that provides not only the I and the being with an existence ("I am thinking, therefore I am") but the supreme being as well.

The knowledge that follows from this mirror operation—that is, the knowledge of traditional (pre-)science—is therefore always a sexualized knowledge, along with the accompanying deadlock. To put it differently, this form of knowledge is merely an attempt to come to terms with the nonexistence of the sexual relationship. As an example, Lacan refers to the relationship between form and matter, as described by Plato and Aristotle. In their theory, they always assume an impossible relationship between two terms which are nothing more than mere replacements for man and woman (ibid., 76). The working through of such an attempt leads to a predictable deadlock: owing to the lack of the sexual relationship, they end in an asexual reasoning: "The Other presents itself to the subject only in an a-sexual form" (ibid., 115). In this reasoning, again, the dreamt-of "two" of the imaginary sexual relationship is brutally reduced to the One. God is a sexless father, and the angels have no sex whatsoever.

The ultimate effect of such reasoning is that it keeps us away from the entrance to whatever may be of our "being," although its impasses could provide us access to it (ibid., 48, 108). Finally, this whole reasoning is only a philosophical development of the mirror stage, through which the ego fosters the illusion of a unified, substantial identity: "m'être/maître à moi-même," to be myself, to be master of myself, to belong to myself (Seminar XVII, 178).

Modern science leaves behind the very idea of a center and thereby also the mirror and sexualization. In mathematics, the concept of the One is not used in a fusional-amorous way anymore (i.e., as what makes up for the nonexistence of the sexual relationship) but indeed as a one. It becomes a letter that can be written down (Seminar XX, 46–47). The difference between that and the One of traditional pre-science is that this letter in modern science does not designate an assemblage—it *constitutes* one. In this way, modern science tries to create an entrance to the Real in a different manner (ibid., 118).

Lacan recognizes the same movement of desexualization and decentering in the very process of analysis. Through the process of free association, a psychoanalytic treatment automatically entails a decentering of the ego. Indeed, free association endorses the splitting of the subject, and it obliterates the idea of any center. Finally, this becomes the goal of analysis, along with subjective destitution. Analytical experience demonstrates that the so-called being is only a para-being, that the agent of every discourse is only an apparent agent, and that the very idea of substance has to be left behind (ibid., 43–44).

At the beginning of an analysis, the analysand "knows" and "understands" everything, through the mirroring process with the Other in the place of the one who is supposed to know. He or she understands everything through the phallic signifier, the $S_1$, which entails a reduction in terms of the One (ibid., 74–75). As a consequence, the a-sexual object *a* becomes sexualized, that is, phallicized, hence, the ever-present confusion between (*a*) and A (ibid., 77). This is the individual implementation of the mirroring process, mentioned above, in traditional science. The articulation of this knowledge leads the subject to talk endlessly about *d'eux* (i.e., "about the two of them"), once again to make up for the nonexistence of the sexual relationship—this with one eye still on the imaginary being in the mirror. But the unconscious also testifies to a knowledge that escapes from this kind of talk, and it is there that there is something to gain (ibid., 125–27).

Analytic treatment drives this articulated, sexualized knowledge to a liminal point where the subject encounters the difference between the truth and the real. The truth can only be half told and is limited by phallic jouissance. The latter is merely a semblance, an envelope around something else. This half telling warns us against the imaginary aspect of the symptom's envelope and refers us to the Real beyond it. This Real, situated beyond and at the same time in the Symbolic, can only be inscribed by a deadlock of formalization. How is it possible to write something that does not belong to the phallicized symbolic order? Again, Lacan refers to the function of the letter without meaning, that is, mathematics as something that permits us to go beyond the brutal reduction in terms of the One (ibid., 85–87).

The question then is: What is there to know about this other knowledge, and how does this other knowledge relate to articulated knowledge? "What we want to know is the status of the Other's knowledge" (ibid., 81). If the Other knows through the articulated signifiers, then we enter the deadlock of the mirror stage again, this time resulting in entelechy, hence, the fact that the last quote has to be rephrased as a question: "Does the Other know?" (ibid., 82). The major difficulty in this respect, says Lacan, has everything to do with the eternal ambiguity of the term *unconscious* and its relation to knowledge (ibid.).

It is at this point in the Seminar that Lacan begins to try to define this "other" form of knowledge. Again, he evokes the idea of traces, inscribed in a contingent way on the body, that come from elsewhere. Psychoanalysis demonstrates that the grounding of this knowledge boils down to the fact that the jouissance of its acquisition is the very same as the jouissance of its experiencing: "For the foundation of knowledge is that the jouissance of its exercise is the same as that of its acquisition" (ibid., 89). The body (or rather parts of that body) "knows" something, because it enjoys this something, and this enjoyment brings about an inscription of both this knowledge and this jouissance on (part of) the body itself. This inscription does not belong to the signifying order (and, hence, not to the Other) but is brought about through what Lacan tries to understand with the "letter." "Use-value" is much more important here than "exchange value" (ibid.), hence, the fact that Lacan, by the end of the Seminar, focuses on what he considers the most important question: learning how to learn; how is learning taught? (ibid., 128–29)

The acquisition of knowledge through "use-value" has nothing to do with being, but has everything to do with the letter. The letter, in this respect, must not be understood as a message. It has to be understood in analogy to a germ cell, the meaningless carrier of a further possible development (ibid., 89). This development will always be an attempt at recuperation of this letter by the articulated signifier, from the objects $a$ (oral, anal, invocative, scopic) to $a/(-\varphi)$ (fellatio, anal penetration, exhibitionism, telephone sex), from "use-value" to "exchange value" with the mother, with the motherly llanguage. As Lacan said at the beginning of the seminar, these traces become secondarily sexualized, but this attempt at recuperation never succeeds completely and thus creates in the signifier and in the Other a part that is not-whole, through which the letter keeps ex-sisting as letter.

As a consequence, Lacan has to accept that the Other of the signifier does not know anything of it. This constitutes the not-whole part in the Other of the signifier: "It is the Other that makes the not-whole, precisely in that the Other is the part of the not-knowing-at-all in this not-whole" (ibid., 90).[13] Hence, the unconscious is not a thinking being but first and foremost an enjoying being who does not want to know anything of it (ibid., 95). This cannot be captured within traditional, articulated knowledge. Beyond the illusion of the mirroring, there is a "relation to being" that cannot be known. There is a discordance, a cleft between being and knowledge, on *our* side, that is, on the side of the subject where it is indeed not-whole (ibid., 108–9).

Having arrived at this point of his reasoning, Lacan feels obliged to question the very idea of being, and thereby the idea of essentialism. Being is a mere supposition, based on articulation: "it is but a fact of what is said" (ibid., 107). Knowledge beyond articulation is literally and figuratively "inter-dit," in the double sense of the French, "prohibited," but also "said, evoked between the sayings as such" (ibid., 108). The question is, to which kind of Real does it give us access? (ibid.) For Lacan, this real takes the place of the ever-presumed being, a presumption based on the mirroring process. Lacan associates this real more and more with the body, albeit not the body constructed through the Other. He concludes: "The real is the mystery of the speaking body, the mystery of the unconscious" (ibid., 118).

This knowledge is an enigma, demonstrated to us by the unconscious. Analytic discourse, on the contrary, teaches us that knowledge is something articulated. Through this articulation, knowledge is turned into sexualized knowledge and functions as an imaginary replacement for the lack of a sexual relationship, but the unconscious testifies especially to a knowledge that escapes the knowledge of the speaking being (ibid., 125–26). This knowledge that we cannot grasp belongs to the order of experience. It is thus effected by *llanguage*, the motherly llanguage that presents us with enigmatic *affects* that go far beyond what the speaking being can articulate through his or her articulated knowledge (ibid., 126).

The unconscious can be considered a way of coping with these affects, coming from the motherly llanguage. This llanguage contains the "stocheion," the primary letter of the alphabet of knowledge (ibid., 130), and it is this stocheion that has to be turned into a sign of the subject. Analysis must aim at reading these letters, beyond what the analysand says (ibid., 29–30). The analysand is supposed to be able to read, and to be able to learn to read these letters, through his or her analysis (ibid., 38). This provides the mysterious bridge between the a-sexual traces and the signifier, between knowledge and the subject. This sign can only be inaugurated through the operation of the master signifier, $S_1$, that ensures the unity of body and subject. The next step brings "exchange value," through which the subject becomes divided between the signifiers, and enters the dialectic of desire. Thus the unconscious is a way of coping with affects, coming from the motherly llanguage, by the application of the signifier One, which does not come from the body but from the signifier as such (ibid., 130–31). "There is One" (*Il y a de l'Un*). Hence, the remaining questions are, what does this One mean? From whence does it arise? (ibid.).

Lacan raises this question several times in the Seminar but does not come up with an answer. Indeed, he researches this question throughout his entire work, especially in Seminar XIX, ". . . ou pire," the one preceding *Encore*.

*Freudian Antecedents* The links to Freud are quite obvious and illuminating, in several respects. In the "Project for a Scientific Psychology," Freud had elaborated on the idea of "Bahnungen," meaning that psychological material receives an inscription through its usage.[14] Exchange value starts only later on.

In this text, Freud expresses this theory in pseudo-neurological terms. The same kind of reasoning reappears right from the very start of his theory of the unconscious, where he puts forward the hypothesis that the psychical material is inscribed in different layers, each time in a different scripture ("Niederschrift"). Each subsequent step in development requires a translation of the previous material into the form of inscription characteristic of the next layer. This in itself creates the possibility of defense: dangerous, unpleasurable material can be left behind in the previous layer with its own inscription. As it is not translated into the new form of inscription, it insists in a strange way.[15]

It is this theory that receives further elaboration with the concept of repression. It is important to acknowledge the fact that with this theory Freud introduces two different forms of unconscious, hence, two different forms of knowledge. Repression proper, literally "after repression" (*Nachdrängung*), targets verbal material, word presentations that have become unpleasurable. The process of repression takes the energetic investment ("cathexis") away from these word presentations, thus making them unconscious in the dynamic sense of the term. This investment is displaced to another word presentation, through which the return of the repressed takes place. This form of "after repression" grounds the "repressed unconscious" or the "dynamic unconscious."[16] Here it is not so difficult to recognize Lacan's, "The unconscious is structured like a language." Indeed, the repressed unconscious involves signifiers coming from the Other during exchange ("The unconscious is the Other's discourse"), based on desire ("Man's desire is the Other's desire"). This is the exchange value of the material. As signifiers, they contain a knowledge, also coming from the Other. This knowledge can be fully known through the return of the repressed. The subject knows "everything" in these matters, but it does not know that it knows. This knowledge concerns sexual, phallic knowledge, which leads Freud to his complaint that interpretation always comes down to the same thing.

This knowledge, which can be known, reaches a limit in Freud's thinking as well. However, beyond "after repression" lurks "primal repression," which belongs to another form of the unconscious and brings with it another form of knowledge. As a process, primal repression is first and foremost a primal *fixation*: certain material is left behind in its original inscription.[17] It was never translated into word presentations. This material concerns the "excessive degree of excitation," that is, the drive, the "Trieb" or "Triebhaft," to which Lacan refers when he interprets the drive as "the drift of jouissance" (Seminar XX, 102).[18] Based on this, Freud develops the idea of the Ucs system. This system exerts a force of attraction on the material of "after repression," that is, the material in the dynamic, repressed unconscious. From a Lacanian point of view, we read: the sexualized, phallicized, articulated material is attracted by the not-whole part within this articulated part, the (a) within the $a/(-\varphi)$.

Contrary to the dynamic, repressed Ucs, there are no word representations in this Ucs system. The central question then is, is it the drive itself that is fixated, or does this fixation involve a primal form of *representation* of the drive?

Furthermore, is there any form of inscription? Freud calls it the "core of our being," the "mycelium," but he also hesitates.[19] Indeed, the question must be raised whether the latent dream thoughts are "present" somewhere, that is, inscribed, or if we should view them as originally nonexistent, meaning that dream formation takes the place of an originally missing process of psychical elaboration.[20] In the latter case, dream analysis does not boil down to the discovery of a hidden inscription. On the contrary, it amounts to an elaboration process involving signifiers, a process that takes the place of something that was originally not there.

It should be noted that Freud presents the same kind of reasoning when he discusses trauma: the traumatic effect of a trauma is caused by the fact that the trauma, when it happened, could not be put into words; it lacked an elaboration in the form of signifiers.[21] This tallies perfectly with Lacan's ideas in Seminar XI, where he understands the unconscious not as a substantial kernel but as a *cause béante*, a causal gap, in which something fails to be realized.

In Freud's work, there is no final discussion of the nature of the drive inscription in the system Ucs. According to Freud, it has to do with the idea of fixation in general and the body in particular, hence, his typical expressions: fixation, constitution, drive root, somatic compliance. These expressions appear in all of his case studies, and they are always associated with a form of infantile pleasure.

From 1964 onward, Lacan takes up the question anew and struggles with it. In the wake of the Bonneval colloquium, and the debate with Ricoeur and with his own students (Laplanche and Leclaire), he tries to elaborate on his answer. Laplanche and Leclaire put forward the hypothesis that the unconscious core contains a representational system: phonemes for Leclaire, imagos (sensory images without signifiers) for Laplanche.[22] Lacan ultimately refuses both answers and presents his own solution by developing a theory of object *a* and the letter. In Seminar XXII, *R.S.I.*, he takes up anew the idea of the letter as drive-representative in the system Ucs. The letter presents us with the particular fixation of the drive for a particular subject, but it cannot be signified in a definite way, meaning the way of the phallic signifier of the One. As a letter, it contains a knowledge, but this knowledge forms part of the not-whole part of the Other, thus making this Other ignorant of it. It is the Other of the body that remembers this knowledge and traces the same tracks each time (Freud's *Bahnungen*) within the economy of jouissance, but this economy of jouissance remains an enigma (Seminar XX, 105).

The importance of this conceptualization has to do with the final goal of analysis. If, in one way or another, the core of the Ucs system is of a representational nature, then it can be verbalized and interpreted during treatment. If not, then the final aim of the treatment has to be reconsidered, because "full speech" would be structurally impossible. In his final theory, Lacan chooses the latter option and elaborates on his theory of identification with the real of the symptom as the final goal of an analysis.[23]

*Conclusion* The other jouissance, which ex-sists as that part in the Other where the Other is not-whole, implies a knowledge that is acquired by the body through experiencing it. At the same time, this experiencing causes its inscription on the body. This knowledge concerns the not-whole part of articulated, phallic knowledge of the Other of the signifier. As knowledge, it does not belong to the Other of language or to a presumed underlying being. It can only be grasped through writing, although we must acknowledge the fact that every formalization meets here with a deadlock.

Associated with this, there are two forms of unconscious and two forms of knowledge. The Ucs system is the unverbalized gap that contains drive fixation and jouissance, thus operating as a cause. The Ucs system ex-sists within the repressed unconscious, where articulated knowledge can be known by the subject. The latter knowledge has to do with exchange value, and thus with the Other's discourse and desire.

The way in which the split is described between other jouissance and phallic jouissance and between articulated knowledge and other knowledge foreshadows a new topology. This topology is new, because it leaves behind the idea of a form of binary opposition. In what way, we might ask, can we elaborate on this new topology, in relation to the classic body/mind deadlock?

BODY/MIND

Ever since Plato, we have been faced with a binary opposition between body and mind. History contains several translations of this deadlock, of which sex/gender is the latest implementation. This last implementation of Plato's deadlock contains another one as well. Indeed, on the side of gender, we find the binary opposition between man and woman, albeit in a strange way. Gender was originally defined in terms of man versus woman, but its further development (by Judith Butler) gave rise to a scattering of gender as such, in a multiplicity of different forms of psychosexual identity. The paradoxical result of this scattering is that a return to the classic, safe male/female opposition within sex has been endorsed. Today, especially within the hard sciences, voices are heard everywhere defending this essential binary opposition in sex (biology, genetics, brain studies). Even more strange is the fact that this man-woman opposition within the original gender idea always brings with it a hidden reprisal of the opposition between sex and gender as such. The female sex becomes identified implicitly with "nature," by the idea of the primal mother, while gender and culture are implicitly understood as belonging to masculinity.

The question is, how can we rethink this binary opposition? Is there an association to be made with gender positions? And, finally, what about ontology?

*Lacan* Without exaggerating, I think I can assert that Lacan's Seminar XX is one long search to escape the deadlocks of this kind of binary thinking. The price to pay for this escape is the loss of the advantages of such an opposition.

Indeed, the latter brings an ever-imaginary clarity, hence, safety; even more so, it provides us with the illusion of a substantial being. Instead of this, Lacan introduces us to a fundamental in-determinism that lies at the heart of the matter itself. His search is not limited to Seminar XX. The problem appears for the first time in his talk on the mirror stage (1948). The innovation of Seminar XX is the association of this question to the problem of knowledge and jouissance. The innovation lies especially in the idea of negation, present throughout the Seminar, the "n'est pas" ("is not"), the "pas-tout" (not-whole), found frequently in sentences in the conditional tense. With this, Lacan delineates a relationship between body and mind that is completely different from the classical opposition. Finally, this relationship is generalized and understood as a basic structure for human beings. Before we go into that, let me summarize Lacan's critique of this binary opposition, based on what I have said above.

His critique becomes quite clear (Seminar XX, 62 ff.) when he answers the critique of his own theory made in *The Title of the Letter*, by Jean-Luc Nancy and Philippe Lacoue-Labarthe. These authors ascribe Lacan an ontology and criticize him for it. Lacan's answer is to the point. He states that, in his theory, there is a clear opposition between "the being of the philosophical tradition" and the experience that we are duped by jouissance (ibid., 66). More particularly, Lacan reads this as an opposition between "the signified of the body" and the "jouissance of being" (ibid., 66–67). Here we must pay close attention to his elaboration of the notion of "being." In his reading, this "being" of jouissance stands in complete opposition to the classic being of the philosophical tradition, as it was elaborated on by Aristotle and Aquinas. Indeed, this classic elaboration always gave rise to the assumption of a supreme being.

Let us focus first on being in classical philosophy, "that is, as rooted in the very thinking that is supposed to be its correlate" (ibid., 66). Thinking grounds itself in the assumption that there is an underlying being that thinks as well—and this underlying thinking of an assumed underlying being has to ground itself in the assumption of a supreme being. If this is not the case, it has to end in an endless mirroring process of ever-more remote underlying beings, who all resemble each other. With this grounding in a supreme being, classical philosophy provides being with consistency.

Aristotle's mistake—a mistake that was repeated by his followers—resides in the assumption that what is thought (*le pensé*) is in the image of thought (*la pensée*) (ibid., 96). The soul is the supposed identity of the body in an identicalness to this body: "being is supposed to think" (ibid., 100, 103), but such an assumption is based on the signifier holding the reins, the *dit-manche* (ibid., 96–97).[24] Lacan had already exposed the fallacy of such reasoning when he criticized the idea of neurological projection of the body onto the brain. If man has a headache, this has to do with the smaller man in his head having a headache, meaning that this small man must have an even smaller man in *his* brain who has a headache, meaning that a still smaller man in the head of the small man . . .[25]

Lacan rejects the idea of a corresponding analogy between body and mind, between being and subject, and he puts forward the idea of a gap "inscribed in the very status of jouissance qua dit-mension of the body" (ibid., 104). He adds that this is precisely what Freud was talking about. There is no being beyond the signifier, "nothing is, if not insofar as it is said that it is" (ibid., 126, 107). The discourse on being is only an assumption that lends it meaning and substance at the same time. In other words, the idea of a presumed correspondence between body and soul is nothing but a philosophical implementation of the mirror stage, by which the infant acquires a supposed identity and unity that originates in the Other of the signifier, the dit-manche. Being always comes down to a signified being, not to an ontological being. Even for analysts, object *a* seems to be being, but it is a mere semblance of being (ibid., 87). In the end, the assumption of such a correspondence is nothing more than a way of coping with the unbearable lightness of being (ibid., 78). It comes down to the creation of a guarantee of the assumed existence of the Other of the Other. The effect of all this is not that we get to know our being; on the contrary, we are shut off from the very possibility of learning anything about it.

Nevertheless, says Lacan, there is another relation to being that cannot be known through the articulation of signifiers, and it is this relation that he wants to investigate. The question is to which kind of real this relationship permits us access (ibid., 108). The aim of such an investigation is not so much to know more about it—indeed, in this respect, knowledge is literally and figuratively "inter-dit," forbidden and said in-between—but that it would grant us better access to jouissance. In other words, it would produce a better agreement between jouissance and its end—this beyond its typical failure, that is, fucking and reproducing (ibid., 109). Lacan hopes to find an entrance to this via the traces "which constitute for the subject his slim chance of going to the Other, to its being" (ibid., 110). With this idea of "trace," he is referring back to the earlier parts of the Seminar (11), and to the idea of the letter. Indeed, as a trace, it must be inscribed, but then again this leads us to the deadlocks of formalization, because there is no metalanguage (Seminar XX, 85, 108, 110). At this point, Lacan builds a bridge to topology, hoping that this will enable him to demonstrate something of this inscription (ibid., 110 ff.).

The above permits us to summarize Lacan's answer to classical binary thinking as follows. The signified being faces a lack-of-being (*manque-à-être*) that is included in this signified being. In this way, Lacan puts forward a new kind of dialectic, beyond the mirroring reasoning of classical binary thinking.

In this reasoning, it is not coincidental that Lacan describes this lack of being systematically in negative terms, that is, negative from the point of view of the Other of the signifier, because it can never be expressed in signifiers. "Negation certainly seems to derive therefrom" (ibid., 101). Seminar XX is full of these negative statements, frequently in the conditional as well: "is not," "not-whole," and so on. Its point of culmination is without any doubt the negative formulations of contingency, necessity, and impossibility. Contingency has to do with the inscription of certain traces on the body (Seminar XX, 86), through which the body enjoys, but these traces cannot be written in the sense of the signifier. Nevertheless, they are not *not* written either, albeit in a contingent way and not understandable or knowable for the Other of the signifier, hence, they "stop not being written." This writing is necessary for the subject, but it should take place through phallic articulation, and precisely this articulation fails in this respect, hence, the never-ending aspect: "It does not stop being written." As a result, we are faced with impossibility: because the traces have to be written on the body but can never be written in a signified way, the sexual relationship "does not stop not being written" (ibid., 85–87; 131–32).

This negative effect has everything to do with a certain characteristic of this impossible to grasp other dimension: its infinity (Seminar XX, 13, 15). This is one of the main differences from the closed symbolic universe of the phallic pleasure principle, which is closed because it reduces everything to the function of the One. So, in a very important remark made by Lacan in an almost offhanded manner (ibid., 93–94), we find the claim that the ever-impossible combination between the phallic and the other dimension, between the symbolic and the real, does not constitute a closed universe. If it were a closed one, this would imply that any particular exception to it could be considered just one exception, meaning reducible to the One. This is not at all the case. On the contrary, we are faced with an open-ended, endless universe in which exceptions do not belong to the order of the one but to the order of the not-whole. Infinity opens a dimension that cannot be caught in the order of the signifier, and it opens a beyond to which object *a* could provide us an entrance way. But even object *a* fails in this respect, "owing to its failure, unable as it is, to sustain itself in approaching the real" (ibid., 87).

In this way, Lacan introduces a totally different dialectic, one between the symbolic dimension of the individual and something that supersedes this dimension, coming from elsewhere. Throughout Seminar XX, he keeps alluding to this latter dimension (11, 32–33, 63, 89, 110), without developing it. Even more so, he demonstrates why it cannot be developed as such. This is why he concentrates on the open-ended dialectic between the two dimensions, between the "advent of the living" and the "advent of the subject," as mentioned in Seminar XI. It has to do with life and death, in such a way that it supersedes mere reproduction, which is always a half-failed way to continue life. At this point, Lacan's theory is a further development of Freud's conceptualization of the life and death drives, Eros and Thanatos.

*Freudian Antecedents* Again, Lacan's theory has obvious links to Freud's. Right from the start, Freud puts forward the idea of an internal splitting, not between a mind and an external body but within a functioning whole. From his first conceptualizations onward, he associates this splitting with the (im-)possibility of representation of certain elements. For example, at the time of the *Studies on*

*Hysteria* (1895) he talks about *bewusstseinsunfägige Vorstellungen,* signifiers that cannot enter consciousness.[26]

This focus on such splitting is without any doubt the major difference between Freud and psychology. The latter always tries in one way or another to reintroduce the subject as a unity. That is the reason psychology is not psychology but egology. The focus on the internal splitting explains the difference between Freud and the post–Freudian "culturalists" (in the large sense of the word) as well, because the latter concentrate on an assumed split between the subject, on the one hand, and a restrictive culture and society, on the other hand. For Freud, this is an effect, not a cause.

The Freudian gap is situated on the inside, and the borderlines are delineated by the (im-)possibility of representation and articulation. "Hypercathexis" of the drive material through the association with word presentations makes consciousness possible, and vice versa; the dividing line has to be situated at that border. Freud's entire work can be studied as an elaboration of this splitting in the representational and articulatory system. His topologies of the mind are attempts to acknowledge this gap: consciousness, preconscious, unconscious; dynamic unconscious, system unconscious; ego, id, superego. Lesser known but even more interesting for the study of Seminar XX is his differentiation between the affectionate current and the sensual one.[27] Indeed, this tallies quite well with Lacan's remarks on love and the drives through all of Seminar XX.[28] Freud's last conceptualization of the gap generalizes this splitting to a universal human characteristic, thus anticipating the idea of Lacan's everdivided subject.[29]

When we study Freud's different attempts to acknowledge this inner split, it becomes obvious that time and again the main theme concerns the gap between the drive, on the one hand, and the (im-)possibility of representation, on the other hand, within the ego or the conscious that is organized in word presentations. In this respect, it is quite interesting to quote one of his attempts to define the drive: "The simplest and likeliest assumption as to the nature of drives would seem to be that in itself a drive is without quality, and, so far as mental life is concerned, is only to be regarded as a measure of the demand made upon the mind to work."[30] The work here is that which is required to insert this drive into the secondary process, into word presentations. This is Lacan's necessity: the drive has to be represented in one way or another.

Thus Freud does not reason in terms of a binary but concentrates on a never-ending dialectical process between the represented and the notrepresented. This is not only present from his very first writings, it receives more and more weight as his work proceeds. Right at the beginning, he talks about the "false connection," meaning a word presentation that is incorrectly associated with another word presentation, for lack of an original correct association with something that is barely expressible.[31] His work on hysteria teaches him that such false connections are not exceptional; on the contrary, the hysterical subject produces them all the time, thus trying to enter this un-expressible into the normal associative chains. This characteristic of hysteria is so obvious that he considers it typical and dubs it the hysterical "compulsion to associate."[32] Much later, he encounters another variant of this compulsion, that is, the repetition compulsion of traumatic neurosis, aiming at the mastering of the trauma by trying to bind it to word representations.[33] Still a bit later in his work, he does not restrict this anymore to hysteria but turns it into a general characteristic of the ego: its proclivity to synthesize, to associate separate things into an ever-larger synthesis. He had met with this proclivity earlier on, when he was studying dreams. Once awake, the dreamer tries to get hold of his or her dream and turns it into a story. This is "secondary revision," that is, the process by which all of the holes and gaps in the original dream are associatively closed and sealed. Furthermore, the dream as such is already an attempt to represent the unrepresentable, its main concern is "considerations of representability." The dream uses different mechanisms (condensation, displacement, and so on) to produce an "Ergänzungsreihe" (complemental series), just like Freud tries to himself, but the navel of the dream, the "Kern unseres Wesen," remains obscure.[34]

In the meantime, his clinical experience taught him that there is no chronological-linear sequence. Indeed, the unconscious does not know time. His famous archaeological metaphor illustrates the simultaneity, through which the so-called "later" contains the "past" in itself, albeit in a different representation.[35] The whole contains the not-whole that ex-sists in this whole. "Nachträglichkeit" ("deferred action") is the rule, foreshadowing Lacan's notion of logical time.

All of these Freudian descriptions of attempts at recuperation through the signifier come down to Lacan's "being of signifierness," which necessarily tries to write the contingent but produces impossibility. In Lacan's theory, not much attention is paid to the underlying motive—why does the subject feel obliged to introduce the drive into the symbolic—what drives him to do so? Freud tries to formulate an explanation by postulating the existence of two primary drives, in combination with the assumption of a basic characteristic of these drives, that is, that they want to return to a previous state.[36]

All of the attempts (from false connection to repetition compulsion) are effects of Eros, with its proclivity to synthesis, to the One, to fusion. For Freud, Eros aims at the reduction of tension through the secondary process, that is, the "abreaction" of bound energy, made possible by association with word presentations. At the other side, he finds another primary drive, which is much harder to get hold of and define, because it operates literally "in silence," that is, outside the dimension of word presentations.[37] It operates as a resistance, the same resistance that Freud discovered at the heart of the Ucs system itself against the conscious, that is, against the association with word presentations. The repetition compulsion collides with the same inertia, hence, its repetitive effect. This other drive, Thanatos, operates like the primary process, that is, unbound, and it causes ever-increasing levels of tension that cannot be "abreacted" for lack of an association with word presentations. Thanatos induces a scattering of Eros, disassembles everything that Eros brought together into the One, and makes this unity explode in an infinite universe. The One of phallic fusion is pitted against the infinity of the beyond. Thanatos implies a pleasure as well, although in this case, it is experienced as an incomprehensible jouissance, as traumatic by the subject who cannot handle it in its usual symbolic way.

Again, it is not a matter of opposition for Freud—quite the contrary. It does not concern the life drive against the death drive; no, the two of them always appear together, in a strange mixture—the "Triebmischung," drive fusion.[38] Defusion, says Freud, is very rare, and it appears only in extreme pathology. In terms of his previous theory, the repressed unconscious is part of the unconscious but does not coincide with it; there is still the Ucs system, the not-whole in the whole. Or, in terms of his earliest theory, the material fended off by the ego to another realm does not lie in an external outside. Instead, it continues to form part of the ego, albeit in such a strange way that Freud thinks it appropriate to use a medical metaphor: they are "Fremdkörper," foreign bodies, present on the inside but foreign to this inside.[39] The real ex-sists within the articulated symbolic.

Finally, Freud has to refer to something that supersedes humankind as such, something that must have to do with the bare properties of life. He refers to Philia and Neikos as a basis for the fusional Eros and the defusional Thanatos, but in this respect, his reference to another classical couple is even more interesting: Anankè and Logos. Logos is, in effect, "reason," but it refers to the signifier as well, and Freud associates it with knowledge. Anankè is the necessity from which we cannot escape.[40]

*Conclusion* For Lacan, there is no binary opposition between body and soul, between being and Other, between man and woman, between phallic jouissance and other jouissance. Each time we meet with an impossible relationship between two terms, in which one tries to regain the other but never succeeds, because this other is already included in the one, albeit by ex-sistence. It is the story of Achilles and Briseis all over again (Seminary XX, 13).

Instead of the binary opposition and its accompanying endless mirroring process, we find both in Freud and Lacan a dialectical process within a whole that contains a part with which it cannot cope, although it is driven to keep trying. The latter part ex-sists with respect to the former, thus turning it into a not-whole. It comforts itself with the illusion of being a finite universe, because it operates based on the principle of the one. The other part functions in a different way, thereby providing an opening to the dimension of infinity. The self-assumed whole amounts to a represented universe, with which consciousness and the pleasure principle coincide. The not-whole part of this whole is not representable in terms of this represented universe and produces another jouissance, which operates in a traumatic way for the representational system.

Thus considered, human ontology has no essential base whatsoever. The hoped-for essence comes down to an inner split, which gives rise to an open-ended dialectic.

## FINAL THOUGHTS

In my introduction, I suggested that Seminar XX cannot be read in an isolated way, because it belongs to a "work in progress." In my conclusion, I address two points from a broader perspective in the hope of better situating them.

First, the best-known theme of Seminar XX is the relationship between phallic pleasure and the other jouissance, which reappears in the relationship between knowledge and that other form of knowledge or, more broadly speaking, in the relationship between the Other and the ever-assumed being. Based on Lacan's work as a whole, it is clear that this relationship comes down to a never-ending attempt of the One to assume that other, but every attempt fails and keeps failing, thereby causing the insistence of the attempt as such. This is called life. As I will demonstrate, this impossible relationship can be written in general terms and provides us, at last, with some kind of ontology.

The second point concerns causality. What is the cause of this insistent failure? Through the discussion of the different implementations of this impossible relationship (jouissance, knowledge, identity), it became clear that it contains a direction and an aim. Freud's axiomatic answer goes back to the drive and its basic aim—to return to a previous state. What is Lacan's answer here?

### CAUSALITY

As long as Lacan was concentrating on the signifier and the symbolic order, all emphasis was placed on the lawful, systematic determination within the chain of signifiers (see his appendix to "The Seminar on 'The Purloined Letter'"). This changes drastically once he no longer takes the real seriously, meaning that he takes the real outside of the seriality of the signifier, the real as such. At that point, he encounters causality as something completely different from determinism.

Determinism belongs to Aristotle's *automaton*, but causality is something different, to be understood as *tuché*. In Seminar XI, Lacan introduces the notion of "cause" as what is to be looked for in something undetermined.[41] "In short, there is a cause only in something that does not work" (Seminar 11, 22; Seminar XI, 25). Later on in Seminar XI, this undetermined cause is understood as the traumatic real, that part of the drive that cannot be represented. In this revised theory, the body occupies a completely new place.[42] As a cause, it obliges and constrains us to "an appointment with a real that eludes us" (Seminar 11, 53; Seminar XI, 53), the real that lies beyond automaton, and that comes down to that part which cannot be assimilated, in the sense of that which is not mediated or represented (Seminar 11, 53–55; Seminar XI, 53–55).

In this sense, the idea of cause implies the idea of failure, of something that does not happen, thus causing something else to fill the scene: a failure of the symbolic to cover over something real. There is an indecision at the heart of the real, that is, a contingency. It implies that the body, through the drive, has a central causal impact on the unconscious as such: "For what the unconscious does is to show us the gap through which neurosis associates with a real—a real that may well not be determined" (my translation; Seminar 11, 22; Seminar XI, 25–26). This real is the drive in its status of unrepresentability (Seminar 11, 60; Seminar XI, 59), hence, its association with trauma. The aspect of failure appears in the negative denominations used by Lacan: "the unrealized" and "the unborn," thus permitting him to make explicit a direct connection with the "un" of the unconscious (Seminar 11, 22–23, 26, 32; Seminar XI, 25–26, 28, 32).

Lacan's theory of causality permits him to develop a status for the unconscious, a status homologous to what takes place at the level of the subject.[43] In the second point of my conclusion, I will discuss this homology more extensively. Indeed, in the wake of this new theory of causality, the unconscious is described by Lacan as *une béance causale*, a causal gap characterized by a pulsating movement. The unconscious is a perpetual opening and closing of a gap in which something fails to be realized. A typical example is a slip of the tongue, but ultimately this goes for every production of the unconscious, the subject as such included (Seminar 11, 130–31; Seminar XI, 119–20), hence, the preontological status of the unconscious: "it" fails to materialize; all emphasis has to be put on this opening and closing (Seminar 11, 29–32; Seminar XI, 32–33).

Thus, the conclusion is that it is not only the symbolic order that has a determining effect; the real as such has a causal function, and the two come together in an ever-impossible relationship.

Of course, this is all merely a description of a rather peculiar process of nonrealization. So far, causality as such is evoked, but not much more than that. How does the real function as a cause? Lacan answers this question by redefining his ideas of the body and lack. His new theory begins when he interprets the real of the body as the cause, because this real implies a primordial lack. This lack or loss is logically prior to the lack in the signifying chain between mother and child (exchange value), although it operates retroactively.

The real of the organism functions as the cause, in the sense that it contains a primordial loss that precedes the loss in the chain of signifiers. Which loss? The loss of eternal life, which paradoxically enough is lost at the moment of birth, that is, birth as a sexed being, because of meiosis (Seminar 11, 205; Seminar XI, 187). In order to explain this ultimate incomprehensibility of the ultimate as such, Lacan constructs the myth of the "lamella," which is nothing but object *a* in its pure form: the life instinct, the primordial form of the libido. As an idea, it goes back to a biological fact: nonsexual reproduction implies, in principle, the possibility of eternal life (as is the case of single-celled organisms, which can be brought about through cloning), and sexual reproduction implies, in principle, the death of the individual. Each organism wants to undo this loss, and each tries to return to the previous state of being. According to

Freud, this was the basic characteristic of the drive, to be read as the life and death drive. With Lacan, the dead facet of the death drive is easier to grasp: indeed, the return to eternal life inevitably implies the death of the sexed individual.

The reaction to this primordial loss—the attempt to return and its defensive elaboration—takes place at the level of the symbolico-imaginary, which is at the same time the level of sexualization, of gender formation. It has to be noted that this sexualization comes down to a "phallicization." This means that the first, real lack is "answered," as was the second lack, the one in the symbolic. Thus the primordial loss at the level of the organism is reinterpreted as a phallic lack in the relationship between the subject and Other. Object *a* becomes associated with the bodily borderlines, the orifices through which other losses take place. Moreover, this phallic interpretation of object *a* implies that this original lack and loss are introduced by the mother/child relationship into the man/woman relationship; this is the effect of the Oedipal passage (Seminar 11, 64, 103–4, 180; Seminar XI, 62, 95–96, 164). From this point onward, the drive becomes a partial drive, containing an ever-present mixture of life and death drives.

As a result, we end with an interaction between a circular but not reciprocal determination (Seminar 11, 207; Seminar XI, 188). Loss at the level of the real is the cause through which individual life—the not-whole—is turned into one elongated, elaborated attempt at returning to the previous eternal life: infinity. This attempt receives an elaboration at another level, in the verbal relationship between mother and child, and still later, at a third level, between man and woman. In the meantime, the original lack is reinterpreted in phallic terms. This attempt to return takes place within the symbolico-imaginary, which means that it is determined in a systematic way (automaton), and that it will run inevitably into the original lack in the real (tuché). The automatic chain can never produce an adequate answer because of this structural incompatibility. This in itself leads the chain to further production, and so on.

It is this kind of failed interaction that brings us to the idea of the not-whole and the accompanying ontological process, instead of the classical binary.

*Homologous Structure: A Circular but Nonreciprocal Relationship* Seminar XX brings us the ever-failing relationship between an articulated whole that contains a nonarticulated part, by which the whole is turned into a not-whole, facing infinity. This description can be recognized quite easily in Lacan's previous theory on the unconscious and causality. It brings us the principle of a homologous structure, described as circular but nonreciprocal (Seminar 11, 207; Seminar XI, 188). This structure contains a kind of development, although it has to be read backwards: the "primary" element becomes delineated retroactively through the operation of the "secondary" element, in which the primary is included, albeit as a foreign body. The relationship does not stop at that point; quite the contrary. The not-whole whole insistently attempts to colonize this

foreign body that ex-sists in the not-whole itself. These attempts produce the
exact opposite effect: instead of assimilation of the "other" part, this other becomes confirmed in its otherness, although at another level. At that other level,
the whole process can start all over again, with the same (lack of) result.

Thus Lacan acknowledges a homologous structure between body, unconscious, and subject.[44] This structure insists in terms of opening and closing, border structure, gap, split, and so on. As a principle, it turns the relation between
life and death into a circular but nonreciprocal interaction. The loss at the level
of the real transforms life into one prolonged attempt to return to the preceding eternal life. From a structural point of view, this leaves us with two elements, one of which serves as a force of attraction, while the other wants to return and move forward at the same time. Their interaction is staged each time
at a different level, which instates and endorses their nonrelationship—the two
borders can never meet. As early as 1948, Lacan had already written that in
mankind there is a primordial discordance in the very core of the organism.[45]
The final result of this primordial cleft is the nonexistence of the sexual relationship.

My attempt to describe and summarize this homologous structure runs as
follows (Seminar 11, 203–13; Seminar XI, 185–93):

1.  The advent of the living: the opening and closing of life at birth.

    The advent of sexually differentiated life-forms implies the loss of
    eternal life. This loss is summarized by Lacan in his concept of object *a*,
    meaning the loss of the life instinct. This eternal life, Zoë in classical
    Greek, functions as a force of attraction for the individual life, Bios, which
    tries to return. The price to pay for this return is the loss of this individual
    life as such, which explains the other tendency, the one that flees from it
    in the opposite direction. The so-called solution implies and endorses a
    structurally defined impossible relationship. Indeed, Bios tries to join Zoë
    through sexual reproduction, thus entailing a necessary failure and even re-
    peating and endorsing the original loss. From this moment onward, life
    and death drives are fused.

2.  The advent of the I: the opening and closing of the body.

    This is the primary alienation of the mirror stage. The living being
    acquires a first mastery, a first identity through the externally imposed,
    unified image of the body. This unified body will be translated in the mas-
    ter signifier, "I," to be understood as "m'être à moi-même/maître à moi-
    même" (to be myself, to belong to myself, to be the master of myself,
    Seminar XVII, 178), the "I" which has a body and has lost its being. This
    "I" will never cease to try to join its body, that is, the being of its body, but
    then again the price to pay for this joining is the disappearance of the "I,"
    hence, the tendency to flee in the other direction as well. Finally, this solu-
    tion will provide the "I" only with the body of the Other, thus endorsing
    the loss of its being.

3.   The advent of the subject: the opening and closing of signifiers.

The ever-divided subject appears and disappears under the signifiers of the Other, aiming at answering the desire of that Other. From a structural viewpoint, such a process has to end in failure, because the answer will be given in terms of signifiers, while object *a* belongs to a different order and is lacking, precisely due to the introduction of the signifier. Again, as a solution, it implies a structurally determined nonrelationship, because the attempt of the subject to join the Other must necessarily pass through the signifier, thus repeating and endorsing the original division of this subject.

Thus considered, the subject comes onto the stage as the last implementation of this homologous structure, containing all of the previous ones. With the former, there is no question of a subject, unless in the form of what Lacan calls "*un sujet acéphale*," a headless subject. If we continue this line of thought, it seems reasonable to expect here a fourth "advent," that is, the advent of gender, through which object *a* and the subject would be provided with a specific gender. This is what the Oedipus complex does, in its own particular way, by interpreting the original loss in terms of castration. As a result, the Oedipal structure inaugurates a gender differentiation that is not a genuine one, because it is based solely on the presence of the phallic One's absence. The phallic interpretation is applied retroactively to all preceding advents, meaning that each loss becomes interpreted phallicly. It is during this process that the body is constructed, the body that we have (not the body that we are), clothed in an ever-secondary gender identity. The originally circular but not reciprocal relationship between life and death, between jouissance and subject, is reproduced and worked over between man and woman.

In this way, the gap between jouissance and Other, between being and sense, is reproduced in the gap between woman and man. Moreover, this repetition produces the same effect: whatever efforts the subject makes to join his or her body via the Other of language, he or she will never succeed, because the gap is precisely due to this Other of language. Whatever efforts the subject (whether male or female) makes to join woman via the phallic relationship, it will never succeed, because the cleft is precisely due to the phallic signifier. The impossible relationship between the subject and its drive reappears in the impossible relationship between a man and a woman, on the one hand, and the not-whole part of woman, on the other hand.

In my opinion, this is the complete elaboration of the ontological structure announced by Lacan in 1949 in "The Mirror Stage."[46] The human being is always divided between something that it is not or does not have and something that it will never be or have—"your money or your life" (Seminar 11, 212; Seminar XI, 193). It is this division that insists as a border structure and corroborates a homology between body, drive, unconscious, and subject. This is the only "ontology" that humans have.

Finally, Lacan's refusal of the binary opposition is a refusal of the reduction by and to the one and an attempt to think beyond this phallus-cy. It is his refusal of the one that always leads to a false "*d'eux*," two, that is, a false binary, and an attempt to think a "*un-en-moins*," a one that is not-whole and faces a never-ending dialectic. This thinking, he says, takes courage and has to do with love. To keep this dimension of the undetermined wide open testifies to Lacan's courage, contrary to the "eyes wide shut" classical attempts of recuperation, which always create a false sense of certainty. Every interpretation of this Lacanian theory that leads to yet another binary misses the point and is merely another form of the return of the repressed.

## NOTES

1. "Hâtez-vous lentement; et, sans perdre courage/Vingt fois sur le métier remettez votre ouvrage," Boileau, *L'Art Poétique* (Paris: Gallimard, 1966), p. 161. In Pope's translation: "Gently make haste, of labour not afraid/A hundred times consider what you've said."

2. All references to Seminar XX given in this chapter are to the original French pagination, included in the margins of the English translation by Bruce Fink.

3. This clinical experience can easily be found in Freud's case studies; in his four actual clinical cases, it is not too difficult to find the infantile drive root, or fixation, as Freud calls it.

4. This idea goes back a long way: "You can see the difficulty of topological representation. The reason is that *das Ding* is at the center in that sense that it is excluded. [It is] something that is *entfremdet*, foreign to me, although it is at the heart of me." In French, "Vous voyez la difficulté de la représentation topologique. Car ce *das Ding* est justement au centre au sens qu'il est exclu. [C'est] quelque chose qui est *entfremdet*, étranger à moi tout en étant au coeur du moi" (Seminar VII, 87/71).

5. "In the psyche, there is nothing by which the subject may situate himself as a male or female being. In his psyche, the subject situates only equivalents of the function of reproduction—activity and passivity, which by no means represent it in an exhaustive way. [T]he ways of what one must do as man or as woman are entirely abandoned to the drama, to the scenario, which is placed in the field of the Other—which, strictly speaking, is the Oedipus complex. [T]he human being always has to learn from scratch from the Other what he has to do, as man or as woman" (Seminar XI, 204/186).

6. The identification made by Lacan between the symbolic order, the master signifier, the phallic signifier, and the One might not be clear to some readers. I understand it as follows. The symbolic order as a system is based on difference (see Saussure). The first signifier to denote difference as such is the phallic signifier, hence, the symbolic order is based on the phallic signifier. As a signifier, it is empty, and it does not create a difference between two different genders. It creates a mere difference between the One and the not-one. This is its major effect on the symbolic order: it operates in a unifying way, by applying a dichotomous reasoning, one or not one. Lacan returns to this at the very end of Seminar XX, when he questions the origins of this idea of one (63–64, 130–31). See also J. Lacan, *Television, a Challenge to the Psychoanalytic Establishment*, trans. D. Hollier, R. Krauss, and A. Michelson, ed. J. Copjec (New York: Norton, 1990), p. 10; J. Lacan, *Télévision* (Paris: Seuil, 1973), p. 22.

7. Lacan's theory of the body is quite complicated; the shift in Seminar XX has to be understood mainly in relation to Seminar XI and Seminar XXII, *R.S.I.* I have commented on this evolution in my paper "Subject and Body—Lacan's Struggle with the Real," in *The Letter: Lacanian Perspectives on Psychoanalysis* 17 (autumn 1999): 79–119.

8. The transition from use-value to exchange value is one of the major themes of Seminar IV.

9. "The common factor of the *a* is the fact that it is associated with the orifices of the body" (my translation; "Le facteur commun du *a*, c'est d'être lié aux orifices du corps" (Seminar XXIII, January 21, 1975, unpublished Seminar).

10. Sigmund Freud, *The Standard Edition of the Complete Psychological Works of Sigmund Freud*, 24 vols., trans. J. Strachey (London: Hogarth Press) vol. XXIII, *Moses and Monotheism*, 71–73, 126, 129. Hereafter, all references to the *Standard Edition* will be given as SE, followed by the title, volume, and page numbers.

11. S. Freud, *Beyond the Pleasure Principle*, SE XVIII, 32–35.

12. All references in this paragraph are to Seminar XI. It should be noted here that Lacan develops his theory on the real in quite a hesitating fashion, the result being that from time to time he speaks about "reality" when he is talking about the real.

13. This is my translation, because the English translation introduces a different interpretation; the original reads: "C'est l'Autre qui fait le pas-tout, justement en ce qu'il est la part du pas-savant-du-tout dans ce pas-tout." Indeed, "pas-savant-du-tout" implies at least two meanings: "not knowing of the whole" and "not knowing at all."

14. S. Freud (1895), "Project for a Scientific Psychology," SE I, 295–397. The idea of "Bahnungen" is used almost constantly in Freud's text. See also *Beyond the Pleasure Principle*, SE XVIII, 26.

15. See Freud's letters to Fliess, dated May 30, 1896, and November 2, 1896 (SE I, 229–40).

16. S. Freud, "Repression," SE XIV, 146; *The Ego and the Id*, SE XIX, 60–62; *New Introductory Lectures on Psycho-Analysis*, SE XXII, 15, 70–72.

17. S. Freud, "Psycho-Analytic Notes on an Autobiographical Account of a Case of Paranoia," SE XII, 66–68; Freud, *The Ego and the Id*, p. 18; Freud, "Repression," p. 146.

18. S. Freud (1926), *Inhibitions, Symptoms, and Anxiety*, SE XX, 94; Freud, *Beyond the Pleasure Principle*, pp. 27 ff. It is fascinating to see how this problem is present right from the start in Freud's theory. As early as in "The Neuro-psychoses of Defense" (1894), Freud struggles with the relationship between what he calls at that time "the memory-traces" of "repressed ideas." Repression takes place at a "traumatic moment" and operates on the "sum of excitation," "the source of the affect." But he is left with the question of whether these processes are of a psychical nature or "are physical processes whose psychical consequences present themselves as if what is expressed by the terms 'separation of the idea from its affect' and 'false connection' of the latter had really taken place" (SE III, 50–53). In later terms, is the drive inscribed psychically, or are we facing right from the start a fundamental incompatibility between the drive and representation as such, thus constituting the nucleus of the unconscious as a gap, a failure operating in a causal way? This is the option that Lacan takes from Seminar XI onward.

19. S. Freud, *The Interpretation of Dreams*, SE V, 525.

20. Freud describes the dream as the externalization of an internal process, in which drive impulses function as the source. The dream tries to express the unconscious impulse, that is, bodily changes, through the preconscious dream-wish. S. Freud, "A Metapsychological Supplement to the Theory of Dreams," SE XIV, 222–26.

21. S. Freud, *Moses and Monotheism*, SE XXIII, 71–73, 126, 129. See also a letter to Fliess, where he states that fantasies go back to "things heard at an early age but understood only later" (April 6, 1897, SE I, 244).

22. J. Laplanche and S. Leclaire, "L'Inconscient: une étude psychanalytique," in *L'inconscient: VIième colloque de Bonneval*, ed. H. Ey (Paris: Desclée de Brouwer), pp. 95–130. In English, see "The Unconscious: A Psychoanalytic Study," *Yale French Studies* 48 (1972): 118–175.

23. For a discussion of this point, see P. Verhaeghe and F. Declercq, "Lacan's Goal of Analysis: Le Sinthome or the Feminine Way," in *Reinventing the Symptom: Essays on the Final Lacan*, ed. Luke Thurston (London: Rebus Press, forthcoming). See also F. Declercq, "Het Reële bij Lacan, over de finaliteit van de psychoanalytische kuur" (Gent: Idesça, 2000).

24. For the explanation of this neologism, "dit-manche," see the excellent comments made by Bruce Fink in his translation of Seminar XX, ed. J.-A. Miller (New York: Norton, 1998), notes 6, 7, 8, 10, 12 (pp. 97–98).

25. J. Lacan, "Propos sur la Causalité Psychique," *Écrits*, pp. 160–61. Lacan's critique of the body/mind impasse is already elaborated on in this paper, dating from 1946.

26. S. Freud, *Studies on Hysteria*, SE II, 286–87.

27. S. Freud, *Three Essays on the Theory of Sexuality*, SE VII, 207; "On the Universal Tendency to Debasement in the Sphere of Love," SE XI, 180 ff.

28. These remarks warrant a fuller study of their own. The most beautiful conclusion on them comes, of course, from Lacan himself: "Only love allows jouissance to condescend to desire" (Seminar X, March 13, 1963).

29. S. Freud, "Splitting of the Ego in the Process of Defense," SE XXIII.

30. S. Freud, SE VII, 168.

31. S. Freud, SE II, 67–70 (note).

32. S. Freud, SE II, 69 (note).

33. S. Freud, *Beyond the Pleasure Principle*, SE XVIII. It should be noted that Freud's discussion of repetition and repetition compulsion is rather confusing, in that he mixes two kinds of repetition: the repetition of the signifier, "automaton," which indeed becomes compulsive when a trauma is concerned (hence, traumatic dreams), as a way of trying to cope with the real of the trauma. On the other hand, there is the repetition of the real as such that time and again reappears in an ex-sistent way, where the chain of signifiers meets its limit. This is tuché. For a discussion, see Seminar XI, chapter 4.

34. S. Freud, *The Interpretation of Dreams*, SE V, 488–508, 525.

35. S. Freud, "Constructions in Analysis," SE XXIII, 259; see also "The Unconscious," SE XIV, 187.

36. Freud, *Beyond the Pleasure Principle*, SE XVIII, 49. *An Outline of Psycho-Analysis*, SE XXIII, 148–49.

37. Freud, *The Ego and the Id*, SE XIX, 46, 59.

38. Freud, *Inhibitions, Symptoms, and Anxiety*, SE XX, 125.

39. Freud, SE II, 290.

40. Freud, "The Economic Problem of Masochism," SE XIX, 168; "The Future of an Illusion," SE XXI, 54–56.

41. J. Lacan, Seminar XI, *The Four Fundamental Concepts of Psychoanalysis*, ed. J.-A. Miller (New York: Norton, 1978), trans. A. Sheridan. All references are given in the chapter itself; "Seminar 11" refers to the English translation, "Seminar XI" to the original French version.

42. New, compared to the body-image, received from the Other during the mirror stage.

43. "At the level of the unconscious, there is something that is homologous on all points to what happens at the level of the subject" (my translation, Seminar XI, 27; the original reads as follows: "au niveau de l'inconscient, il y a quelque chose en tous points homologue à ce qui se passe au niveau du sujet"; see also Seminar 11, 20–23; Seminar XI, 23–25).

44. "Well! It is insofar as something in the apparatus of the body is structured in the same way, it is because of the topological unity of the gaps in play, that the drive assumes its role in the functioning of the unconscious" (Seminar 11, 181; Seminar XI, 165).

45. This ontology can be summarized by one sentence of his first paper on the mirror stage: "In man, however, this relation to nature is altered by a certain dehiscence at the heart of the organism, a primordial Discord" (*Écrits*, 96/4).

46. The implications of this principle go very far indeed. While writing this chapter, my thoughts went back and forward all the time. To give but a few examples: What about racism? Sexism? And heteronormativity, as its latest implementation? (To be continued.)

# THE ONTOLOGICAL STATUS OF LACAN'S
# MATHEMATICAL PARADIGMS

*Andrew Cutrofello*

> Show that the median, hce che ech, intersecting at royde angles the
> parilegs of a given obtuse one biscuts both the arcs that are in
> curveachord behind.
>
> —James Joyce, *Finnegans Wake*

Readers of Lacan's work have disagreed over what to make of his forays into
the mathematical field of topology. Some, such as Jeanne Granon-Lafont, have
taken quite seriously two ideas: that topology provides the only proper model
for developing the insights of metapsychology, and that metapsychological insights into topological structures can be useful to mathematicians.[1] Others,
such as Joël Dor, have argued that Lacan's topological models serve merely as
"metaphorical illustrations" of psychoanalytic discoveries.[2] Dor is concerned
with absolving Lacan of having indulged in a disastrous enterprise; Granon-
Lafont maintains that Lacan's theses make no sense apart from the topological
manner in which he articulated them. The aim of this chapter is to try to specify the precise ontological status that Lacan assigns to his topological models,
focusing in particular on the Borromean knots that make their first appearance
in Seminar XX.

## LACAN'S APPEAL TO MATHEMATICAL FORMALIZATION

In chapter 10 of Seminar XX, Lacan writes:

> Mathematical formalization is our goal, our ideal. Why? Because it alone is
> matheme, in other words, it alone is capable of being integrally transmitted.

> Mathematical formalization consists of what is written, but it only subsists if
> I employ, in presenting it, the language (*langue*) I make use of. Therein lies
> the objection: no formalization of language is transmissible without the use of
> language itself. It is in the very act of speaking [*C'est par mon dire*] that I make
> this formalization, this ideal metalanguage, ex-sist. (119)

Lacan's first sentence here is straightforward: the telos of psychoanalytic theory
is a mathematical formalization of some sort. The justification of this claim is
that "it alone is matheme." But what exactly is a matheme? Lacan gives a partial
answer to this question by suggesting that mathemes are "capable of being integrally transmitted," or are "capable of transmitting themselves [*se transmettre*] integrally." It is useful to recall here that the Greek word *mathesis* means learning.
If by "integrally transmitted" Lacan means something like "passed on from
teacher to student," then a matheme would be that which a teacher gives a student, or that discourse in which learning can be passed on.

But Lacan immediately goes on to suggest that, by themselves, mathemes
cannot transmit anything, since "no formalization of language is transmissible
without the use of language itself." To formalize a language would be to translate its terms into a set of fixed symbols and to specify a finite number of axioms that would govern the production of sentences in that language. Such a
formalized language would itself be a matheme—that is, a discourse that could
serve as the repository of a *mathesis universalis*. Leibniz presented perhaps the
purest ideal of such a discourse in his conception of a "universal characteristic,"
into which all languages could be translated. In the future, Leibniz hypothe-
sized, people would settle all disputes by saying, "Let us calculate."

I take it that by "metalanguage" Lacan has in mind something very close
to Leibniz's universal characteristic. To say that there is no such thing as a metalanguage is to say that the task of constructing such a universal discourse could
never be completed. At a minimum, Lacan suggests, it would always be necessary to motivate the metalanguage through some other discourse. Thus the attempt to translate everything into a formal discourse is subject to either of two
possible failures: on the one hand, the translation is completed, with the result
that the symbols become hermetically inscrutable; on the other hand, one retains a discourse that can motivate the symbols, in which case the translation is
never completed.[3] Take *Finnegans Wake*. Unlike, say, *Principia Mathematica*,
Joyce's text seeks not univocity but plurivocity, and rather than constituting a
pure symbolic language that would be distinct from natural languages, it aspires
to the condition of being written in all languages simultaneously.[4] In this sense,
*Finnegans Wake* might seem to be the very opposite of a formalized text, but
if we take Lacan's point seriously, the relationship between *Finnegans Wake* and
*Principia Mathematica* can be read in terms of the logic of the Möbius strip. Insofar as it is written in English, *Principia Mathematica* is itself not written in the
formalized language it defines. Suppose Russell and Whitehead had tried to go
one step further by writing the whole thing in the formalized language itself.
The result would have been an inscrutable text that we could not read at all—

unless perhaps the authors had adopted the strategy of using English words in necessarily unfamiliar ways. The "English" words of *Principia Mathematica* would then be mere homonyms with English words, so that reading the text would give one the uncanny feeling that one was understanding something that made no sense at all—exactly the feeling we get reading *Finnegans Wake*. Or, to turn the point around, in writing *Finnegans Wake*, Joyce deliberately made his text inscrutable—but not so inscrutable that it was altogether impossible to read, whence, the proliferation of scholarly guides to the book that indicate where one might identify the various linguistic roots of all of the portmanteau words. When I pick up a book such as *A Guide to the Use of Finnish in Finnegans Wake*, I get something like *Principia Mathematica* in Finnish: a text that shows me how to interpret Joyce's highly "formalized" language. So it is as if the effort to subject *Finnegans Wake* to a rigorous reading turns Joyce's text into something resembling *Principia Mathematica*, just as the effort to write a *completely* rigorous *Principia Mathematica* would have turned that text into *Finnegans Wake*. Given Lacan's view that psychoanalytic theory aspires to the condition of a formalized language, it is no wonder that he was drawn to Joyce's text. The moral of this story is that if psychoanalysis aspires to the condition of mathematical formalization, we should not expect to be able to say whether the results will more closely resemble mathematics or poetry.

One type of complaint against Lacan's thesis as I have formulated it so far would be a Derridean sort of objection. Lacan says that a matheme must be written; it has the form of an *écrit*, but it only "subsists" as matheme through a motivating discourse that has the character of spoken language (*"mon dire"*). Hence, the Derridean argues that Lacan is here repeating the classical philosophical gesture par excellence by treating writing as "dead" language and speech as "living" language. The only warrant for such a distinction would seem to be a clandestine metaphysics that grants what Lacan is officially supposed to deny, namely, subjectivity's self-presence to itself. In other words, Lacan seems to repeat his earlier distinction between full and empty speech, a distinction that comes under attack in Jean-Luc Nancy's and Philippe Lacoue-Labarthe's *The Title of the Letter*, a book that Lacan mentions several times in Seminar XX.[5]

Leaving aside the hermeneutic question of the relationship between Seminar XX and Lacan's Rome discourse (in which the distinction between full and empty speech is taken up), there are a number of reasons Lacan's account of the relationship between written mathemes and spoken discourse need not succumb to the Derridean objection. In claiming that mathemes are incapable of functioning without a motivating discourse, Lacan can be read as making a point about the relationship between an "object language" and a "metalanguage," as these terms usually are understood in mathematical logic. When an attempt is made to "formalize" a language, as in *Principia Mathematica*, the language that is to be formalized often is called the "object language," while the language in which we describe the object language is what is called the "metalanguage."[6] So in *Principia Mathematica*, we would say that everyday English is the metalanguage in question, not the formalized language that Russell and Whitehead define. One of the crucial results arising out of Tarski's work was the suggestion that an adequate theory of truth for a formal language could be presented only if one distinguished between the object language *for* which we define a truth predicate and the metalanguage *in* which we define this predicate.[7]

When Lacan says that no formalization of language is possible without a motivating discourse, he seems to be invoking this result, so his use of "metalanguage" would be the inverse of what we would expect.[8] If so, and provided we take into account the idiosyncrasies of his terminology, there is no reason the motivating language needs to be a spoken discourse. The point that Lacan is making is not to oppose the written to the spoken but to oppose that which is written in a formal language to that "other language" in terms of which the formal language can be presented as such. Admittedly, Lacan does say that a formal language must be written, for reasons I will come back to, but this in itself says nothing about how we are to conceive of the relationship between speech and writing. Moreover, there is no reason to think that the motivating discourse is "complete" in contrast to the "incompleteness" of the object language. More plausibly, we could read Lacan as making a point about what Derrida calls "supplementarity," namely, that no formalization of a language can take place except by a supplementary language, which in turn would require a supplementary language for its own formalization.

If anything, in claiming that there is no such thing as a metalanguage, Lacan is making the eminently Derridean point that language is not the medium through which the presence of being reveals itself. More precisely, Lacan has this to say:

> When I say that [there's no such thing as a metalanguage], it apparently means—no language [*langage*] of being. But is there being? As I pointed out last time, what I say is what there isn't. (Seminar XX, 118)

That which I say is that which is not: *ce que je dis, c'est ce qu'il n'y a pas*. If Lacan prefers to use the term *metalanguage* to refer to the ideal of a formalized language, it is in part because he associates that ideal with the dream of metaphysics. Metalanguage, as the formal discourse of metaphysics, would be the language in which being could be said. But, Lacan argues, being is precisely that which is not said in any language, whence again the impossibility of a metalanguage. Indeed, just to push the juxtaposition with Derrida a bit further, as Lacan construes the ideal of a written metalanguage, it coincides with what Derrida discerns as the philosophical ideal of living speech. Just as Derrida exposes the manner in which that ideal cannot be articulated without an appeal to writing, so Lacan is making a comparable point when he argues that the ideal of a metalanguage cannot be articulated without an appeal to the discourse that would motivate such a language.

It should be noted, of course, that the post–Fregean project of constructing a pure formalized language has not always been associated with metaphysics. Frege's *Begriffsschrift* does tie the two together, but *Principia Mathematica* and especially Carnap's *The Logical Syntax of Language* explicitly separate the function of constructing a formal language from any metaphysical pretensions. Of all twentieth-century philosophers, perhaps no one would agree more readily with Lacan than Carnap that what I say has nothing whatsoever to do with being.

But there is a difference between Carnap and Lacan. For Carnap, metaphysics is something that can be dispensed with entirely. The Gordian knot can be cut once and for all, thereby separating scientific discourse from metaphysics. Lacan, in contrast, suggests that the knot in question has a convoluted structure, and he goes so far as to suggest that the proper task for psychoanalytic theory is to investigate the gesture by which modern science claims to break from metaphysics.[9]

Lurking in the background of Lacan's discussion in Seminar XX is his important essay, "Science and Truth," presented in 1965, a year after Seminar XI.[10] In Seminar XI, Lacan advances the thesis that the subject with which psychoanalysis is concerned is none other than the Cartesian cogito. In "Science and Truth," he expands on this thesis, identifying the cogito as "the subject of science." Drawing on the work of Alexandre Koyré (whom he invokes again in chapter 7 of Seminar XX), Lacan argues that the "position of the subject" undergoes a radical shift with the rise of modern science, and he identifies the Cartesian cogito as that which emerges from this shift. What I would like to call attention to here is the importance that Lacan ascribes to a certain Cartesian *scene*:

> Descartes' approach is, singularly, one of safeguarding the ego from the deceitful God, and thereby safeguarding the ego's partner—going so far as to endow the latter with the exorbitant privilege of guaranteeing the eternal truths only insofar as he is their creator.[11]

In the last part of this sentence, Lacan is referring to the fact that, according to Descartes, if God had so chosen he could have made it the case that $2 + 2 = 5$. In Seminar XI, Lacan comments on "the extraordinary consequences" of this "handing back of truth into the hands of the Other," going so far as to suggest that the Cartesian algebraization of geometry, along with all of its consequences in the subsequent history of mathematics, is somehow dependent on this gesture by which God is granted the power to make what is true be true.[12] I will return to this topic, but for now I would simply note that the Cartesian thesis here is radically opposed to that of Plato. In the *Euthyphro*, we are clearly expected to conclude, with Socrates, that the holy is not holy because the gods love it; rather, the gods love it because it is holy. For Descartes, in contrast, if God never makes a mistake balancing his checkbook, it is because whatever he tallies is correct.[13]

The passage from Seminar XI discussed above gives us reason to think that psychoanalysis might have something to say about the rise of modern mathematics and modern science, though the details of that story still need to be worked out. But it does not seem to explain why metapsychology itself might tend toward its own type of mathematical formalization. In Seminar XI, Lacan takes great pains to defend the idea that psychoanalysis is, or aspires to be, a science. In order to make that claim, he finds it necessary to distinguish between a science that takes *reality* as its object and a science that takes *the real* as its object. In Seminar XX, he claims that "Mathematization alone reaches a real . . . that has nothing to do with what traditional knowledge has served as a basis for, which is not what the latter believes it to be—namely, reality—but rather fantasy" (131). For Lacan, "reality" always refers to something framed by fantasy, while "the real" names—or gestures in the direction of—that which we never encounter *as such*. By distinguishing between these two senses of science, Lacan is able simultaneously to criticize those psychoanalysts for transforming Freud's discourse into a science of reality and for failing to transform it into a science of the real. At the same time, I suggest, he wants to distinguish between two levels of the Cartesian discourse. By appealing to a benevolent God who guarantees the correctness of my clear and distinct perceptions of objects, Descartes conjures an "objective" reality that is always supported by an appeal to fantasy. But the advent of Cartesian science lies not there but rather at the level of the mathematical signifier whose proper destination is to yield not a science of reality but a science of the real. It is the completion of that destiny that interests Lacan.

## MODERN SCIENCE AND THE LOSS OF
## THE SEXUAL RELATIONSHIP

In order to bring out what is at stake here, I propose an analysis of the Cartesian scene that Lacan calls to our attention.

> Accordingly, I will suppose not a supremely good God, the source of truth, but rather an evil genius, supremely powerful and clever, who has directed his entire effort at deceiving me. I will regard the heavens, the air, the earth, colors, shapes, sounds, and all external things as nothing but the bedeviling hoaxes of my dreams, with which he lays snares for my credulity. I will regard myself as not having hands, or eyes, or flesh, or blood, or any senses, but as nevertheless falsely believing that I possess all these things.[14]
>
> Am I so tied to a body and to the senses that I cannot exist without them? But I have persuaded myself that there is absolutely nothing in the world: no sky, no earth, no minds, no bodies. Is it then the case that I too do not exist? But doubtless I exist, if I persuaded myself of something. But there is some deceiver or other who is supremely powerful and supremely sly and who is always deliberately deceiving me. Then too there is no doubt that I exist, if he is deceiving me.[15]

It would be impossible for me to exist, being of such a nature as I am (namely, having in me the idea of God), unless God did in fact exist. God, I say, that same being the idea of whom is in me: a being having all those perfections that I cannot comprehend, but can somehow touch with my thought, and a being subject to no defects whatever. From these considerations it is quite obvious that he cannot be a deceiver.[16]

How should this scene be interpreted? One way would be to adopt the method of Lévi-Strauss.[17] Instead of attempting to interpret each of the elements of the Cartesian scene, we could treat it like a myth whose significance lies in its relationship to other myths. Lévi-Strauss sees in myth the articulation of the transition from nature to culture. At issue in the Cartesian scene for Lacan is not so much the transition from nature to culture as from a dogmatic metaphysics to science. Instead of classifying such a discourse as a myth, we might better characterize it, for reasons I will elaborate on below, as a thought experiment. In the manner of Lévi-Strauss, I will call the Cartesian thought experiment not $M_1$ but $C_1$.[18]

"Thought experiment" would have a double sense: on the one hand, it would name any experiment carried out *in thought*; on the other hand, it would name an experiment carried out *on* thought itself. Conceived in this double way, it is perhaps fair to say that thought experiments are to the advent of modern science precisely what myths are to the advent of culture. Galileo provides us with an exemplary instance of the former. It is *in* thought that I imagine a frictionless space where, once moved, a body will continue in its course indefinitely. The Cartesian thought experiment has this character too (i.e., it is in thought that I imagine the possible existence of an evil deceiver, etc.). It also is an experiment on thinking as well, for to carry out the experiment is precisely to isolate my thought as object of inquiry, to experiment on it, as when I ask myself, suppose I really believed in this evil deceiver—what then would be the status of my thinking?

One might be tempted to say that thought experiments predate modern science. After all, what do we get in Plato's cave analogy if not a thought experiment? But there seems to be a difference. At stake in the cave analogy is a question about the relationship between the objects of perception, or *aisthesis*, and the intelligible forms that make them what they are. It is not the reality of these objects that Plato questions but their degree of reality. In contrast, the Cartesian thought experiment breaks with *aisthesis* altogether ("I shall consider myself as having no hands, no eyes, no flesh, no blood, *nor any senses*"). The cogito that emerges from this radical break with *aisthesis* is a subject of pure *noesis* ("I am therefore precisely nothing but a thinking thing; that is, a mind, or intellect, or understanding, or reason—*words of whose meanings I was previously ignorant*").[19] Koyré offers a similar reading of Galileo. Calling attention to the radicality of the Galilean break with premodern science, he writes, "We must choose: either to think or to imagine. . . . For it is thought, pure unadulterated thought, and not experience or sense-perception, as until then, that gives the basis for the 'new science' of Galileo."[20] For Plato, the difference between *aisthesis* and *noesis* is a difference of degree (whence, the metaphor of the line); for Descartes and Galileo, it is one of kind.

In Seminar XI, Lacan figures Cartesian subjectivity as forcing a choice between being and thinking. As the passage from Koyré suggests, we might better figure the forced choice as between perceiving and thinking, but the two models can be put together. In Aristotelian metaphysics, *aisthesis* is that faculty through which the being of beings is disclosed to the soul; *noesis* is that faculty through which the truth of beings is discerned. The audacity of Descartes and Galileo is to repudiate the assumption that a homology exists between the being of beings, as revealed in *aisthesis* and the truth of beings, as revealed in *noesis*. It is not through my senses that I perceive what truly belongs to the wax: "I perceive it through the mind alone."[21]

One way of identifying the elements of $C_1$ would be to isolate the narrative "events" of the *Meditations*, of which the encounter with (the problem of) the evil deceiver would be one. Another way would be to isolate the series of truths accumulated in the course of the thought experiment, since each of the important narrative events gives rise to the articulation of one such truth. These truths invariably concern one of two things. The first is the existence of an object of a certain sort (sometimes a singular object, such as my soul or God, and sometimes a class of objects, such as other bodies or other souls in general). The second is the causal relations that hold among the objects whose existence has been established. We could therefore take the elements of $C_1$ to be the set of distinct types of objects whose existence is established and construe the posited causal interaction between any two of these objects (not necessarily a commutative operation) to be something like a binary relation that operates on them. I say "something like" a binary operation, because the operation need not yield a third object that is itself a "group" member, and it need not be the case that the operation can be indifferently applied to all members of the group. But if we take the elements to be fixed and the operation of causal connection to specify a particular way of *linking* the elements, then we can consider any particular stipulated pattern of causal connections to be one possible instance of a larger set of possible transformations.

For example, we could identify the principal elements of $C_1$ as:

> *my soul*
> *God*
> *my body*
> *other bodies*
> *other souls*

—all of which are brought together in an elaborate causal nexus by the end of the *Meditations*. Using arrows to signify the relationship between a cause and the object acted upon by that cause (allowing for bi-directional arrows, where commutativity is permitted), we would have:

**FIGURE 8.1**

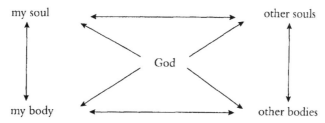

Figure 8.1 illustrates Descartes' conclusion that my soul and body are in causal interaction with each other, as is the soul and body of any other ensouled being; that all bodies are in causal interaction with one another; that the souls of ensouled bodies may enter into causal interactions as well; and that God acts on everything, but that nothing acts on God. Strictly speaking, it is unclear whether Descartes held to all of the details of this "interactionist" model, but this question is in a way immaterial for our purposes, since what matters is not who held which view but what the possible transformations of this basic framework in early modern thought were.[22] Thinkers such as Malebranche, Leibniz, Newton, Wolff, and so on were deeply concerned with describing the causal nexus among just these five elements in the right way. In Malebranche, for example, we get the so-called "occasionalist" ontology, which can be represented (see Figure 8.2) as follows:

**FIGURE 8.2**

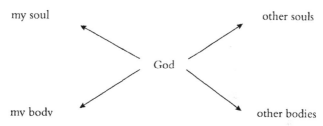

For the occasionalists, God is the only real agent. Malebranche denies that soul and body interact, famously arguing that God arranges things so that changes in the one correspond to changes in the other. He also denies that there is any real physical interaction between bodies, a view represented in Figure 8.2 by the absence of any arrows connecting "my body" and "other bodies." Finally, he denies that souls can enter into any real interaction with one another. I will call this structural product of the occasionalist thought experiment $C_2$.

The Leibnizian thought experiment (see Figure 8.3), in contrast, yields $C_3$:

**Figure 8.3**

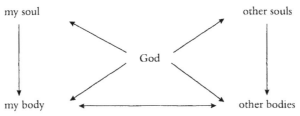

For Leibniz, as for Malebranche, there is no genuine causal interaction between souls, but there is causal interaction between bodies. Where Malebranche conceives of the soul as passive, even with respect to its own states, Leibniz takes the soul to be active so that in order to coordinate the states of souls, God must arrange for some sort of preestablished harmony.

My claim is that in order to see what is at stake in the Cartesian thought experiment, we need to consider the series of early modern thought experiments ($C_1$, $C_2$, $C_3$, etc.) as a set of structural transformations.[23] Before proceeding to an analysis of this series, I would like to attenuate matters just one step further by taking a suggestion of Slavoj Zizek's. In *Looking Awry*, Zizek advances the thesis that certain aspects of theoretical positions (such as thought experiments) can only be revealed by staging them, an act that enables us to "look awry" at the positions in question.[24] I will return to the question of why it should be the case that staging a thought experiment can reveal something that we would not otherwise detect, though already we have reason to suspect that it has something to do with the split between *aisthesis* and *noesis*. For now, I will implement Zizek's strategy by briefly considering a series of films, each of which stages a variant of the fundamental Cartesian problematic—that is, the implication of the disjunction between reality and the real—in an obvious way.

In *Total Recall*, a man named Doug Quaid is haunted by a dream in which he finds himself on Mars involved with a woman other than his wife, a fact that apparently makes his wife jealous. ("I can't believe you're jealous of a dream." "Who is she?" "Nobody." "Nobody? What's her name?") He goes to a clinic called "Recall Incorporated," where for recreational purposes they implant artificial memories. Quaid asks for a memory sequence in which he will go to Mars, meet a "sleazy" and "demure" woman, and save the planet. In the middle of the memory implant, things go wrong, as he suddenly remembers that his previous identity (as Quaid) was itself a false memory implant; he is really a man named Hauser. He is sedated, and when he awakens again, he thinks of himself as Quaid, but as events transpire, he has reason to think that he might really be Hauser—particularly after his "wife" tells him that they are not really married. ("Sorry Quaid. Your whole life's just a dream.") Eventually he ends up going to Mars, meeting a woman remarkably like the woman of his dreams, and saving the planet. At the end of the film, standing next to his sleazy and demure partner, he says, "I just had a terrible thought. What if this is a dream?" To which she responds, "Well then kiss me quick before you wake up."

In *The Matrix*, a computer programmer named Thomas Anderson who goes by the hacker name "Neo" finds the words "Wake up" typed onto his computer screen one morning. Following the instructions on the screen, he ends up meeting a woman called Trinity and, through her, a man named Morpheus. Through them Neo discovers that all of his life he has been immersed in some sort of embryonic fluid, attached to an immense computer created by AI (artificial intelligence) forms of life that "grow" humans for the energy output of human brains. Everything that Neo had "experienced" until then had only been the false virtual reality world of "the matrix." Freed from his prison, he trains to reenter the virtual world to be able to save others from it, but it is uncertain whether he is the prophesied "One" who can do this. The prophetess tells him that he is not, but she also tells him that he does not believe in fate. Neo in fact performs an act (saving Morpheus' life) that the prophetess had predicted he would not be able to do. But he gets "killed" in the matrix, the death of his mind there entailing the death of his body as well. Trinity whispers to his dead body that he cannot really be dead, since she loves him and the prophetess has predicted that she would fall in love with the One. After she kisses him, Neo comes back to life (both outside of the matrix and inside of it). He is now able to alter events in the matrix at will and to lead a human rebellion against the AI forms of life.[25]

In *13th Floor*, Douglas Hall is part of a team of computer programmers who have created a virtual reality world into which they can enter and "interact" with the virtual "subjects" who "live" in that world. After Fuller, the head of the programming team, is murdered, Hall enters the virtual world and finds a message that Fuller had left for him. The message says that if he leaves town and drives far enough, he will discover that the world is "incomplete," thereby revealing its virtuality. He is puzzled, because he knows that this is true of the virtual reality world in which he has received the message and thinks that the message is referring to it. Eventually he discovers that the message in fact refers to what he had thought was the "real" world, which he now learns is itself a virtual world created by computer programmers living in the *real* world. He learns this when he drives to the visually literalized limits of his world, directly encountering, as it were, the fantasy frame of reality. A woman from the "real" world, who has entered his world posing as Fuller's daughter Jane, falls in love with him. Hall eventually joins her in her world after her husband, Hall's "higher" world "user," is killed as he tries to kill his wife while inhabiting Hall's body. The film ends with Hall united with his partner in her world, which turns out to be a utopian California of the future (a newspaper headline reads, "2024 Crime Rates at All-Time Low").

It is obvious that each of these films stages a variation on the key Cartesian thought experiment, and it is instructive to consider which of the variations is at stake.[26] *Total Recall*, for instance, might be described as staging the Male-branchian thought experiment, since occasionalism is in effect the doctrine that everyone's experiences are "memory implants." If everything that happens to Quaid is just a dream, then he has not really acted at all; he has merely passively experienced the events that have been "downloaded" into him by the big Other.[27] In contrast, *The Matrix* might be said to stage the Leibnizian doctrine of preestablished harmony.[28] Outside the matrix, human bodies really do interact, but inside the matrix, their "souls" only appear to interact, since each mind merely experiences events that are "in synch" with the events experienced by others. These experiences are not merely passively received, though, since each "soul" is capable of effectively altering its condition in the matrix. Thus we have all of the ingredients of $C_3$. In *13th Floor*, finally, we have the staging of the interactionist doctrine—that is, the view that there is real interaction between soul and body, soul and soul, and body and body, for the suggestion is that the subjects who live in their respective virtual worlds are *not*, as in *The Matrix*, merely living in a dream; both they and their worlds are "just as real" as any higher-level reality, a point insisted on by characters who ask higher-world users to leave them alone and let them live their own lives. The fact that only some of these souls (apparently) have bodies while others do not only shows that there is room for nonstandard forms of embodiment (or perhaps angels) in the interactionist doctrine.

What exactly do these films reveal about the early modern thought experiments that they stage? I suggest that each of the films discussed has as its central topic a worry about the ontological status of the sexual relationship. We have already seen this to be the case in *Total Recall*, a film that begins and ends with the suggestion that a successful sexual relationship exists only within the realm of fantasy. Trying to placate his wife, who is jealous of the woman he's been dreaming about, Quaid says to her, "Come on, baby, you know you're the girl of my dreams," but the fact that he still wants to go to Mars indicates that his relationship with her is not fulfilling. Later, when he points a gun at her after she has tried to kill him, she says, "Sweetheart. Be reasonable. After all, we're married"—at which point he shoots her in the head and says, "Consider that a divorce." The idea that he would have to kill his wife *because* she was trying to kill him is obviously an element of the fantasy that enables Quaid to be with the (sleazy and demure) girl of his dreams in a guilt-free way. *Total Recall* could thus be said to stage the thesis that the sexual relationship takes place only at the level of fantasy.[29]

In *The Matrix*, the sexual relationship is figured in terms of the feminine relation to the divine. In effect, the film stages the transition from a world governed by the evil deceiver to a world governed by a benevolent God. The Christian symbolism that recurs throughout the film places Neo in the position of Jesus and Trinity in the position of Mary Magdalene. When Trinity kisses Neo's corpse, thereby causing his resurrection, the possibility of their sexual relationship is guaranteed solely insofar as he is "the One." Once again, it is a fantasy of a certain sort that sustains the sexual relationship.

The connection between fantasy and the sexual relationship is evident in *13th Floor* as well. Fuller enters the virtual world for the sole purpose of having sex with prostitutes. His position in the film therefore corresponds to Quaid's in *Total Recall*, and his murder early on indicates that the film has another agenda, one that concerns the relationship between Hall (who, notably, has the same first name as Quaid) and the woman claiming to be Jane Fuller. Earlier I suggested that this film can be read as staging the doctrine of interactionism. At the end of the film, the happily united couple have entered a supposedly "real" world that is obviously fantasmatic. In this sense, what is being staged is the fantasy that the sexual relationship could really exist outside of fantasy. Of course, this is to say that the role of fantasy is not absent even here, but it is to call attention to the difference between fantasy as that which provides an "escape" from reality and fantasy as that which seeks an idealized transformation of reality.[30]

Read in this way, our films suggest that just as for Lévi-Strauss, the myths of South America are "really" about cooking as that which marks the transition from nature to culture, so the early modern thought experiments of Europe are "really" about the loss of the sexual relationship as that which marks the transition from Aristotelian metaphysics to modern science. In fact, Lacan suggests as much in the passage from "Science and Truth," cited above, where he speaks of Descartes as "safeguarding the ego's partner."

One of the recurring themes of Seminar XX concerns the difference between an Aristotelian approach to the divine and a post–Cartesian approach. For Aristotle, the subject's relationship to the prime unmoved mover is precisely a relationship of love, and that relationship in turn serves as a kind of guarantee of the sexual relationship. After Descartes and Galileo, Lacan suggests, that relationship becomes problematic. As long as science remained Aristotelian, that is, as long as it was concerned solely with "reality," as Lacan understands this term, it remained within the confines of fantasy. What happens in modernity is that a science of reality gives way to a science of the real, where the real is that which can be approached only by way of a pure *noesis*. Because the rise of modern science depends upon an extrusion of *aisthesis* from the domain of the real, the cogito (or subject of science) finds itself without a world—that is, without the fantasy frame that sustained the Aristotelian cosmos. If fantasy is that which alone makes the sexual relationship possible, then the anxiety associated with modern science arises from the disclosure of the subject's relationship to a "real" radically other than reality.

Consider again the scene in *13th Floor* where Hall appears to "traverse the fantasy," discovering the literal fantasy frame of his world. ("I know the truth." "Where are you?" "You could call it the end of the world.") One way of reading this scene would be to say that it mimics the Galilean and Newtonian gesture whereby the subject discovers its subordination to the signifier. What is traumatic in $F = ma$, I suggest, is that the equation in question is a way of *naming* the real—that is, of disclosing the subject's *agalma*, as Lacan puts it elsewhere. Galileo said the book of nature was written in mathematical symbols. To discover that this is so is exactly akin to discovering that "my whole world" is a simulacrum conjured by a bunch of computers, a discovery that gives rise to a certain "aphanisis" of the subject, where this term connotes both a sense of despair and a concomitant loss of sexuality.[31] In *The Metastases of Enjoyment*, Zizek associates aphanisis with what he calls "feminine depression," the suggestion being that it is feminine subjectivity that perpetually runs the risk of despair and loss of world.[32] What *13th Floor* brings out is that it is the masculine Cartesian subject who is especially prone to this "feminine" depression. Hall's interest in Fuller's daughter disappears after his discovery, and the possibility of their having a sexual relationship comes to hinge on her bringing him within her fantasy frame—or, in the terms of ego psychology, on his being able to reconstruct a sense of reality (i.e., a fantasy) that matches hers. ("From the moment this simulation was created, I've watched you . . . I fell in love with you before I even met you." "How can you love me? I'm not even real. You can't fall in love with a dream." "You're more real to me than anything I've ever known.") Note the reversal of the problematic staged in *Total Recall*. For Doug Quaid, the problem is that his ideal sexual partner may exist only in his dreams; for Doug Hall, the problem is that he may exist only in the dreams of his ideal sexual partner. To the extent that the film ends with Hall's reintegration into the frame of his original fantasy—he is again a "real" person with an identity confirmed by the paternal presence of Fuller's higher-world "user"—we could say that he does not truly traverse the fantasy in Lacan's sense. We also could say that the passage from Hall's aphanisis to his recovery of reality marks the passage from his worrying that he lives in an occasionalist world to his belief that he lives in an interactionist world.

What then can we conclude about $C_1$? The Cartesian subject "loses its world" when it discovers itself qua cogito or subject of the signifier in the second Meditation, but it attempts to reestablish that world, rather in the manner that Freud describes the psychotic's attempt to recreate reality. Thus we can read the Cartesian thought experiment as exhibiting three crucial features: (1) it enacts the passage from reality to the real, thereby giving rise to the problem of the evil deceiver; (2) it reestablishes reality insofar as the transition from evil deceiver to benevolent God is effected; and (3) it bears witness to an ongoing anxiety about how to reconcile the new mathematical physics, a science of the real, with the familiar parameters of reality. That anxiety, Lacan argues, *is* the anxiety over the sexual relationship.

Thus what Lacan means when he says "there's no such thing as the sexual relationship" is that, after the rise of modern science, the split between *noesis* and *aisthesis* corresponds to the subject's aphanisis, where that aphanisis is to be understood primarily in terms of the loss of world. The various thought experiments, $C_1$, $C_2$, $C_3$, and so on, are ways of trying to rethink the ontological status of the sexual relationship.

It needs to be kept in mind that the early modern thought experiments are metaphysical in character. The elements of the Cartesian "group" are *beings* whose mode of being is at issue. In other words, far from drawing the consequences of the rise of modern science, the early modern thought experiments are ways of "not wanting to know anything about it," to cite a Lacanian phrase. Modern metaphysical thinking seeks a way of identifying the real with a reality of spatial bodies revealed in *aisthesis* while at the same time separating the subject (the soul) from the realm of spatial bodies. In this way, not only does modern science seek to identify the real with reality, it simultaneously tries to exempt the subject from the realm of the bodily, that is, from the realm of the mathematizable. This last point, of course, is a truism: mind/body dualism and its kindred alternatives are ways of "saving" the subject; in particular, it seems as though the only way of preserving the autonomy of the subject is to show that the subject's position within the causal nexus—this nexus now known to be governed by mathematical laws—somehow exempts the subject from being reduced to an object of these laws. All of the thought experiments above are ways of wrestling with this problem in one way or another.

Thus if the subject of science emerges as that which is capable of thinking the truth of beings in mathematical terms, it simultaneously appears as that which resists the reduction of its own truth to those same terms.[33] This, I take it, is what is staged in the films discussed above, each of which proposes a different way of "saving" the subject, of refusing to allow the subject to be reduced to the signifier. By insisting that there is always something in a subject that is "more" than the signifier (or computer program) that constitutes it, both *The Matrix* and *13th Floor* affirm the autonomy of the subject; in both cases, it is the subject's ability to "wake up" that saves it from the signifier. In *Total Recall*, it is the exact opposite: the subject precisely does not want to wake up or, again, "doesn't want to know anything about it." But even here, the subject is the site of a certain excess, in this case, of enjoyment ("Kiss me quick").[34]

## LACAN'S MATHEMATICS OF THE SIGNIFIER

It is not enough to say that modern science is mathematical, since Aristotelian science could already accommodate a certain mathematization of *aisthesis*, as, for example, in the Ptolemaic model of the heavens. What distinguishes modern science is a certain type of mathematics, one based not on the sign (object of *aisthesis*) but on the signifier (object of *noesis*). For Aristotle, mathematical entities are mere abstractions derived from our perceptions of the visible world. Understood in this way, our sense of the necessity of mathematical truths— such as that the shortest distance between two points is a straight line, that the sum of the angles of a triangle is 180°, that $2 + 2 = 4$—is grounded in our perception of the visible world. We know that Euclid's axioms are true *because we see*, that is, because the evidence of *aisthesis* reveals that this is so. Descartes repudiates this type of justification. We do not know because we see; we know because we think. If it is true that $2 + 2 = 4$, we can determine that it is true not by counting apples but simply by *counting*.[35]

Lacan suggests that the consequences of the liberation of *noesis* from *aisthesis* are incalculable:

> What does this imply, if not that we will be able to begin playing with the small algebraic letters that transform geometry into analysis, that the door is open to set theory, that we can permit ourselves everything as a hypothesis of truth?[36]

To be sure, Lacan is not explicitly speaking here of the separation of *noesis* from *aisthesis* but of that "handing back of truth into the hands of the Other" by which Descartes affirms that God could have made it the case that $2 + 2 = 5$. But what does it mean to ascribe such a capacity to God? It means, I suggest, that *everything which can be thought must be possible*, so when Lacan says that Descartes paves the way for the algebraization of geometry, the development of set theory, and so on, he is pointing out that post–Cartesian mathematics is freed from the constraints of *aisthesis*. That there are truths concerning, say, numbers whose square is equal to $-1$ does not require that the being of such numbers be demonstrated. This is precisely what it means to say that a mathematics of signs has given way to a mathematics of the signifier. To motivate truths about complex numbers, all that is needed is a certain mathematical formalism of the sort that Viète and Descartes articulate. The algebraic letters with which they write equations do indeed appear within *aisthesis*, but only insofar as they make possible the articulation of truths, not insofar as they stand in for beings. Here we see why Lacan requires that a mathematical formalism be written: it is not because he reinstates a metaphysics of signs, as the Derridean suggests, but because he thereby marks the advent of modern science as something precisely other than a metaphysics of presence.[37] The fact that nothing in reality corresponds to negative, complex, or transfinite numbers, that I cannot intuit Lobachevskian or Riemannian or n-dimensional space, does not in the least compromise the truths I can grasp by thinking such objects.[38]

The gap between modern science and Aristotelian science might not seem so great, for it is easy to imagine that an "educated" *aisthesis* might come to perceive the new truths revealed by the new science, as when we learn to "see" not the sun rising but the earth turning. But as Koyré points out, for Galileo we do *not* see that the law of gravity is true, nor do we *confirm* the law of gravity through physical experiments, since all genuine justification takes place at the level of the thought experiment: "Good physics is made *a priori*."[39] For Lacan, the gap is completely radical, since it is not a question of substituting one "picture" of the world for another but of substituting mathematical equations for pictures.[40] It is thus the truth of beings—not necessarily the being of beings revealed in *aisthesis*—that modern science reveals. This means that there is a radical disjunction between the order of the mathematical and the order of perception—or, to invoke Lacan's dispute with phenomenology, that the order of the signifier is radically other than the order of "lived experience."

Of all modern philosophers, no one has been more aware of the fact of this disjunction than Heidegger, whose sole philosophical enterprise was to summon thinking back to what he takes to be its proper (essentially Aristotelian) task, namely, to think the being of beings as this is revealed in *aisthesis*.[41] Lacan's strategy is the exact opposite. His aim is to show that the split between *aisthesis* and *noesis* has not been sufficiently appreciated.[42] If Heidegger can be said to attempt to reclaim the being of beings by thinking the history of the truth of beings in terms of the way in which that truth itself unfolds within *aisthesis*, Lacan attempts to accentuate the encounter with the real that thrusts subjectivity within the domain of the truth of beings (i.e., the symbolic order), thereby definitively exiling the subject from the being of beings. It is the difference between an attempt to reestablish reality and an attempt to confront that loss of reality, which is the true consequence of modern science. Or, put otherwise, it is the difference between a discourse that sees in anxiety the mark of the subject's being-in-the-world and a discourse that sees in anxiety the mark of the subject's not-being-in-the-world.[43] From a Lacanian perspective, the Heideggerian enterprise would be a way of attempting to reclaim the possibility of a sexual relationship, despite the rise of modern science. As such, it has the character of a refusal.

## TOWARD A SCIENCE OF THE REAL

One of the difficulties associated with the Cartesian thought experiment is that we seem to be faced with a choice: either souls and bodies are different in kind, in which case it is difficult to conceive of how they could interact (this is the line of argument that seems to lead directly from Cartesianism to occasionalism), or they interact, in which case it is not clear that they differ in kind at all. If we opt for the latter alternative, we can do so from either an idealist (Berkeleyan) or a materialist (Hobbesian) perspective. The Berkeleyan position requires that we give up the domain of bodily interaction altogether, but the Hobbesian position implies that the cogito is just as subject to the signifier—that is, to the Newtonian laws of nature—as any physical object.

In his earliest writings, Kant attempted to address this dilemma by bringing together Newtonian physics and Leibnizian metaphysics. Against the doctrine of preestablished harmony, he maintains that souls can have real interactions with one another, just as bodies do. He also claims that souls interact with bodies. But he preserves the subject's independence from the signifier by suggesting that the spatiality of bodies is a consequence of a repulsive force exercised by simple substances (including souls) in their repelling of one another. What we might call the "space of intercorporeality" thus ends up being an extension of a metaphysically prior "space of intersubjectivity," so rather than having to face the deterministic implications of Newtonian physics (which grants autonomy to the space of intercorporeality), Kant can affirm the autonomy of subjects, despite their participation in the space of intercorporeal-ity. The two spaces are governed by different sorts of laws, the space of inter-subjectivity by moral laws, and the space of intercorporeality by mathematical laws. By insisting on the fundamental difference between these two spaces, or between the moral and the mathematical, Kant is able to fully accept the sub-ject of science while maintaining a proper "distance" between the subject and the signifier. We might diagram this position (see Figure 8.4) as follows:

**FIGURE 8.4**

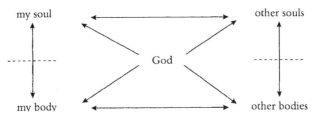

The dotted line is intended to indicate the difference in kind between the (upper) space of intersubjectivity and the (lower) space of intercorporeality.

Why did Kant ultimately find this resolution of the problem unsatisfac-tory? One way of putting the answer to this question would be to say that, like Doug Hall in *13th Floor*, he discovered its fantasmatic character. In particular, reading Emanuel Swedenborg's *Arcana coelestia* obviously had a profound effect on Kant, as we can tell from his "Dreams of a Spirit-Seer." In this essay, Kant chides himself for having advocated metaphysical theses strikingly close to what he takes to be the obviously fantasmatic visions described by Swedenborg (whose first name, perhaps not incidentally, was the same as Kant's). Like Kant, Swedenborg holds that there is a community of souls distinct from the com-munity of bodies, and that the former exhibits spatial relations of exactly the same sort as the latter. Kant rebels against this view, and he does so in a manner that is highly instructive. He does not deny that there might be a community among souls distinct from the community among bodies. What he denies is the idea that any of the sensible properties that characterize the space of intercor-poreality can be presumed to hold for the space of intersubjectivity, and yet he does this without giving up on the idea that some sort of causal interaction might nonetheless take place between the two spheres (this is the crucial point he will defend in the third and fourth antinomies of the first *Critique*). Because the space of intersubjectivity is merely something that we conceive of without being able to perceive, we can approach it only through fantasy:

> All judgements, such as those concerning the way in which my soul moves my body, or the way in which it is now or may in the future be related to other beings like itself, can never be anything more than fictions—fictions which are, indeed, far from having even the value of those which feature in natural science and which are called hypotheses.[44]

What exactly is Kant doing when he insists here, as he will later in the first *Critique*, that a sharp distinction be drawn between science and metaphysics? I can only briefly indicate a proper answer to this question, but I suggest that Kant's crucial philosophical gesture is to think even more rigorously than Descartes the radical difference between *aisthesis* and *noesis*. For Descartes, this distinction did not prevent the subject of science from being capable of drawing metaphysical conclusions: the discovery of the truth of beings entitles the cogito to say something about the being of beings. Kant's doctrine is much more austere. To say that intuitions and concepts are radically different in kind, that the being of beings revealed in sensibility and the truth of beings revealed in thought are utterly heterogeneous, is to say that nothing whatsoever can be known about the being of beings. At first, this sounds paradoxical, since if sensibility discloses the being of beings to us, why should that disclosure not count as a knowing? This is precisely the objection that Heidegger levels against Kant, for reasons I have already indicated, but Kant's thesis is arguably more radical than Heidegger appreciates. Yes, the being of beings is in some sense disclosed in sensibility, but *aisthesis* does not count as a knowing. In Lacanian terms, what Kant argues for is the imaginary character of objects of *aisthesis*, a consequence of their being located in a kind of "pure fantasy frame" (the forms of intuition). This is why it is necessary to distinguish between the ersatz knowledge that can be attained in science (through the application of categories of the understanding to objects given in sensibility) and that foreclosed metaphysical knowledge for which reason strives in vain. Kant never gives way on the thesis that the radical heterogeneity between *aisthesis* and *noesis* marks a fundamental split between science, by which the subject can acquire knowledge of the space of intercorporeality, and metaphysics, by which the subject can only think problematic thoughts about the character of a "space" of intersubjectivity among (themselves problematic) souls.

The Kantian thought experiment thereby institutes something new. It cannot be represented as another permutation of the Cartesian group, because *its elements are not beings*—or, to put the point in Lacanian terms, because it "puts a bar" through each of its terms. In other words, what had been the Cartesian group represented below (in Figure 8.5)

**FIGURE 8.5**

my soul                                    other souls


God


my body                                    other bodies

might now be schematically represented something like this (see Figure 8.6):

FIGURE 8.6

$$\frac{\text{S}}{\text{S}_1} \qquad \text{S}(\cancel{A}) \qquad \frac{\text{a}}{\text{S}_2}$$

Here S is no longer a soul but the subject that can only think itself problematically as soul, $S_1$ is my body (as object of both inner and outer intuition) insofar as this is how I appear (i.e., "am represented") within reality; $S_2$ represents
other bodies or the sum-total of these as the locus of the space of intercorporeality; "a" stands for that in these bodies which I take to be "more" than their
bodies, that is, their souls, which do not appear in *aisthesis* but which I think
problematically as I do my own soul (the sum-total of these constituting the
problematic space of intersubjectivity); and S($\cancel{A}$), finally, is the Kantian God
whose very possibility is itself merely problematic.

To say that the subject-in-itself now appears only as problematic for a
body that takes itself as object of inner sense is to suggest that it would be more
proper to invert the top and bottom levels of the diagram (i.e., for reasons anal-
ogous to those for which Lacan inverts Saussure's diagram of the relationship
between signifier and signified). This gives us

FIGURE 8.7

$$\frac{\text{S}_1}{\text{S}} \qquad \text{S}(\cancel{A}) \qquad \frac{\text{S}_2}{\text{a}}$$

—which of course is basically Lacan's discourse of the master.

In saying this, I do not mean to imply that Lacan is merely restating the
Kantian discourse. Elsewhere, I have argued that metapsychology can be construed as the perverse "flip side" (*envers*) of transcendental philosophy.[45] Each of
the judgments Kant construes as synthetic a priori is read by psychoanalysis as
belonging to a class of statements that Kant forecloses, namely, the analytic a
posteriori. Instead of repeating or correcting the details of that analysis, what I
would like to do here is show that when Lacan poses the problem of the math-
ematizability of psychoanalysis, he is addressing a problem explicitly thematized
by Kant.

Kant separates the subject from the signifier in two different ways. On the
one hand, he does so by equating the subject with the "I" of apperception
which, as such, cannot become an object of intuition at all. No rational psychology can yield knowledge of the soul, since the soul is itself merely problematic: if Kant does not "save" the subject, he thereby saves the possibility of
saving the subject. But Kant also argues that not even the subject qua object of
inner sense can be understood in mathematical terms. His brief argument turns
not on some radical incompatibility between inner intuition and mathematics
but solely on the presumed poverty of the mathematical properties of lines:

Mathematics is inapplicable to the phenomena of the internal sense and their laws, unless one might want to take into consideration merely the law of continuity of the flow of this sense's internal changes. But the extension of cognition so attained would bear much the same relation to the extension of cognition which mathematics provides for the doctrine of body, as the doctrine of the properties of the straight line bear to the whole of geometry.[46]

Kant's idea is this. As object of inner sense only, I appear to myself in time but not in space. For this reason, the only mathematical concepts that could possibly be applicable to a science of inner sense would be the concepts of arithmetic—or, equivalently, those geometrical concepts that concern the properties of a one-dimensional object (i.e., a line). But *lines lack mathematical structure*, and for this reason any purported mathematical psychology would be a poor cousin of mathematical physics.

Actually, lines have a much richer mathematical structure than Kant realized, and much of topology—particularly knot theory—can be construed as an elaboration of just this.[47] For this reason, it is tempting to suggest that Lacan is taking up the Kantian gauntlet when he appeals to the theory of knots and links to spell out the details of his metapsychology. Obviously it is not a question of saying that psychoanalysis is a science of "inner sense," but one of challenging Kant's argument that mathematical concepts have no possible employment beyond the limits of possible experience.[48] One of the first thinkers to challenge this Kantian claim was Frege. In *The Foundations of Arithmetic*, Frege grants to Kant his well-known thesis that geometric statements are synthetic a priori, but he denies that the same holds for arithmetic statements. Frege's argument is worth quoting at length:

> Empirical propositions hold good of what is physically or psychologically actual, the truths of geometry govern all that is spatially intuitable, whether actual or product of our fancy. The wildest visions of delirium, the boldest inventions of legend and poetry, where animals speak and stars stand still, where men are turned to stone and trees turn into men, where the drowning haul themselves up out of swamps by their own topknots—all these remain, so long as they remain intuitable, still subject to the axioms of geometry. Conceptual thought alone can after a fashion shake off this yoke, when it assumes, say, a space of four dimensions or positive curvature . . . For purposes of conceptual thought we can always assume the contrary of some one or other of the geometrical axioms, without involving ourselves in any self-contradictions . . . The fact that this is possible shows that the axioms of geometry are independent of one another and of the primitive laws of logic, and consequently are synthetic. Can the same be said of the fundamental propositions of the science of number? Here, we have only to try denying any one of them, and complete confusion ensues. Even to think at all seems no longer possible . . . The truths of arithmetic govern all that is numerable. This is the widest domain of all; for to it belongs not only the actual, not only the intuitable, *but everything thinkable*.[49]

Read through a Lacanian lens, Frege is here suggesting that, while geometry pertains to the realm of fantasy (i.e., to any possible intuitable reality), arithmetic pertains to the order of the real. He grants to Kant that geometric concepts may not be applicable beyond the fantasy frame of reality but maintains that it is otherwise in the case of numerical concepts.

It was Jacques-Alain Miller who called attention to the relevance of Frege's text to Lacanian theory, arguing that the subject's relationship to the signifier could be understood in terms of Frege's account of the ontological status of numbers.[50] Here I would only add to that analysis the observation that it is Frege's understanding of the radical difference between geometry, a science that belongs to *aisthesis*, and arithmetic, construed by Frege to be a science that belongs solely to *noesis*, that makes possible the further claim that the concepts of number are applicable even beyond what Kant identifies as the limits of possible experience.[51]

How might it be possible to develop a mathematical account of the subject? I will not rehearse the details as Miller lays them out but will instead suggest that there are two possible options here. The first would be to include the "soul" within the realm of reality—that is, to reduce the space of intersubjectivity to the space of intercorporeality. We deny that the unity of apperception indicates the irreducibility of subjectivity to the physical and seek within empirical reality a way of understanding the genesis of subjectivity in strictly empirical terms. For example, suppose we take the Kantian distinction between outer and inner intuition to mark the difference between an organism's awareness of its environment and its awareness of its internal bodily states. Suppose we account for the organism's awareness of this difference by assuming that it is susceptible to two different sorts of sensations—those it can alter through bodily movements and those it cannot. Suppose the organism has a tendency to discharge the energy conveyed to it through its internal sensations, but it is impossible to eliminate these entirely, and so on. Obviously, I am reconstructing the analysis that Freud presents both in his 1895 "Project" and in *Beyond the Pleasure Principle*. We know that Freud never entirely gave up the idea that an adequate science of the mind might one day reduce metapsychology to a chapter of empirical psychology. To say this is to say that Freud took his cue from the idea of a science of reality.

The second alternative would be to accept the subject's noninclusion in empirical reality and to take seriously the Koyrean idea that modern science is essentially a science not of reality but of the real. To pursue this line of thought is to begin not with an organism embedded in a pregiven space but to begin with the problematic idea of a subject that cannot be described in terms of any empirical properties whatsoever. Suppose we take seriously the idea that such a subject belongs first and foremost to something like a space of intersubjectivity—a space, however, whose character can be conceived of only in numerical, not geometrical, terms. Such a space might be conceived of as a network of signifiers, and the way to propose a mathematization of the subject would be to seek a model for understanding the advent of subjectivity in the linking of signifiers.

The Borromean link provides Lacan with precisely such a model.[52] In Seminar XX, this model plays many different, though interrelated, roles. First it serves as a way of diagramming a particular discourse, as when Lacan cites his earlier use of the model to illustrate the sentence, "I ask you to refuse what I offer you" (126). This is a particular statement supposed to characterize a particular subjective symptom, and the aptness of the Borromean model lies with the supposed homology between the symptom in question and the topological features of the link. Once we see how the Borromean link can serve as a model for a particular symptom, we also see how, second, it can serve as a model for the symptom in general. In order to fulfill this double requirement, Lacan will turn in later seminars to a variety of links, each meant to illustrate a particular type of symptom; in Seminar XX, the Borromean link serves both functions. It also represents, third, not just the particular discourse mentioned above but discourse in general. In particular, Lacan associates a Borromean chain of some finite number of rings with a sentence, each link in the chain being a particular signifier (128). Fourth, the Borromean link is used to represent "the social link," which enables us to think of each ring as a particular subject, or of each ring as the signifier of a subject. Thus in chapter 5 he says:

> In the final analysis, there's nothing but that, the social link. I designate it with the term "discourse" because there's no other way to designate it once we realize that the social link is instated only by anchoring itself in the way in which language is situated over and etched into . . . speaking beings. (Seminar XX, 54)

Finally, the Borromean chain provides Lacan with a model of the unconscious. In *The Ego and the Id*, Freud provides a diagrammatic model of the psychic apparatus. This model is intended to map the "space" of the subject precisely insofar as that space is modeled on the organism's location in physical space. Lacan reverses Freud's strategy. His Borromean diagrams, particularly in the later seminars, also are intended to map the spatiality of the subject, but precisely not on the model of the organism's location in physical space. On the contrary, the Lacanian gamble is to wager the reverse: that only if we begin with a topological representation of the subject, insofar as it is "located" within the linking space of signifiers, will we be able to give an account of how the subject accedes to that imaginary representation of physical space that will forever after count for the subject's ego as the locus of the subject's existence. Only if we read Lacan in this way can we appreciate the radicality of his strategy, for it literally requires us to assume that all of phenomenal "reality" has the character of a dream whose hidden ground—the real—can only "appear" as a problematic x, as a signifier, as a stain within *aisthesis*.[53]

Recall that Kant transforms the Cartesian thought experiment by distinguishing between a space of intersubjectivity and a space of intercorporeality, arguing that the space of intercorporeality is itself generated by relations of force that souls—or, in Leibnizian terms, monads in general (i.e., simple substances, only some of which are souls)—exert on one another. That there are spatial relations among bodies would be a consequence of the fact that there are relations *of another kind* between subjects.[54]

But suppose we take the relations in question to be not relations of force (which is to remain within Freud's geometrical model) but, precisely, *linking* relations:

> The signifier as such refers to nothing if not to a discourse, in other words, a mode of functioning or a utilization of language qua link. . . . *The link . . . is a link between those who speak.* (Seminar XX, 30, emphasis added)

Because the spatiality of these linking relations would not be understood in terms of a pregiven space, it would be necessary to conceive of the genesis of intersubjective "space" in terms of the linking of signifiers. Moreover—and here is where the thought experiment becomes especially audacious—if *aisthesis* itself is to be explained as a consequence of the genesis of that space, then one of the tasks of such a project would be to try to establish how the social link might give rise to something like forms of intuition, that is, to the conditions under which the space of intercorporeality can appear in *aisthesis*. I take it that this is the sort of question Lacan has on his mind when he says:

> What is important is not that there are three dimensions in space. What is important is the Borromean knot and that for the sake of which we accede to the real it represents to us. (Seminar XX, 132–33)

When Freud proposes his (Newtonian) model, he explicitly characterizes it as speculative. Similarly, Lacan claims that the subject can only be supposed—by which I read him as calling attention to a certain irreducibly speculative character of his topology. In his essay on Poe, Lacan had already focused on the way in which the linking of signifiers gives rise to a structuring of the real that would otherwise not exist.[55] In Seminar XX, he has found a way of illustrating how the linking of signifiers can give rise to a structure that is spatial in character. The space of intersubjectivity would be, as it were, the condition for the possibility of the appearing of the real within the (imaginary) space of intercorporeality. To say this is not to say that the subject literally moves about in some Swedenborgian moral space, but to explain how discourse can be thought of as a textured surface, whose warp and woof are the site of the appearance of subject and world.

This is why psychoanalysis has as its goal a mathematical formalization. But such a formalization, as we have seen, tends toward the production of (Joycean) nonsense. That is not a criticism but an assessment of the way in which psychoanalysis approaches the limits of thought.

Earlier I promised to return to the question of why it should be the case that "staging" theoretical positions might bring out something in them that we could not otherwise see. One way of answering this question would be to suppose that theoretical positions such as thought experiments are never truly "pure," because they always bear within themselves some "stain" of *aisthesis*. To take this view is to suggest that the split between *aisthesis* and *noesis* is never truly radical, that the very idea of a pure cogito is a symptom of something amiss. Staging the cogito's attempts at pure *noesis* would then be a way of unmasking the cogito's pretension to autonomy. This kind of explanation assumes that the split between *aisthesis* and *noesis* is something secondary in relation to the subject's being-in-the-world.

Following Zizek, I would like to suggest another explanation. By insisting on the difference between reality and the real, Lacan invites us to take seriously the distinction between *aisthesis* and *noesis*. If the two are different in kind, then to stage a thought experiment is to subject the cogito to something wholly other. Understood in this way, it is not the discovery of a secret affinity that makes possible a moment of insight in the staging of theoretical motifs but something that happens in the revelation of a radical dis-affinity. The same could be said of the staging of any written play. When it is staged, what surprises is not the discovery of "something that was there all along in the text" but the discovery of something that, although it precisely does not belong to the text, although it is something that the text might even resist, nonetheless belongs to it as an uncanny "other" that it cannot entirely disavow. A slip of the tongue is, of course, the classic psychoanalytic example of such a "staging."

I suspect that something similar can be said about the relationship between the Lacanian thought experiment and the various attempts that Lacan and others have made to stage it in mathematical terms. If so, this would explain why Lacan can say both that mathematical formalization is the goal of psychoanalysis and that, "The analytic thing will not be mathematical" (Seminar XX, 117). For what is a matheme if not an object of *aisthesis*?

## NOTES

1. Jeanne Granon-Lafont, *La Topologie Ordinaire de Jacques Lacan* (Paris: Point Hors Ligne, 1985). Cf. the articles collected in *Littoral* 5 (June 1982).

2. Joël Dor, "The Epistemological Status of Lacan's Mathematical Paradigms," trans. Pablo Nagel, in *Disseminating Lacan*, eds. David Pettigrew and François Raffoul (Albany: State University of New York Press, 1996), pp. 109–21.

3. Note that for Lacan the same point would presumably hold for any attempt to "translate everything," that is, whether or not one is translating into mathemes, since "*on ne saurait tout dire*" (39). Cf. pp. 22 and 26, as well as Bruce Fink's notes on the translation of *tout dire*.

4. See Derrida's introduction to Husserl's "Origin of Geometry," where the contrast between Joycean plurivocity and Husserlian univocity is drawn. Jacques Derrida, *Edmund Husserl's Origin of Geometry: An Introduction*, trans. John P. Leavey Jr. (Stony Brook, N.Y.: Nicolas Hays, 1978), p. 100ff.

5. Jean-Luc Nancy and Philippe Lacoue-Labarthe, *The Title of the Letter: A Reading of Lacan*, trans. François Raffoul and David Pettigrew (Albany: State University of New York Press, 1992).

6. Quine, for example, refers to a metalanguage as "the ordinary unformalized language in which I describe and discuss the object language." See W. V. Quine, *Philosophy of Logic*, 2d ed. (Cambridge: Harvard University Press, 1986), p. 36. Instead of "metalanguage," Carnap refers to the "syntax language."

7. In this way, it becomes possible to block certain paradoxes such as that of the Cretan liar. The strategy is to stipulate that in the object language it is impossible to construct sentences of the type, "This sentence is false." One then appeals to the metalanguage to define "is true" and "is false" for the language in question. Note that in Seminar XI, Lacan discusses the paradox of the Cretan liar, appealing to his distinction between the "subject of the enunciation" and the "subject of the enunciated" to make sense of it. See Jacques Lacan, *The Four Fundamental Concepts of Psycho-Analysis*, trans. Alan Sheridan (New York: W.W. Norton, 1978), pp. 138–42.

8. The term also is used by Hjelmslev. See the discussion in Oswald Ducrot and Tzvetan Todorov, *Encyclopedic Dictionary of the Sciences of Language*, trans. Catherine Porter (Baltimore: Johns Hopkins University Press, 1979), p. 23. Lacan seems to have picked it up by way of Jakobson.

9. In this respect, Lacan—again like Derrida—suggests that there is no simple way of getting beyond metaphysics.

10. Jacques Lacan, "Science and Truth," trans. Bruce Fink, in *Newsletter of the Freudian Field* 3 (1989): 4–29.

11. Ibid., p. 14.

12. Lacan, *The Four Fundamental Concepts*, 36.

13. Incipit Marx. Or one might think of a joke about Moses and Jesus playing golf. Jesus just barely misses a putt, but then uses his miraculous powers to make the ball go into the hole anyway, at which point Moses says, "Do you want to fuck around, or do you want to play *golf?*" One could similarly imagine Gauss asking God, "Do you want to fuck around, or do you want to do *math?*" Incidentally, or not so incidentally for psychoanalysts, at a young age Gauss corrected a mistake in his father's accounting book.

14. René Descartes, *Meditations on First Philosophy*, 3rd ed., trans. Donald A. Cress (Indianapolis: Hackett, 1993), pp. 16–17.

15. Ibid., p. 18.

16. Ibid., p. 35.

17. Slavoj Zizek does something similar in a fascinating reading of Kafka's *The Trial*. See his *Looking Awry: An Introduction to Jacques Lacan through Popular Culture* (Cambridge: MIT Press, 1991), p. 147ff.

18. Consigning a pun to an end note, not the "key myth" of the Bororo but the "key thought experiment" of the Borromo.

19. Descartes, *Meditations on First Philosophy*, p. 19; emphasis added.

20. Alexandre Koyré, "Galileo and the Scientific Revolution of the Seventeenth Century," *The Philosophical Review*, vol. LII, no. 310 (July 1943): 346.

21. Descartes, *Meditations on First Philosophy*, p. 22.

22. For a discussion of both the debate in Descartes scholarship and the dispute in early modern thought about how to conceive of the proper nexus of causal relations, see Kenneth Clatterbaugh, *The Causation Debate in Modern Philosophy 1637–1739* (New York: Routledge, 1999). A discussion of the three principal early modern positions I will be discussing (as well as of the Kantian intervention) can be found in Alison Laywine, *Kant's Early Metaphysics and the Origins of the Critical Philosophy*, North American Kant Society Studies in Philosophy, vol. 3 (Atascadero, Calif.: Ridgeview, 1993).

23. Strictly speaking, I am only sketching a way of beginning such an analysis, which would need to consider a wider class of thought experiments—for example, those of Spinoza, Berkeley, Hume—and clarify the precise logic of a thought experiment in general.

24. "What is at stake in the endeavor to 'look awry' at theoretical motifs is not just a kind of contrived attempt to 'illustrate' high theory, to make it 'easily accessible,' and thus to spare us the effort of effective thinking. The point is rather that such an exemplification, such a mise-en-scène of theoretical motifs renders visible aspects that would otherwise remain unnoticed" (Zizek, *Looking Awry*, p. 3).

25. The credits at the end of the film roll to the tune of Rage against the Machine's "Wake Up," and so the film ends, in a sense, with the same two words that *Total Recall* ended with.

26. Obviously many other films (as well as early modern thought experiments) could be taken up in this context. The recent film *Existenz* is one.

27. There is, however, one crucial scene that suggests another reading. In a hotel room on Mars, a man from Recall Incorporated tries to convince Quaid that he is still having a dream. Quaid points a gun at the man and is uncertain whether or not to believe him until he sees a single bead of sweat falling down the man's face. That "stain" of the real—the palpable presence of the man's fear—convinces Quaid that what he is experiencing is *not* a dream. He then kills the man. One could read this gesture as a kind of *passage à l'acte* (acting out) by which Quaid definitively renounces the fantasmatic character of his world.

28. But for an equally plausible reading of *The Matrix* as staging the Malebranchian doctrine, see Slavoj Zizek, "*The Matrix*, or Malebranche in Hollywood," *Philosophy Today* 43, supplement (1999): 11–26.

29. Thus as a last-ditch effort to convince her "husband" that they really do have a sexual relationship, Quaid's wife has this exchange with him: "If you don't trust me, you can tie me up." "I didn't know you were so kinky." "Maybe it's time you found out." In other words, she tries to reestablish the illusion of their sexual relationship by shifting fantasies.

30. In this respect, the politics of *13th Floor* are naively utopian. It is interesting, too, that the film "exorcises" that which prevents the married couple in *Total Recall* from being able to have a sexual relationship; it does this by having the woman's "real" world husband (a double of Hall) get killed after violently trying to kill her. The situation here is exactly the inverse of that in *Total Recall*: there I suggested that it is as though Quaid fantasizes that his wife wants to kill him so that he can justify killing her to be with the sleazy and demure girl of his dreams; here, it is as though the woman fantasizes that her husband wants to kill her so that he can be killed—not to be with *another* partner but to be with an idealized version of him.

31. Lacan's discussion of aphanisis occurs in *The Four Fundamental Concepts*, p. 207ff.

32. Slavoj Zizek, *The Metastases of Enjoyment: Six Essays on Woman and Causality* (New York:Verso, 1994), chapter 5.

33. As Jean-Claude Milner puts it, "precisely because the modern universe is defined by a boundless (mathematically infinite) relevance of the letter, the being that speaks and lives in the modern universe insistently asks that a limit be imposed on that infinite relevance." See Jean-Claude Milner, "Lacan and the Ideal of Science," in *Lacan and the Human Sciences*, ed. Alexandre Leupin (Lincoln: Nebraska University Press, 1991), p. 37.

34. Indeed, one might say that the politics of *Total Recall* and *The Matrix* are totally different for precisely this reason. In one we have the willfully ignorant "cynical" attitude, while in the other we have the stirrings of a youthful rebellion finally throwing off the yoke of years of political quietism. Indeed, *The Matrix* stages and condemns the cynicism of someone who does not care whether or not it is all just a dream, in the figure of the traitor—Cipher is his code name, but the AI man calls him "Mr. Reagan"—who agrees to betray the liberated humans in exchange for a hedonistic series of virtual pleasures inside the matrix. In *Total Recall*, trying to get his mind off Mars, Quaid's wife says to him, "No wonder you're having nightmares.You're always watching the news." This sort of reading could be pursued by considering the different political positions embodied in the writings of Descartes, Malebranche, Leibniz, and so on.

35. Lacan later modifies this idea, suggesting that the subject is a consequence of the fact that "there is counting." See Lacan, *The Four Fundamental Concepts*, p. 20. I return to this point below.

36. Lacan, *The Four Fundamental Concepts*, p. 36.

37. Of course, if a signifier is a type rather than a token, further issues would need to be addressed, a point Derrida makes in slightly different terms in his "Signature Event Context," in *Margins of Philosophy*, trans. Alan Bass (Chicago: University of Chicago Press, 1982).

38. Obviously something needs to be said here about the Kantian intervention, which seems to proscribe unintuitable mathematical truths. In the account I have presented, one might see Kant as a "reactionary" figure, and then see thinkers such as Bolzano and Frege as "revolutionaries" who again took up the Cartesian gauntlet, but I think that this picture would be something of an oversimplification. I will have something to say about Kant in what follows, but I will not address this particular topic.

39. Koyré, "Galileo and the Scientific Revolution," p. 347.

40. One way of reading Lacan here would be to see him as reiterating the sort of thesis advanced by Eddington, according to which everyday objects such as tables do not "really" have any of the sensible properties that we ascribe to them, since it is the table as described by science—as a swarm of electrons, for example—that is truly real. Critics of this thesis have argued that if our scientific theories are about anything, they must be about the objects that we perceive, in which case Eddington's concern is somewhat misplaced.Whether the same objection might be raised against Lacan is a question I cannot take up here, but I would suggest that the question turns on how the relationship between the being of beings and the truth of beings is conceived.

41. See especially Heidegger's own discussion of Galileo in Martin Heidegger, *What Is a Thing?*, trans. W. B. Barton Jr. and Vera Deutsch (Chicago: Henry Regnery Company, 1967).

42. Zizek offers a similar reading in his *Tarrying with the Negative* (Durham: Duke University Press, 1993).

43. Again, I draw on the work of Zizek. See his *The Ticklish Subject: The Absent Centre of Political Ontology* (New York: Verso, 1999), p. 63.

44. Immanuel Kant, "Dreams of a Spirit-Seer Elucidated by Dreams of Metaphysics," in *Theoretical Philosophy, 1755–1770*, trans. and ed. David Walford (New York: Cambridge University Press, 1992), p. 357.

45. Andrew Cutrofello, *Imagining Otherwise: Metapsychology and the Analytic A Posteriori* (Evanston: Northwestern University Press, 1997).

46. Immanuel Kant, *Metaphysical Foundations of Natural Science*, in *Philosophy of Material Nature*, trans. James W. Ellington (Indianapolis: Hackett, 1985), p. 8.

47. Strictly speaking, the lines that knot theorists study are closed curves embedded in a containing space; the study of knots can in fact be thought of as the study of the spaces themselves. More precisely, if K is a knot embedded in the space S, knot theory would study the space that remains when K is eliminated from it, that is, one studies the space $S - K$. Kant would no doubt protest that, insofar as they imply spatiality, knots cannot provide us with a mathematical basis for a psychology of inner sense, whose temporal character precludes all spatial structure. Moreover, the linearity of time for Kant would imply that the time of inner sense does not close on itself—that is, my time line is not a closed curve but a sequence whose end points (my birth and my death) are distinct. Lacan's alternative understanding of time, particularly the retroactive character of symptom formation (his take on Freud's notion of *Nachträglichkeit*), lends itself to an alternative view here, though one whose details would need to be carefully spelled out. See Seminar I, the "Logical Time" essay, and a careful analysis of the latter in Bruce Fink, "Logical Time and the Precipitation of Subjectivity," in *Reading Seminars I and II: Lacan's Return to Freud*, ed. Bruce Fink, Richard Feldstein, and Maire Jaanus (Albany: State University of New York Press, 1995).

48. Kant's fullest discussion of this point occurs in the chapter on the "Discipline of Pure Reason" in the first *Critique*. See Immanuel Kant, *Critique of Pure Reason*, trans. Norman Kemp Smith (New York: St. Martin's Press, 1929).

49. Gottlob Frege, *The Foundations of Arithmetic: A Logico-Mathematical Enquiry into the Concept of Number*, trans. J. L. Austin (Evanston: Northwestern University Press, 1980), pp. 20–21; emphasis added.

50. Jacques-Alain Miller, "Suture (Elements of the Logic of the Signifier)," trans. Jacqueline Rose, in *Screen*, vol. XVIII, no. 4 (winter 1977/1978): 24–34.

51. Thus, citing Leibniz with approval, Frege notes that it is true to say, for instance, that the set consisting of "God, an angel, a man, and motion" is one containing exactly four members. See Frege, *The Foundations of Arithmetic*, p. 31. It also is worth noting that, according to Frege, it is a mistake to think that contradictory concepts do not exist. A contradictory concept is simply one with the empty set as its extension (p. 87). Frege's idea here suggests a way of clarifying my earlier discussion of Descartes. To say that God could have made it the case that $2 + 2 = 5$ is equivalent to saying that we can think the concept of $2 + 2$ equaling 5.

52. Although Lacan refers to the Borromean rings as a knot, they are typically classified by knot theorists as a link. A knot can be loosely defined as "a closed curve in space that does not intersect itself anywhere." See Colin C. Adams, *The Knot Book: An Elementary Introduction to the Mathematical Theory of Knots* (New York: W. H. Freeman and Company, 1994), p. 2. The simplest knot is a ring, often called the "trivial knot," or the "unknot." A link is generally defined as two or more knots intertwined in such a way that they cannot be separated without at least one of the knots being cut. "A *link* is a set

of knotted loops all tangled up together" (p. 17). Raymond Lickorish defines a link as a collection of closed curves, without stipulating that they be connected in any particular way. He then defines a knot as a link with only one component. See W. B. Raymond Lickorish, *An Introduction to Knot Theory* (New York: Springer-Verlag, 1997), p. 1. The Borromean link has the additional property that no two of its rings are linked: it is only in relation to the third that any two are inseparable. Knot theorists usually classify only a three-ring link of this sort as a Borromean link. Lacan treats the three-ring Borromean link as the simplest instance of a more general type, which would be an arbitrary number of rings linked in such a way that cutting one would release all. Arbitrary links that have this property are sometimes referred to by knot theorists as "Brunnian" rather than "Borromean." See Adams, *The Knot Book*, p. 22.

53. The proximity between this thesis and Kant's should be clear. The principal difference would be that transcendental philosophy assumes the existence of pure limits of reality separated from an inaccessible real, whereas psychoanalysis begins from the hypothesis that the real irrupts within reality.

54. It is noteworthy, moreover, that Kant never entirely reneges on this view. Even in his critical period, he continues to think (albeit, "problematically") of physical space as generated by forces of repulsion and attraction that substances (including souls) exert on one another. These relations of force can be understood in geometrical terms. Kant goes so far as to suggest that we can know the law of gravity a priori.

55. See not only the essay in *Écrits*, but also Bruce Fink's illuminating discussion in the second appendix to his *The Lacanian Subject: Between Language and Jouissance* (Princeton: Princeton University Press, 1995), pp. 165–72.

# TONGUES OF ANGELS: FEMININE
# STRUCTURE AND OTHER JOUISSANCE

*Suzanne Barnard*

"Strange" is a word that can be broken down in French—*étrange,*
*être-ange* . . .

—Lacan, Seminar XX

In *Encore*, Lacan poses—in the form of a series of questions—the possibility of
a certain being beyond the fault line of sexual difference, an intimation of a real
incarnation that, while not external to the symbolic, cannot be contained
within it. Indeed, he even refers mysteriously to some sense in which the symbolic is not indifferent to this being but is affected by it—troubled, unsettled by
its strangeness. The being that Lacan is concerned with here would hence be a
question of a materialization across a division, across the "gap" between the
symbolic and the real. To understand what Lacan might have in mind in these
cryptic interrogatives requires some understanding of the transformation in the
relationships between feminine structure, other jouissance, and knowledge that
he effects in Seminar XX. These specific themes emerge in the context of
Lacan taking up the cultural knot between sexuality and epistemology that
Freud had, years earlier, marked as central to the question of culture itself. In
his earlier work, Lacan had approached the relationship between sexuality and
knowledge primarily in terms of its symbolic and imaginary coordinates. In
*Encore*, however, he comes to formulate the relationship between feminine
sexuality and knowledge more explicitly in terms of the relationship between
the symbolic and the real.

Lacan's first sustained attempt to articulate the relationship between the
real and the symbolic is found in Seminar XI, the Seminar in which he most

171

clearly elaborates his by now well-known shift in emphasis from the subject of desire to the subject of drive. This shift reflects, among other things, Lacan's increasing preoccupation with understanding how the gap between the real and the symbolic affects the functioning of the symbolic itself. Just as Freud's confrontation with the enigmas of traumatic war neuroses led him to the "beyond" of pleasure, so too did Lacan's recognition of a certain morbid recalcitrance of the symptom to interpretation lead him to the "beyond" of desire. Lacan formulates this "beyond" in terms of the function of the real in the subject's relation to object $a$ and the implications of this relation for the structure of the drive. However, in his return to the question of sexuality and knowledge in Seminar XX, one can discern another shift in focus, this time from the structure of drive to the structure of sexual difference. Thus in Seminar XX, Lacan's questioning of the relationship between the real and the symbolic is sustained more explicitly in relation to the relevance of sexual difference in understanding the nature of the gap between them.

In his formulas of sexuation, Lacan suggests that because women (feminine subjects) and men (masculine subjects) are "in" the symbolic differently, they each have a different relation to the Other. While man is coupled to the Other via object $a$, woman is "twice" related to the Other—coupled via the phallus and "tripled" via S($\cancel{A}$), the signifier of the lack in the Other. The feminine subject's "other" relation to the Other correlates with a jouissance "beyond" the phallus, a jouissance that belongs to that part of the Other that is not covered by the fantasy of the "One"—that is, the fantasy sustained by the positing of the phallic exception. As such, this form of jouissance is inscribed not in the repetitive circuit of drive but in what Lacan calls the *en-corps*, an "enjoying substance" which insists in the body beyond its sexual being (Seminar XX, 26/23). It is in the traces of jouissance inscribed in this en-corps that we can, perhaps, discern something of the *poesis*—the something coming from nothing—that Lacan links to the contingency of being and, ultimately, to the path of love.

## THE UNDEAD

> Regarding [the germ cell, one] can't say that it's life since it also bears death, the death of the body, by repeating it. That is where the *en-corps* comes from. It is thus false to say that there is a separation of the soma from the germ because, since it harbors this germ, the body bears its traces.
>
> —Lacan, Seminar XX

As early as 1957–1958, Lacan began to consider unconscious desire in terms not of a transformative subversive force vis-à-vis the symbolic but as itself inescapably bound up with symbolic law. This position becomes explicitly articulated in Seminar XI, where Lacan claims that as a superego formation, paternal Law invokes a subject motivated by an inherently transgressive desire (hence, his famous description of the superego as the imperious agent of enjoyment). Lacan credits Freud as one of the first to link the libidinal body with death, in other words, to suggest that the superego does not derive from social or psychological sources exclusively but is itself a structural component of desire. Desire is, therefore, always inextricably caught up with the symbolic Other that brings it into being and, as a result, within a morbid circuit of prohibition and transgression.

While the subject of drive also is "born" in relation to a loss, this loss is a real rather than a symbolic one. As such, it functions not in a mode of absence but in a mode of an impossible excess haunting reality, an irrepressible remainder that the subject cannot separate itself from. In other words, while desire is born of and sustained by a constitutive *lack*, drive emerges in relation to a constitutive *surplus*. This surplus is what Lacan calls the subject's "anatomical complement,"[1] an excessive, "unreal" remainder that produces an ever-present jouissance. He locates the loss correlative with the emergence of the subject of drive within the structure of sexual reproduction:

> Sexuality is established in the field of the subject through the way of lack. Two lacks overlap here. The first emerges from the central defect around which the dialectic of the advent of the subject to his own being in relation to the Other turns—by the fact that the subject depends on the signifier and that the signifier is first of all in the field of the Other. This lack takes up the other lack, which is the real, earlier lack, to be situated at the advent of the living being, that is to say, at sexed reproduction. The real lack is what the living being loses, that part of himself *qua* living being, in reproducing himself through the way of sex. This lack is real because it relates to something real, namely, that the living being, by being subject to sex, has fallen under the blow of individual death. (Seminar XI, 189/205)

Here Lacan is complicating his earlier account of sexuality in which he had focused primarily on the role of the symbolic in the generation of sexuality and sexual difference. In Seminar XX, he returns to this conundrum of overlapping lacks, suggesting that—beyond the structuring effect of the symbolic—sexuality has *also* to do with another splitting, this time involving a "real" deduction in being. This deduction is no simple subtraction, however, as it also produces something that while no longer "real" cannot be completely inscribed within the symbolic.

In *Encore*, Lacan elaborates on the significance of this deduction, this "blow of individual death," through recalling Freud's use of the distinction between germ and soma cells. Freud invokes this distinction in *Beyond the Pleasure Principle* to illustrate the tension between Eros and Thanatos. While Lacan claims that Freud was indeed attempting to trace an alternative trajectory of drive, he also suggests that Freud failed to recognize a certain loss inherent in sexual reproduction. More specifically, we see that in Freud's account of that which exceeds or is "beyond" the pleasure principle, the life and death drives are maintained in a relatively oppositional, binary relationship. Hence, his account of the role of germ cells in reproduction ultimately suffers from an emphasis on their generative and recuperative role, to the exclusion of what Lacan underscores is a "real" loss represented in the process of meiosis. Whereas Freud valorizes the germ cell's role in "work[ing] against the death of the living substance and succeed[ing] in winning for it what . . . can only be regard[ed] as potential immortality,"[2] Lacan attends to genetic theory's account of the "dominant function, in the determination of certain elements of the living organism, of a combinatory that operates at certain of its stages by the expulsion of remainders" (Seminar XI, 139/151). Hence, Lacan describes Thanatos—the force that thwarts the telos of Eros toward the One—as

> obviously a metaphor that Freud is able to use thanks to the fortunate discovery of the two units of the germ, the ovum and the spermatozoon, about which one could roughly say that it is on the basis of their fusion that is engendered what? A new being. Except that that doesn't happen without meiosis, a thoroughly obvious subtraction, at least for one of the two, just before the very moment at which the conjunction occurs, a subtraction of certain elements that are not superfluous in the final operation.[3] (Seminar XX, 63/66)

Thus the germ cell cannot be exclusively associated with "Life" because—with the expulsion of its meiotic remainders—"it also bears death, the death of the body by repeating it" (Seminar XX, 11/5). As a result, Lacan says, Freud's disjunctive pairing of "germ" with Life and "soma" with Death is false.

It is important to note here that by invoking the process of meiosis to illuminate the structure of the libidinal subject, Lacan is not mobilizing a biologism or any (other) foundational form of materialist discourse. Rather, we can broadly understand his move here as a reframing of Freud's opposition between Eros and Thanatos in terms of the impact of the gap between the real and the symbolic on the functioning of the symbolic itself. Within this frame, then, he is using meiosis as a trope to suggest a way in which the drive is not the fundamental ground of the subject but a *short circuit* of any closed loop of reproduction, of any fulfillment of Eros through a joining of complementary halves. In fact, the drive comes into being as the *disjunction* between sexuality and the accomplishment of Eros, the disjunction between sexuality and the union of the two in the One.

In addition, the death-in-life attending the "birth" of the subject of drive is not the whole story, for when Lacan states that the subtracted meiotic elements are "not without their place in the final operation," he is referring to the way in which these elements do not disappear but serve to condition the status of the drive in an important way. This is so because the detritus of meiosis, its "waste," returns to haunt the libidinal subject in the form of object *a*. Object *a* is a remainder *in excess* of the being produced via sex, a "scrap of the real" that ex-sists as a residue of a strange form of life. This is what allows Slavoj Zizek to say that "for Lacan, the death drive is precisely the ultimate Freudian name for the dimension traditional metaphysics designated as that of *immortality*—for a drive, a 'thrust' that persists beyond the (biological) cycle of generation and corruption . . . a strange, immortal, indestructible life that persists beyond death."[4] Thus the drive and the object are made of the same stuff and function together in this domain of "indestructible life"—the drive as an immortal *pulsion* that "circles around" the object as a scrap or remainder of asexual, "undead" life.

In both Seminar XI and "Position of the Unconscious," Lacan refers to object *a*, this excessive, residual scrap of the real as the lamella—an "organ" without a body,[5] which is, in the end, none other than libido itself. Several points of Lacan's discussion of the lamella are worthy of note here. Shifting the terms of his origin myth from the germ cell to the fertilized egg, Lacan proposes to supplant Aristophanes' myth of the androgynes with a less symmetrical scene.

> Consider the egg in a viviparous womb where it has no need of a shell, and recall that, whenever the membranes burst, a part of the egg is harmed, for the membranes of the fertilized egg are offspring [*filles*] just as much as the living being brought into the world by their perforation. Consequently, upon cutting the cord, what the newborn loses is not, as analysts think, its mother, but rather its anatomical complement. Midwives call it the "afterbirth" [*délivre*].
>
> Now imagine that every time the membranes burst, a phantom—an infinitely more primal form of life . . . takes flight through the same passage. ("Position of the Unconscious," 273)

Here, then, as in meiosis, there is a remainder, a third term that "falls out" of the structure only to reemerge from within. The novelty of this second cycle of the origin myth is Lacan's linking of the detritus of sexed reproduction to the trope of the placenta. He underscores that the lost object—the maternal Thing—is *not* the mother herself but the placenta. As such, the placenta is the "organ" that mediates the relationship between the mother and developing organism that is neither a "One" (it is not a matter of fusion or complementary unity) nor a "two" (it is not a matter of autonomy). Each inhabits or is inhabited by the other in a strange relationship that confounds counting and hence the boundaries between "inside" and "outside." Thus Lacan suggests here that what is lost is not what it is retrospectively fantasized to be—that is, a union or whole—but rather a certain strange relation to the Other. This relation is not the "One" of undifferentiated fusion; neither is it the "One" formed by the union of two complementary halves; but it is, perhaps, . . . "not not One."

In what is a more familiar Lacanian vignette, we find yet another turn in Lacan's mythical cycle, this time in a further elaboration of the role of object *a* in the constitution of the body. In his rereading of Freud's account of the *Fort-Da*, Lacan rejects the "old hat" interpretation that sees in little Ernst's juxtaposition of phonemes with the action of the spool "an example of primal symbolization" (Seminar XI, 216/239). Rather, the spool "is not the mother reduced to a little ball . . . it is a small part of the subject that detaches itself" (ibid.,

60/62) from him while still remaining his, still retained. It is a split-off piece of
the subject that allows him to traverse the "ditch" that his mother's absence
creates. Here Lacan explicitly links the production of object *a* to the emergence of the body "proper," that is, to the subject marked by sex that gains significance at the point of entry into the symbolic. In other words, of particular
interest in this version of the myth is the structural linkage between the to and
fro action of the spool and Ernst's articulation of phonemes—"letters"—that
are taken as first signifiers. As signifiers, they are—like Ernst in his corporeality—split into two registers simultaneously, the registers of being and truth.

While in Seminar XI Lacan describes the lost object as an indestructible
fragment of asexual, nonsymbolized libido that both masculine and feminine
subjects lose with the advent of sexual being, in Seminar XX the object plays
an important role in his account of sexual difference. What the two sexes lose is
not their complementary lost half but an asexual "sameness," libido not yet
marked by castration or the cut of sexual difference. How is sexual difference
related to this "death-in-life" that object *a* represents? In Seminar XX, Lacan
suggests that men and women are ultimately positioned differently vis-à-vis
this "death-in-life." There would be, then, a different kind of jouissance for
those with feminine structure than that produced and maintained in relation to
object *a*. The feminine subject's relation to S($\cancel{A}$) would produce an "Other
jouissance" related to a different kind of "knowledge" of death-in-life.

Masculine and feminine structures are, in some sense then, distinguished in
terms of the structure of the drive in relation to the Other. More specifically,
the formulas of sexuation must be read in terms of how they inscribe the masculine and feminine subject's relation to the real, how masculine and feminine
structures are—each in its own way—a manifestation of the subject as an answer from the real. Thus Lacan's account of sexual difference in Seminar XX
can be understood as emerging from his progressive understanding of the
impact of the gap between the real and the symbolic on the symbolic itself and,
hence, on the structuration of the subject in its possible modes of relation to
the real; in this context, his elaboration of feminine sexuality can be read as a
manifestation of his preoocupation with the nature of this gap and the feminine subject's relation to it.


## INFINITY

Infinity: the limit that a function *f* is said to approach at $x = a$ when
for *x* close to *a*, *f(x)* is larger than any preassigned number.
—*American Heritage Dictionary*


In Lacan's formulas of sexuation (Seminar XX, 73/78), one gets a glimpse of
something that he will make more explicit later in the same Seminar, namely,
that phallic jouissance and Other jouissance are produced within different logical frameworks that have a strange internal relationship to each other. He

begins his exposé of the formulas with the claim that "the lower line—
∀xΦx—indicates that it is through the phallic function that man as whole
acquires his inscription" (ibid., 74/79).[6] Thus this formula, ∀xΦx, defines masculine subjects as "wholly" subject to the phallic function, which is the function of lack or of alienation within the symbolic. However, this "whole" is itself
founded on the logical exception represented by the foreclosure of the phallic
function from the set, "man," that it determines. This is represented in the top
line of the formulas for man, ∃x$\overline{Φx}$. In other words, the negation of the phallic
function provides a limit that produces man "wholly" with respect to it, which
anchors the masculine subject firmly in the symbolic order. Hence, masculine
or phallic jouissance is produced within the structure of a *finite logic*—as a
closed set determined by a fixed limit that remains outside of or "extimate" to
the set itself.

This latter formula of masculine sexuation suggests that the phallic function is itself limited by a certain functioning in fantasy of the exception that
grounds it—the nonphallic exception of the primal father.[7] Thus while man is
"whole" within the symbolic, the exception that delimits him precludes him
from fully identifying with castration. One could say that while man is wholly
subject "to," and hence "in," the symbolic, he is "in it with exception," that is, he
"takes exception" to it in some way. As a result, the fantasy of a subject not
subjected to Law—the fantasy of no limit—determines masculine structure in
an essential way. The point here is that the masculine subject is effectively
"caught" in the phallic function, ironically because he does not fully identify
with it but maintains a kind of distance toward it through believing in an
exception to symbolic Law.

In Seminar XX and elsewhere, however,[8] Lacan suggests that the fullness
of presence that the negation of castration represents is itself an illusion. In fact,
it is in this light that Lacan's equation of woman with the phallus can be perhaps
most easily understood; the phallus is at once *both* the signifier of enjoyment
and its negation. Hence, what the masculine subject does not recognize is that
because Woman does not exist, phallic jouissance is limited by the remainder
that forever escapes, that forever eludes his pursuit; this is the significance of the
paradox of Achilles and the tortoise that Lacan invokes in Seminar XX (13/8).
Paradoxically then, the figure that lends the symbolic its seeming integrity, its
automatic and "Law-like" functioning, is only an illusion. Thus the deterministic, repetitive character of desire as it plays out in and through the symbolic
functions only within the frame of a certain finite logic, one fixed by a constitutive exception. Moreover, it is an illusion that Woman as man's symptom
(e.g., the Lady, the Virgin Mother, etc.) is put to work in support of.

In turning to the formulas of feminine sexuation, however, Lacan suggests
that it would be a mistake to read them strictly in accordance with Aristotelian
logic, in other words, to assume, for example, that the laws of noncontradiction
must apply. This sort of logic is only adequate to inscribing the symbolic constituted as finite through the postulate of the phallic exception. In *Encore*, Lacan

suggests that the structure of the not-whole Woman requires another sort of logic, a logic of the infinite rather than the finite. He states:

> [Because] one can write "not-every (*pas tout*) x is inscribed in $\Phi$x," one deduces by way of implication that there is an x that contradicts it. But that is true on one sole condition, which is that, in the whole or the not-whole in question, we are dealing with the finite. Regarding that which is finite, there is not simply an implication but a strict equivalence. . . . There is an exception. But we could, on the contrary, be dealing with the infinite. . . . When I say that woman is not-whole and that that is why I cannot say Woman, it is precisely because I raise the question of a jouissance that, with respect to everything that can be used [encompassed] in the function $\Phi$x, is in the realm of the infinite. (Seminar XX, 94/102–3)

Here Lacan suggests that feminine structure (and hence, Other jouissance) is produced in relation to a "set" that *does not* exist on the basis of an external, constitutive exception. In other words, it is produced in relation to a set not haunted by a figure operating as a limit. Hence, feminine structure can be understood to undermine the functioning of the symbolic as structured by a founding limit or anchoring point. Perhaps another way of saying what amounts to the same thing is that the not-whole Woman—as "radically Other in the sexual relationship, or what can be said of the unconscious" (Seminar XX, 75/81)—has a view to the contingency of the signifier of the Other in its anchoring function. This means that she has a relation to the Other such that she "knows" that *neither she nor it knows*—in other words, she "knows" that the signifier of phallic power merely lends a certain mysterious presence to the Law that veils its real impotence.

However, this does not mean, in turn, that the not-whole of feminine structure is simply outside of or indifferent to the order of masculine structure. Rather, she is in the phallic function *altogether* or, in Lacan's words, "She is *not* not at all there. She is there in full [*à plein*]" (Seminar XX, 71/77). Here Lacan seems to be playing with the way in which the double negation—"not not at all there"—works to effect a kind of affirmation, a strange form of positivity. The feminine subject inhabits the symbolic in this form, not as a simple absence but as a mode of presence that emerges from "beyond the veil" of phallic presence. In other words, the feminine subject is (wholly) alienated in the symbolic in such a way as to have a different relation to its limit. By being in the symbolic "without exception" then, the feminine subject has a relation to the Other that produces another "unlimited" form of jouissance.

Hence, Lacan claims that feminine and masculine subjects have a different relation to infinity. For man, the infinite is placed in the service of producing the One—finite and totalizable. For the feminine subject, it is a limit of "realization," a relation to the contingency of Law that produces, engenders something new rather that keeps the "idiotic," repetitive circuit of the drive going. This is effected not in relation to Law and lack but rather in relation to S($\cancel{A}$), the signifier of the lack in the Other. It is, in other words, effected in a relation to "undeath." For woman, hence, the object does not haunt subjectivity as a promised but necessarily avoided plenitude but as a nontraumatic signifier of the lack in the Other. This other relation to the Other (via S(Ⱥ)) is one that although not unrelated to Law recognizes the contingency and failures of the law and, one could even say, both exhorts from and returns to the Law a certain strange corporeality.

What the paradoxical structure of the feminine subject ultimately reveals is the way in which the consistency of the symbolic, and of the gap between the symbolic and real, is susceptible to the "unsettling" effect of the real. In other words, it reveals that insofar as one "is" in the symbolic via the limit placed by an unsymbolizable element, the symbolic and real are separated by a traumatic gap—a "ditch" that the subject relies on object *a* to "play at jumping" (Seminar XI, 60/62). However, while this gap holds within the universe of masculine structure—a universe in which the phallic exception is instituted *from the outside*—for feminine structure there exists the possibility for a provisional "master" signifier that is not instituted from without but from *within*; this institution of a master signifier from within would be produced through a contingency, via *tuché* as encounter.[9] Another way of saying this is that without the constitutive illusion of the phallic exception as limit, the *symbolic becomes*, in a sense, *real*. One way of conceptualizing feminine jouissance consistent with this claim might be to say that in feminine jouissance, the real finds a signifier.

## ANGEL-BEING

> It is a truly miraculous function to see, on the very surface emerging from an opaque point of this strange being, the trace of these writings taking form, in which one can grasp the limits, impasses, and dead ends that show the real acceding to the symbolic.
>
> —Lacan, Seminar XX

How might we understand feminine jouissance as correlative with the real finding a signifier? In *Encore*, Lacan introduces two figures that, while he does not explicitly elevate them to the status of myth, are reminiscent of the mythical figurations of object *a* in Seminar XI. These two figures of being "beyond" the symbolic—the strange being of the angel and the spider—suggest the nature of the materialization across the gap between symbolic and real that the real "finding" a signifier represents. Returning to the notion of object *a* as an unsymbolizable scrap of the real, we could, perhaps, represent the real finding a signifier through the denotation S(a).[10] Hence, one can retroactively (re)read Lacan's account of the object in Seminar XI through the lens of his later account of sexual difference as a means of grasping what is at stake in the feminine subject's relation to S(Ⱥ) or to S(a).

In Seminar XI, Lacan suggests that the lamella—as organ of an indestructible, infinitely proliferating life—is the libido itself. The objects *a* are "merely its representatives, its figures. The breast . . . as an element characteristic of the mammiferous organization, the placenta for example . . . certainly represents that part of himself that the individual loses at birth, and which may serve to symbolize the most profound lost object" (Seminar XI, 198/180). The libido and its objects *a* can be understood to function like organs in the everyday sense of the term, in that they operate both semi-autonomously and in support of metabolic and (at least in the case of phallic jouissance) regulatory processes. However, Lacan's meaning diverges from popular usage in that he describes these organs not as hierarchically organized or structured systems but as *surfaces* without centralized functions or any "proper" demarcation of inside and out-side. With this definition, Lacan clearly distinguishes his account of the object as organ from traditional psychoanalytic notions of the object, notions that assume, above all, an "affinity of *a* to its envelope" (Seminar XX, 85/93).

In emphasizing the difference between his account of the object and those of other psychoanalytic accounts, Lacan underscores the importance of con-ceptualizing the organ-libido as a *surface*. He states, "[T]his image [the lamella] shows 'libido' to be what it is, namely, an organ, to which its habits make it far more akin than to a force field. Let's say that it is *qua* surface that it orders this force field" ("Position of the Unconscious," 274). Additionally, the libido (as surface-organ) and the objects *a* (its figures) exist in an *ectopic* rather than an internal relation to the subject.

In standard biomedical terms, an ectopia represents an abnormal positional and functional relation between a body (as signified) and one of its organs or parts. This reading of the libido-organism coupling can be seen as exemplary of the paradoxical tension inscribed in masculine structure. Within masculine structure, the drive remains haunted by the image of phallic presence, despite the fact that the masculine subject's place in the symbolic is fixed by its *exclu-sion*. Hence, one consequence of the masculine subject's attempts to realize the object of desire (to make it exist)[11] is the (paradoxical) risk of dissolving the order within which *he* exists. As a result, he must remain at a certain distance from the object of his desire in order to maintain his sexual position. This is what Lacan refers to as the risk of annihilation that the masculine subject takes in approaching the object. In other words, for the masculine subject, the flip side of the fantasy of the "One" is the horror of a loss of being (existence) evoked, ironically, by a recognition of lack in the Other. Hence, within the logic of masculine structure, the gap between the symbolic and the real must be maintained in order to protect the subject from a loss of being. To use the terms that Lacan deploys in Seminar XX to distinguish between the symbolic and real "faces" of the Other, one could describe the masculine subject's rela-tion to object *a* as the site of an irreparable disjunction between being and truth.

However, while the masculine subject struggles to maintain a proper dis-tance with respect to the object, he nevertheless suffers from an excess jouis-sance produced within the trajectory of his vacillation, within the to and fro of the repetitive circuit of drive. This is the "pathological" jouissance of the object as representative of the organ-libido; missing from its proper position the object reappears "out of place," as a foreign body, an enjoying substance that threatens the integrity of the signified (sexual) body. In other words, within the logic of masculine structure, object *a* can be thought of as an organ out of place and out of proportion, an organ that has no proper boundaries and hence no internal relation to "its" organism but, rather, functions in a manner that destabilizes the boundary between the sexual (symbolic) body and the "flesh" of the real.

In its potential for a dual reading, Lacan's invocation of such a relation between the libido and the subject foreshadows his later account of the character of the feminine subject's relation to S($\cancel{A}$). From the Lacanian postulate that the feminine subject is "in" the symbolic without exception (hence, her failure to exist within it), we can conclude that she has the potential for a relation to the object that is absent the traumatic dimension of semblance that characterizes the masculine subject's relation to the object. In other words, given her not-whole relation to the Other, the feminine subject can have a different relation to the lack in the Other. Lacan's account of this potential relation allows for a "nonpathological" reading of ectopia. What appears within the phallic economy of masculine structure as a threat to the subject's existence emerges here as the possibility of a contingent encounter, of a heterogenous coupling that produces an "other" jouissance—one inscribed in the en-corps and, hence, which insists in the body beyond its sexual being.

Here Lacan's description of the peculiar qualities of the organ-libido as an infinitely proliferating, regenerative, and heterogeneous surface evokes the characteristics of contiguous space as defined within elliptical (Riemannian) geometry. In Riemannian space, relations between its heterogeneous elements (or, more accurately, *vicinities*) are not predetermined and can be effected in an infinite number of ways. We could, then, understand the contingent encounter between the feminine subject and the lack in the Other—the encounter manifest as Other jouissance that produces what Lacan calls "being effects"—in terms of the properties of Riemannian surfaces. In this case, the coupling of heterogenous elements represented by the organ-libido and the subject can be understood to produce, via Other jouissance, a strange signifier—a letter—one we might perhaps signify as S(a).

Ultimately, Lacan more explicitly suggests that the feminine subject's "ex-sistent" relation to the symbolic allies her jouissance, not with the signifier as signifying, but instead with the signifier's *ex-sistence*. Thus she has a (potential) relation to the real face of the Other that he elaborates on in Seminar XX as the *signifierness* of the signifier, or the "being" of the letter. Here he attempts to transmit something of this being of the letter via the letter of mathematical formalization, or the matheme.

It is useful to remember that Lacan defends his use of mathemes on the basis of their role in transmitting psychoanalysis as a *praxis*, or a particular practice of learning, rather than as a static corpus of knowledge. For example, in

"The Subversion of the Subject and the Dialectic of Desire," he claims that mathemes are not "transcendent signifier[s]," but are instead indices of "an absolute signification," designed to "allow for a hundred and one different readings, a multiplicity that is acceptable as long as what is said about it remains grounded in its algebra" (*Écrits*, 313–14/816).[12] Hence, while the "letter-al" quality of the matheme will always be secondarily caught up in a "will to truth," as manifest in knowledge that aims at the One, in its *stupidity* and *opacity* (its "absolute signification") it also bears a particular relation to being, to being as a corporeal effect of the Other's jouissance. In Seminar XX, Lacan evokes the image of a spider web to suggest the nature of the material surface of language that the letter represents in its potential for producing such being-effects. He suggests that it is as a "surface" with the "dimensions that writing requires" that the "textual work" of the spider web can illustrate a certain relation between feminine structure and S($\text{Ⱥ}$) (Seminar XX, 86/93). The figure of the web renders an example of a network of letters, of material marks or tracings that do not in and of themselves "mean" anything but nevertheless—like the heterogeneous, contingently juxtaposed elements in Riemannian space—have certain discernible effects on *what can be known*. The web as a network of letters also emerges from an "opaque" or nonsignifying corporeal locus, one "beyond" and yet paradoxically internal to the body as signifying.

Combined with the alternative reading of the libido-subject ectopia that I have sketched above, this feminine figure of the spider web allows for a retroactive (re)interpretation of the myth of the lamella. To begin with, the figure of the web reorients the drama of the lamella around the "tripled" relationship between the subject-to-be and the (m)Other. In this tripled figuration, the lamella can be seen to function—like the web—as a nonsignifying material mediation corresponding to the corporeal being of the letter. Rather than the pathological ectopic coupling of the object and subject associated above with masculine structure, the tripling of the feminine subject to the (m)Other presents a figure of material jouissance that cannot be reduced to the metaphysical "One" of Aristophanes, or even to the "countable" one of the modern science of the real. Rather, the tripled figure of the *(m)Other-placenta-subject-to-be* is one that confounds counting, that prevents a rehabilitation of the One via any form of biunivocalization. As a "not not One," it can only ex-sist in the domain of the infinite. As this strange, irreducible form of positivity, it also evokes a strange jouissance that is simultaneously "inside" of and yet beyond the body. Lacan describes this jouissance as produced by the way in which libido—as "this lamella that the organism's being takes to its true limit"—goes further than the body's limit and, in so doing, prefigures a certain being yet to come ("Position of the Unconscious," 275). However, in this "feminine" reconstruction of the scene, the lamella "meets up" with the real Other at the point of the (m)Other's lack, calling forth an asexual jouissance that could be described as of the "body" of the Other but precisely at the point at which it is not whole.

Finally, Lacan invokes the angel as yet another iteration of the material mediation of the feminine subject's contingent encounter (*tuché*) with the real face of the Other. The angel—neither a "being" nor of Being—is an asexual creature who inhabits the space between life and death and who is outside of time and hence immortal. The "angel-being" which Lacan alludes to throughout Seminar XX represents another figure of the strange positivity of the letter's "being." As an emissary of the real Other (or, as Lacan says, the "God-face" of the Other), the angel is engaged as a response to the Other's lack, taking leave from the point at which the Other is not whole in relation to the subject. As such, the angel does not carry a message but rather a "pro-clamation," which in its Latin origin suggests a "crying forth." Like the flesh of the placenta and the opaque textual surface of the spider web, the angel functions as a nonsignifying corporeal mediation between the feminine subject and the "other" face of the Other. As such, the angel is not simply real nor symbolic but a form of undead or "not not being" that serves as a figure of the possibility for a "real-izing" of the gap between the symbolic and the real.

While Lacan does not explicitly link this figure to the lamella or the spider's "letters," these three figures can be understood to come together in his notion of *lalangue*, or llanguage. In his earlier work, Lacan relied on the distinction between the statement and the enunciation in his attempts to articulate the relationship between language and the unconscious. In "The Subversion of the Subject and the Dialectic of Desire," for example, he associates the statement with the ego and the conscious dimension of speech; in contrast, the enunciation corresponds to the subject of the unconscious and its speaking (via slips of the tongue, etc.). In Seminar XX, however, Lacan presents us with a further refinement of this earlier distinction, as his preoccupation with the feminine subject's relation to S(A̶) leads him increasingly to consider the function of the written in psychoanalysis. Writing, or the production of letters, "constitutes a medium that goes beyond speech" (Seminar XX, 86/93) and, consequently, beyond enunciation. The locus of this beyond is not to be found in language but in llanguage. Consider Lacan's statement that, "If I have said that language is what the unconscious is structured like, that is because language, first of all, doesn't exist. Language is what we try to know concerning the function of llanguage" (Seminar XX, 126/138). And llanguage is associated not with the unconscious meaning or signifying effects discernible in the symbolic but with affects or "being-effects" of the (m)Other tongue. Thus Lacan here describes the speaking being not simply in terms of the ego and the subject of the unconscious but as

> that being [which] provides the occasion to realize just how far the effects of llanguage go, in that it presents all sorts of affects that remain enigmatic. Those affects are what result from the presence of llanguage insofar as it articulates things by way of knowledge that go much farther than what the speaking being sustains by way of enunciated knowledge. (Seminar XX, 126–27/139)

Hence, Lacan understands llanguage—as the (m)Other tongue—to be the
language of the being that ex-sists in Other jouissance. This jouissance can be
heard in the "body" of language—the letter of the body—just as it was first
heard in the tone and rhythm of the mother('s) tongue. This jouissance also is
associated with what we might call the "navel" of the unconscious, that is,
the absent origin of the unconscious beyond which interpretation and knowledge proper cannot reach. While it does not "know," that is, does not signify
any-*thing*, Lacan suggests that this jouissance "creates," that it engenders being
nonetheless.[13] As the materialization in the body of the angel's enigmatic
heralding, Other jouissance leaves its traces of a future being. Perhaps it is in
this way that we can hear it, as in the tongues of angels, as *annunciation*—
knowledge of *a*-being, of incarnation yet to come.

## NOTES

1. Jacques Lacan, "Position of the Unconscious," in *Reading Seminar XI: Lacan's
Four Fundamental Concepts of Psychoanalysis*, trans. Bruce Fink (Albany: State University
of New York Press, 1995), p. 273.

2. Sigmund Freud, *Beyond the Pleasure Principle* (New York: W. W. Norton & Co.,
1961), p. 48.

3. Lacan is referring here to the process of cell division entailed in the formation
of gametes (ova and sperm). In meiosis, a germ cell with two pairs of double-stranded
DNA undergoes two divisions, with the consequent production of four haploid cells.

4. Slavoj Zizek, *The Ticklish Subject: The Absent Center of Political Ontology*
(New York: Verso, 1999), p. 294, emphasis added.

5. See Lacan, "Position of the Unconscious," p. 275.

6. See the schema of the formulas of sexuation in the Introduction to this book.

7. The primal father is only one of the figures Lacan uses to invoke the status of
the exception that conditions the symbolic; there are other "Names-of-the Father," perhaps most notably in this context the figure of the Lady in courtly love. For a discussion
of the Lady as a "Name-of-the Father," see Slavoj Zizek, *The Metastases of Enjoyment: Six
Essays on Woman and Causality* (New York: Verso, 1994), chapter 4.

8. See *The Seminar, Book VII, The Ethics of Psychoanalysis*, trans. Dennis Porter
(New York: W. W. Norton & Co., 1992), chapter XI.

9. Lacan links *automaton* to the symbolic order, or "network of signifiers," and as
such, he relates it to the effects of the signifier that appear to be arbitrary but are ultimately determined by the insistence of the signifier in the trajectory of the subject's desire. In contrast to *automaton, tuché* as causality is a wholly arbitrary, incalculable, and
purely heteronomous form of chance. As such, it is beyond both consciousness and the
unconcious effects of language in the structuring of desire. Lacan refers to it as a *cause*,
because it produces being-effects.

10. I am indebted to Bruce Fink for this particular nomenclature and the way of
conceptualizing S($\cancel{A}$) that it implies. He refers to S(a) as a notation for the real finding a
signifer in a footnote to chapter 8, "There's No Such Thing As a Sexual Relationship,"
in *The Lacanian Subject: Between Language and Jouissance* (Princeton: Princeton
University Press, 1995), pp. 115, 195, n.36.

11. One could perhaps understand this (ultimately halfhearted) attempt at "making" the object exist as something the masculine subject "plays" at—as in Ernst's to and fro game with the spool.

12. J. Lacan, *Écrits: A Selection*, trans. A. Sheridan (New York: Norton, 1977). All translations have been modified to reflect the new forthcoming translation of *Écrits* by Bruce Fink.

13. A recent news article in the *Manchester Guardian* contained an uncanny example of the perversion of such an engendering within masculine structure. Genetic engineers have been working to isolate the DNA fragment from spiders responsible for the resiliency of their web filaments and to exponentially magnify its potency. It will then be combined with the DNA of goats to produce goats whose milk will contain pliable fibers with a tensile strength much greater than that of steel. This new fiber will be marketed for use in surgical suturing and, perhaps more interesting for the subtending fantasy that it reveals, to "catch" jets landing at high speeds on aircraft carriers.

# CONTRIBUTORS

SUZANNE BARNARD is Associate Professor of Psychology at Duquesne University in Pittsburgh, Pennsylvania, a practicing clinical psychologist, and an experimental media artist. She has authored numerous articles on Lacanian and French feminist theory in journals such as *Gender and Psychoanalysis* and *Theory and Psychology*, as well as several book chapters. She is currently co-directing a digital video (with C. Griggers) titled *The Fantasy of Weightlessness: A Video on Women, Embodiment, and Food.*

ANDREW CUTROFELLO is Associate Professor and Graduate Program Director in the Philosophy Department at Loyola University of Chicago. His most recent book is *Imagining Otherwise: Metapsychology and the Analytic A Posteriori.*

BRUCE FINK is a practicing Lacanian psychoanalyst, analytic supervisor, and Professor of Psychology at Duquesne University in Pittsburgh, Pennsylvania. He is a member of the *École de la Cause freudienne* in Paris, and obtained his Ph.D. from the Department of Psychoanalysis at the University of Paris VIII. He has authored three books on Lacan, *The Lacanian Subject: Between Language and Jouissance*, *A Clinical Introduction to Lacanian Psychoanalysis: Theory and Technique*, and *Lacan à la Lettre: Reading* Écrits *Closely*, and has edited two collections of papers on Lacan's work: *Reading Seminar XI: Lacan's Four Fundamental Concepts of Psychoanalysis* and *Reading Seminars I and II: Lacan's Return to Freud.* He has also translated Lacan's Seminar XX, *Encore: On Feminine Sexuality*, and has completed a retranslation of *Écrits: A Selection.*

GENEVIÈVE MOREL is a Lacanian psychoanalyst in Paris and Lille, who completed her early training in mathematics at the École Normale Supérieure, and has taught in the Department of Psychoanalysis at the University of Paris VIII. She has published numerous articles on Lacanian theory and practice, and recently published a book entitled *Ambiguïtés sexuelles: Sexuation et psychose* (Sexual Ambiguities: Sexuation and Psychosis).

RENATA SALECL is Senior Researcher at the Institute of Criminology, University of Ljubljana and Centennial Professor at the London School of Economics. She has authored two books, *The Spoils of Freedom* and *(Per)versions of Love and Hate,* and has edited two collections of papers, *Sexuation* and (with Slavoj Zizek) *Gaze and Voice as Love Objects.*

COLETTE SOLER is a Lacanian psychoanalyst in Paris, who completed her early training in philosophy at the École Normale Supérieure, and has taught in the "Section Clinique" of the Department of Psychoanalysis at the University of Paris VIII. She has published many articles on Lacanian theory and practice in journals such as *Ornicar? La Cause freudienne, La Lettre mensuelle, Lacanian Ink,* and *Newsletter of the Freudian Field,* recently coauthored a book entitled *La Psychanalyse, pas la pensée unique,* and is currently organizing an international coalition of *Forums of the Lacanian Field.*

PAUL VERHAEGHE is Professor and Chair of the Department of Psychoanalysis at the University of Ghent in Belgium. He is also a practicing psychoanalyst and a member of the European School of Psychoanalysis. He has authored two books on psychoanalysis, *Does the Woman Exist? From Freud's Hysteric to Lacan's Feminine* and *Three Essays on Drive and Desire: Love in a Time of Loneliness,* as well as numerous papers on Freudo-Lacanian psychoanalysis.

SLAVOJ ZIZEK is a Senior Researcher at the Department of Philosophy, University of Ljubljana, Slovenia, and Research Project Coordinator at the Kulturwissenschaftliches Institut, Essen, Germany. He has been a guest lecturer at Columbia University, Princeton University, University of Michigan, and the University of California. He is the author of numerous books on Lacan, politics, and film including *Enjoy Your Symptom: Jacques Lacan in Hollywood and Out, Metastases of Enjoyment: Six Essays on Woman and Causality, The Sublime Object of Ideology,* and *The Ticklish Subject.* His most recent publications are *On Belief* and *The Fright of Real Tears.*

# INDEX

16747137R00106

Made in the USA
Lexington, KY
08 August 2012